Y0-DEM-662

RHETORIC,
THROUGH EVERYDAY THINGS

RHETORIC, CULTURE, AND SOCIAL CRITIQUE

Series Editor
John Louis Lucaites

Editorial Board
Jeffrey A. Bennett
Barbara Biesecker
Carole Blair
Joshua Gunn
Robert Hariman
Debra Hawhee
Claire Sisco King
Steven Mailloux
Raymie E. McKerrow
Toby Miller
Phaedra C. Pezzullo
Austin Sarat
Janet Staiger
Barbie Zelizer

RHETORIC,
THROUGH EVERYDAY THINGS

EDITED BY
SCOT BARNETT & **CASEY BOYLE**

THE UNIVERSITY OF ALABAMA PRESS
Tuscaloosa

The University of Alabama Press
Tuscaloosa, Alabama 35487-0380
uapress.ua.edu

Copyright © 2016 by the University of Alabama Press
All rights reserved.

Inquiries about reproducing material from this work should be addressed to the University of Alabama Press.

Typeface: Scala and Scala Sans

Manufactured in the United States of America
Cover design: Michele Myatt Quinn

∞

The paper on which this book is printed meets the minimum requirements of American National Standard for Information Sciences—Permanence of Paper for Printed Library Materials, ANSI Z39.48-1984.

Cataloging-in-Publication data is available from the Library of Congress.
ISBN: 978-0-8173-1919-9
E-ISBN: 978-0-8173-8994-9

Contents

List of Illustrations   vii

Acknowledgments   ix

Introduction: Rhetorical Ontology, or, How to Do Things with Things
Scot Barnett and Casey Boyle   1

I. THE NEW ONTOLOGY OF PERSUASION

1. Listening to Strange Strangers, Modifying Dreams
Marilyn M. Cooper   17

2. Implicit Paradigms of Rhetoric: Aristotelian, Cultural, and Heliotropic
John Muckelbauer   30

3. Rendering and Reifying Brain Sex Science
Christa Teston   42

4. Alinea Phenomenology: Cookery as Flat Ontography
Katie Zabrowski   55

II. WRITING THINGS

5. Writing Devices
Donnie Johnson Sackey and William Hart-Davidson   69

6. The Material Culture of Writing: Objects, Habitats, and Identities in Practice
Cydney Alexis   83

7. The Things They Left Behind: Toward an Object-Oriented History of Composition
Kevin Rutherford and Jason Palmeri   96

8. Object-Oriented Ontology's Binary Duplication and the Promise of Thing-Oriented Ontologies
S. Scott Graham   108

III. SEEING THINGS

9. Materiality's Rhetorical Work: The Nineteenth-Century Parlor Stereoscope and the Second-Naturing of Vision
Kristie S. Fleckenstein   125

10. Circulatory Intensities: Take a Book, Return a Book
Brian J. McNely   139

11. On Rhetorical Becoming
Laurie Gries   155

12. So Close, Yet So Far Away: Temporal Pastiche and *Dear Photograph*
Kim Lacey   171

IV. ASSEMBLING THINGS

13. Assemblage Rhetorics: Creating New Frameworks for Rhetorical Action
Jodie Nicotra   185

14. Objects, Material Commonplaces, and the Invention of the "New Woman"
Sarah Hallenbeck   197

15. Encomium of QWERTY
James J. Brown Jr. and Nathaniel A. Rivers   212

Afterword: A Crack in the Cosmic Egg, Tuning into Things
Thomas Rickert   226

Works Cited   233

List of Contributors   255

Index   259

Illustrations

5.1. A network map of how Mike realizes bighead carp's non/invasive identity 74

5.2. Three patterns of information flow among patients and care providers 80

6.1. Diana's primary writing site (kitchen) 89

6.2. Diana's alternative writing site (library/living room) 89

8.1. The two-world of modernity and postmodernity 110

8.2. The four-world of new materialisms 112

9.1. The Holmes-Bates Stereoscope 131

9.2. The Brewster Stereoscope 133

10.1. The Little Free Library placard and credo 139

10.2. Current holdings, December 21, 2012 148

10.3. The Little Free Library, looking down Maxwell toward an eagle's perch 152

10.4. Circulations, disclosures, and attunements in rhetorical situatedness 153

11.1. Obama Hope poster 156

11.2. Beacon by OVO 162

11.3. Obama in Ghana bag 162

11.4. Obama for Presidente poster 163

11.5. Obama mural in Los Angeles 164

11.6. Obama Biscuits 166

11.7. PhotoFunia montage of Pimp Obamico 168

11.8. *Yes We Scan*, Rene Walter 169

12.1. The image that launched *Dear Photograph*   175

12.2. AT&T Twitter advertisement   176

12.3. Siblings on steps   181

14.1. Pope advertisement, 1885   203

14.2. Damascus Bicycle Company Gentlemen's Safety Bicycle   205

14.3. Damascus Bicycle Company Ladies' Safety Bicycle   205

14.4. Damascus Bicycle handlebar options for male and female riders   207

14.5. "The New Woman Wash Day"   209

15.1. Sholes and Glidden Type-Writer   218

15.2. Engelbart's NLS, featuring the chord keyset, the mouse, and QWERTY   221

Acknowledgments

Any book is a patchwork of voices and interests. This one is no exception. First and foremost, we thank the contributors to this volume, who each brought tremendous faith, creativity, and patience to a collaborative project. We would also like to thank the many fine scholars who submitted proposals for the collection and who have expressed interest and support for the project over the past three years. Although not necessarily reflected in the table of contents, your voices and perspectives are present throughout these pages in many important ways. We also extend our gratitude to Byron Hawk and Thomas Rickert, who shared our interest in this project and provided much feedback in the book's initial planning stages.

We would also like to thank the fine staff at the University of Alabama Press for their support and careful attention throughout this book's various stages of production: Jon Berry, Kristie Henson, John Lucaites, Jonathan Lee Pattishall, Dan Waterman, and JD Wilson, as well as the anonymous reviewers who offered invaluable feedback.

For the editors, this project's life has spanned four academic institutions, numerous academic pursuits and publications, and the birth of two children. It is impossible to do justice to the many people who have supported us professionally and personally during this time. However, we offer the following in the hopes of capturing something of the essence of these complex networks we call our lives:

Scot

This project began while I was a new Assistant Professor at Clemson University. While at Clemson, I received tremendous support from my department chair, Lee Morrissey, as well as my colleagues and friends in the Department of English: David Blakesley, Erin Goss, Cynthia Haynes, Jan Holmevik, Steve Katz, Michael LeMahieu, Brian McGrath, Sean Morey, and Victor Vitanza. My new department at Indiana has been equally supportive. In particular, I thank my department chair, Paul Gutjahr, and numerous friends and colleagues in the department: Michael Adams, Dana Anderson, John Arthos, Christine Farris, Justin Hodgson, John Lucaites, John Schilb, Rebekah Sheldon, Katie Silvester, Kathy Smith, and Robert Terrill.

Finally, I offer my sincerest thanks and appreciation to Jhondra, Pierce, and Sam. Whatever small part of this book belongs to me, I dedicate it to you.

Casey

We began this project when I was a newly appointed Assistant Professor at the University of Utah in what was then known as the University Writing Program. I cannot express the amount of gratitude I have for my Utah colleagues and their support in this project and me in general. Jenny Andrus, Jay Jordan, and Maureen Mathison each have impacted me and this project by offering words of encouragement and simply serving as fine scholarly models. In addition, I want to thank members of my Utah writing group ("Will This Get Me Tenure?"), especially Rob Gehl, Michael Middleton, Danielle Endres, and Sean Lawson (who, though not an official writing group member, might as well have been). While the collection was accepted in just my first semester at Texas, my colleagues here have been equally supportive and encouraging: Jeff Walker, Diane Davis, Clay Spinuzzi, Trish Roberts-Miller, Mark Longaker, Davida Charney, Daniel Smith, Linda Ferreira-Buckley, and Rasha Diab. Also, I'd be remiss not to send my thanks to a number of friends and colleagues who are always willing to read work and offer advice, much of which concerned this volume: Christian Smith, Jonathan Maricle, Jenny Rice, Nathaniel Rivers, Collin Brooke, Jim Brown, and Jeff Rice.

Finally, I offer my deepest gratitude to Tracey, my ultimate collaborator, along with our shared projects, Owen and Parker. More than a few nights and weekends were taken up by this collection, and your support made my contributions possible.

Introduction

Rhetorical Ontology, or, How to Do Things with Things

Scot Barnett and Casey Boyle

> The thing, matter already configured, generates invention, the assessment of means and ends, and thus enables practice.
>
> Elizabeth Grosz

In disciplines across the humanities and social sciences, the first decade of the twenty-first century has been characterized by a return to things. In fields such as philosophy, archaeology, anthropology, science and technology studies, literary studies, and rhetoric and writing studies, things increasingly attract attention as scholars attempt to understand the roles things play in their disciplines, from archaeologists studying the interdependence of things and humans in ancient cultures (Hodder) to technology theorists exploring the moral and political agencies of things such as Robert Moses's highways and overpasses (Winner; Verbeek). While important differences remain, the interdisciplinary reassessment of things recognizes that we do not simply point *at* things but act *alongside* and *with* them. Indeed, the difficulty in teasing apart the *them* (things, technologies, objects, animals, etc.) from the *us* (humans) makes all the more urgent our turning back to things. As literary theorist Bill Brown suggests, "the story of objects asserting themselves as things . . . is the story of a changed relation to the human subject and thus the story of how the thing names less an object than a particular subject-object relation" (4). Things provoke thought, incite feeling, circulate affects, and arouse in us a sense of wonder. But things are more than what they mean or do for us. They are also vibrant actors, enacting effects that exceed (and are sometimes in direct conflict with) human agency and intentionality.

Things are rhetorical, in other words. Understanding them as rhetorical, however, requires more than a leap of imagination; it requires a shift in some of rhetoric's most entrenched critical, methodological, and theoretical orientations. As we argue below, perhaps more than anything else, things challenge—and potentially exhaust—epistemological understandings of rhetoric that ground rhetoric's scope and meaning in terms of human symbolic action. In their introduction to a special journal issue on extrahuman rhetorical relations, Diane Davis and Michelle Ballif recall that "traditionally, rhetorical theory has been defined as the study of human symbol use, which posits at the center of 'the rhetorical situation' a knowing subject who understands himself (traditionally, it is a *he*), his audience, and what he means to communicate" (347). Among other things, this emphasis on the knowing human subject relegates nonhuman things to a secondary—and perhaps even arhetorical—status, because, as Debra Hawhee notes, nonhumans such as animals and things "invite those of us (human ones) interested in questions of rhetoric and communication to suspend the habituated emphasis on verbal language and consciousness" (83). For Davis, Ballif, and Hawhee, the answer to this conundrum is not simply to advocate for the inclusion of nonhumans into existing frameworks for rhetoric. While such a move may work in the short term, it likely will not prove sustainable enough over time, since many of these frameworks have already determined in advance what belongs in the realm of rhetoric and what does not. Instead, what is called for, they argue, are new theoretical orientations that, though recognizably rhetorical, enable us to begin our inquiries from different places, with different attunements and different assumptions about what it means to be—*to be rhetorically*—in the world.

Put simply, things pose a significant challenge for rhetoric in its current forms. Responding to the recent declarations of a *nonhuman turn* (Grusin) invites rhetoricians to rethink, among other things, rhetoric's epistemic tradition. While undeniably useful, the epistemic paradigm constrains our ability to grasp the "thingness" of things—the way things *are* and the rhetorical force they wield in relation to us and other things. As we argue below, and as this volume's contributors further attest, understanding things as active agents rather than passive instruments or backdrops for human activity requires different orientations on rhetoric, orientations inclusive of human beings, language, and epistemology, but expansive enough to speculate about things ontologically. With this in mind, we introduce the concept of *rhetorical ontology*, a relational framework that harnesses the energies of past and present theories of materiality in rhetoric but also anticipates possibilities for new rhetorical approaches to materiality going forward. Rhetorical ontology builds on the philosophical definition of ontology as the study of being, or "what is," to develop an inclusive rhetorical theory and practice. Rhetorical ontology highlights how various material elements—human and nonhuman alike—interact suasively and agentially in rhetorical situations and ecologies.

Although not always taken up by name, rhetorical ontology informs and unifies the wide-ranging essays in this collection. Taking inspiration from the interdisciplinary turn toward things, as well as ontological work already underway in rhetoric, communication, and writing studies, the essays in *Rhetoric, Through Everyday Things* explore the many ways that things both occasion rhetorical action and act as suasive rhetorical forces. From the nineteenth-century stereoscope and women's bicycle to contemporary food culture and the QWERTY computer keyboard, the essays in this volume invite us to see things as vibrant actors whose existence matters for—and in many cases catalyzes—rhetorical being-in-the-world.

To echo Ian Hacking, we recognize that rhetorical ontology "is not, at first sight, a happy phrase; it is too self-important by half" (1). Notwithstanding the concept's possible self-importance, the essays included here demonstrate that rhetorical ontology is indeed rhetoric, albeit rhetoric conceived differently from—although in relation to—the dominant epistemic and linguistic traditions that have defined rhetorical scholarship for much of the past century. In enabling us to see and theorize things as actors that occasion and hold sway in rhetorical relations, rhetorical ontology offers rhetoricians new circumferences from which to engage rhetorical theory and new questions to ask about the history and practice of rhetoric.

The Gathering Power of Things

Crystalized in Robert L. Scott's 1967 declaration that rhetoric is a knowledge-making art, rhetoric over the past decades has largely been defined as an epistemic practice—a discursive mode for constructing and evaluating knowledge and truth claims. Recently, however, rhetoricians have begun to question the primacy of epistemology in the field's understandings of rhetoric. The issue, as always, is emphasis. In epistemic paradigms, the human subject occupies a privileged and central position in the rhetorical scheme of things. While epistemic frameworks allow for inquiry into nonhuman actors (e.g., objects, places, media, technology), such inquiry invariably begins and ends in the same place. From the epistemic point of view, the world matters, but only insofar as it matters *for us*. While useful in helping direct attention to the discursive and epistemic natures of reality, the fixation on rhetoric as "a way of knowing" comes at a loss: namely, a lack of attunement to the nondiscursive (or not exclusively discursive) things that occasion rhetoric's emergence. Jack Selzer captures well some of the limits of the linguistic turn for rhetoric:

> In history, textualized accounts of historical events have come to count as much as the historical events themselves; in anthropology and sociology, cultures have been understood as intangible webs of discourse more than as aggregates of people and things, the substance of tangible realities; in studies of gender and ethnicity, the emphasis has been on constructions of identity through language and other symbol systems; in science, biology and chemistry and physics are now understood as collections of texts as much as they are efforts to engage and describe the physical world through discrete material practices. Things in themselves, consequently, are sometimes being reduced to a function of language: genes, genders, jeans, and

genetics have all been reconceived recently through the prism of language. Words have been mattering more than matter. (4)

Language matters, of course. How bodies, genders, and genetics are constructed discursively has material consequence, particularly for people whose identities have been defined a priori through processes of cultural inscription and social regulation. And yet, when we assume that words matter more than matter, we assume that things matter only in the metaphoric or symbolic sense. The essays in this volume argue that one of the major challenges facing rhetoric today is how to attune ourselves to the "ontological weight and rhetorical agency of things" (Bay and Rickert 213). If we continue to think of things exclusively in terms of language, appearance, or representation—as epistemological objects—we will likely go on believing that human beings alone determine the scope and possibilities of rhetoric and that humans, as a consequence, are the only true legislators of nature. This to the peril of all things.

The good news is that rhetoricians have already begun to explore the rhetoricity of things and the thingness of rhetoric. In "Evocative Objects: Reflections on Teaching, Learning, and Living in Between," for example, Doug Hesse, Nancy Sommers, and Kathleen Blake Yancey remind us that everyday things matter and exert rhetorical power with and over us. In their discussions of a son's craft project for his father, a family photograph, and an image of tectonic plates, Hesse, Sommers, and Yancey demonstrate how things serve both as "companions to our emotional lives" and as "provocations to thought" (Turkle 5). "We think with the objects we love; we love the objects we think with," Sherry Turkle says (5). For Hesse, Sommers, and Yancey, exploring these highly personal objects enables them "to summon a network of associations and evoke cross-disciplinary inquiries" (325). As their self-described "writing experiment" illustrates, things occasion traditional rhetorical actions such as composing an essay for a scholarly journal. Things are also rhetorical in how they gather forces and communities around shared concerns and interests. The child's art project, posted proudly on the refrigerator door, gathers family members and in so doing reinforces the bonds of sentimentality that keep their relationships strong and meaningful.

The sense of things as suasive and agential that we find in Hesse, Sommers, and Yancey echoes other recent accounts of things in the emerging area of "thing theory." Contemporary theorists such as Elizabeth Grosz, Bill Brown, Barbara Johnson, Bruno Latour, and Jane Bennett have each forwarded new conceptions of things that foreground their material agencies and transformational power. Much of this recent work builds on Martin Heidegger's influential writing on the "thingness of things." In his widely cited essay "The Thing," Heidegger poses the seemingly simple question, "what is a thing?" ("Thing" 164). Whereas the word "object" etymologically suggests an opposition between subject and object, with the object construed as "that which stands before, over against, opposite us" (166), Heidegger notes that in the Old High German word *Ding* we find a different meaning rooted in the ancient idea of "thing" as a "gathering" (171), specifically, "a gathering *to deliberate* on a matter under discussion, a contested matter" (172). "Thing," in this sense, denotes "a matter of discourse," a meaning likewise found in the Roman word *res* ("discourse"), which itself is derived from the Greek *eiro* from which we get the word *rhetos*, meaning to "speak about something, to deliberate on it" (172). Largely forgotten in both German and English, this sense of thing as a gathering around matters of public concern can still be found in some Nordic languages that continue to use the word *Althing* for their parliaments (Iceland being a notable example) (Latour, "Dingpolitik"; "Critique"). Echoing Heidegger, Bruno Latour finds in this other meaning of thing a strong rhetorical dimension. A politics built around the idea of things as gatherings, Latour claims, devises "methods to bring into the center of the debate the proof of what is to be debated" ("Dingpolitik" 157). In Latour's view, the ancient art of rhetoric is perfectly suited to bringing in the "object of worry" (157). Rhetoric enables those assembled to make "matters of concern" visible and salient and to "bring into the center of the debate the proof of what is to be debated" (157). As Latour reminds us, "After all, when Aristotle—surely not a cultural relativist!—introduced the word 'rhetoric' it was precisely to mean *proofs*, incomplete to be sure but proofs nonetheless" (158). Following Heidegger and Latour, we might say that rhetoric *"things."* In other words, rhetoric facilitates the gathering of people and things around *matters of concern and matters of interest*. "Interest," deriving from the Latinate *inter* and *est*, literally means "being between." Rhetoric, too, might well designate the art of being between: of being between things and yet also being their means of connection. These things that we find ourselves between possess a certain "thing power" in the way they gather forces and actors and in so doing "affect other bodies, enhancing or weakening their power" (Bennett, *Vibrant* 3).

While some of the vocabulary may be new, the idea of thing power and interested connection is not new to rhetoric. One of the ways Aristotle distinguishes artistic and nonartistic proofs, for example, is on the basis of their thingness and material reality. Artistic proofs are those the rhetor herself invents, and they include, most prominently, syllogisms and enthymemes. The forms of nonartistic proof, on the other hand, Aristotle defines as laws, witnesses, contracts, tortures, and oaths. Although each of these has a clear discursive dimension, what distinguishes them from artistic proofs is the fact that they "are not provided by 'us' but are preexisting" (1.2.2). Things also factor into Quintilian's understanding of rhetoric. In the eleventh book of the *Institutes of Oratory*, he describes in detail the proper dress necessary for excellence in delivery. We are told, for example, that wrapping the toga around the left hand "makes an orator look like a madman," and that throwing one's robe over the right "indicates effeminacy and delicacy" (11.3). Far from constituting the "mere style" of rhetoric, small things such as folds in a garment affect delivery by enabling the body to move and express itself in different ways. The history of rhetoric as told through fashion is yet to be written.

For their part, modern rhetoricians have continued to explore the rhetoricality of things and the thingness of rhetoric. Digital rhetoricians, for example, often emphasize how digital images, advertisements, and social networking sites function as vibrant rhetorical agents that contribute to the gathering of social, political, and technological worlds (Bay and Rickert; Cooper, "Agency"; Edbauer; Jenny Rice; Spinuzzi, *Network*; Trimbur). Likewise, rhetorical theorists have taken increasing interest in the rhetoricity of spaces such as monuments and museums. Far from the inert spaces or blocks of granite we sometimes take them to be, monuments and museums are rhetorical agents that enact a suasive "drawing power," gathering, for example, the material-aesthetic composition of a thing such as the Vietnam Veterans Memorial together with the political and deliberative rhetorics of the Vietnam War and its aftermath (Blair, Jeppeson, and Pucci; see also Bernard-Donals; Dickinson, Blair, and Ott). Importantly, these and other studies have not attempted to remove the human rhetor from consideration. Instead, they seek more inclusive and ecological frames—more "interested" frames, we could say—that move rhetoric beyond the familiar humanist triad of speaker-audience-purpose. Human beings are still relevant here; however, they are no longer singularly spotlighted on the rhetorical stage. As these studies help us to see, turning our attention back to things may constitute a *post*human turn, but it need not be an *anti*human one.

Things, Objects, and the In-Between

Accounting for the co-constitutive relations between humans and things is critical to any rhetorical understanding of things. However, it is important for us to not limit ourselves to the human-thing relation alone, even if this relation is typically the most pressing form of relationality for us. If things have their own ways of being in the world, and if we understand these ways of being as vibrant and rhetorical, then we should also be interested in relations between things themselves, how things interact with and have effects on other things. In other words, we should consider how "things depend on other things" as well as on us (Hodder 64–87). As a field, we sometimes find it difficult (if perhaps even misguided) to imagine rhetorical action as occurring anywhere except in the conscious, intentional, and symbolic activities of human speakers and writers. As the essays in the volume collectively argue, the various and at times competing accounts of things in object-oriented ontology, actor-network theory, and feminist new materialism offer fruitful pathways for us to develop rhetorical understandings of relationality that account for our co-belonging and co-responsibilities with things. In the case of object-oriented ontology, relationality between things is typically conceived in asymmetrical terms, with things (or "objects" in this case[1]) relating to each other on some levels of their being but not others. In one of Graham Harman's oft-repeated examples, when fire encounters cotton it "relates" to the cotton primarily by way of its flammability. All of the other aspects of cotton's being—its color, usability, smell, etc.—withdraw from the fire's relation with cotton. Thus for Harman and other object-oriented theorists, things have a depth to their being that is never fully revealed or exhausted in their dealings with other things or human beings. "Every object is a private reality that withdraws from any attempt to perceive, touch, or use it," Harman says. "An object cannot be fully translated or paraphrased; it simply is what it is, and no other object can replace or adequately mirror it" (*Guerilla* 222).[2]

Harman's asymmetrical theory of object relations is a response in part to theories of relationism that define things in terms of their connections to other things rather than by their "lonely kernel of essence" (Harman, *Prince* 75). Latour's work is exemplary here, however it should be noted that Latour has rebuffed Harman's charges of relationism in his work.[3] While Latour accepts the idea of things interacting independent of human beings, he argues that things are what they are because of their relations and alliances with other things. In other words, Latour minimizes the problems of withdrawal that Harman foregrounds by emphasizing *symmetrical* models of relationality. In one of his more controversial examples, Latour asks whether microbes existed before Pasteur first discovered them. His answer is that "After 1864 airborne germs were there all along" (*Pandora's* 173). Although the claim at first glance reads like an extreme social constructivist argument, it actually emphasizes how mutual relations, in this case between Pasteur and the microbe, "articulate each other more fully" (Harman, *Prince* 125). In 1864 Pasteur retroactively brings microbes into focus through the various symptoms he finds and interprets, and, in turn, microbes "bring Pasteur into focus as a genius and national hero. Pasteur and the microbes need one another" (125). To be clear, Latour is not suggesting that Pasteur and microbes are equal or equivalent actors but that relations in this case are characterized by gradations of agency and influence, with some actors proving to be stronger than others. "To be symmetric," then, "simply means *not* to impose a priori some spurious *asymmetry* among human intentional action and a material world of causal relations" (*Reassembling* 76). For Latour, symmetricality is the necessary precondition for network analysis. Actor-network theory's methodological slogan—"to follow the actors themselves," whatever they are and wherever they take you—depends on the researcher's ability to bracket divisions between humans and nonhumans in order to "learn from them what the collective existence has become in their hands" (12). While things in Latour may lack the dark, subterranean essence Heidegger, Harman, and object-oriented ontologists champion, his method has the advantage of enabling us to trace the suasive nature of things as they materialize relationally within larger networks and systems of meaning.[4]

In the work of feminist new materialists, we find still more productive attempts to bring together the symmetrical and asymmetrical approaches to relationality. While benefiting from the linguistic and social constructivist paradigms in feminist thought—such as Judith Butler's performative theory of embodiment and related accounts of difference and alterity—a new generation of feminist theorists has turned its focus from writings about materiality toward the persuasive effects of materiality itself. This slight difference is a difference that matters. Donna Haraway's classic essay "A Cyborg Manifesto" in many respects anticipated this shift in the way it problematized essentialist thought in feminist theory and humanities scholarship in general. In part a commentary on technology's increasing role in everyday life, Haraway's essay carves out a space for thinking about things in ways that avoid the prevailing masculine-feminine and linguistic-materialist dichotomies. While the intervening years have brought some criticism to Haraway's essay—critiques of a simple, supplemental dynamic between human and nonhuman actors—what remains prescient and still key to this essay is Haraway's emphasis on materiality as relational. Building on Haraway's work, Karen Barad develops an understanding of things rooted in what she calls *intra-activity*, in which things are defined by their relations with other things rather than language and signification alone. These theoretical insights compound the pressing case that humans and nonhumans are co-constitutive and co-emerging, all involved together in composing our shared worlds. Blending philosophies of gender, science, and materiality, feminist new materialists such as Elizabeth Grosz, Sara Ahmed, and Rosi Braidotti similarly explore the "situatedness" of materiality and the ways difference and differentiation constitute the plane from which relationality and intra-activity emerge in the first place.[5] Through these blended philosophies, we find once more that we are turning from epistemological and cultural paradigms of rhetorical theory and into discussions of ontology.

Rhetorical Ontology

Whereas epistemology emphasizes knowledge *about* things, and thus about their meaning and cultural significance for us, ontology stresses relational *being*. To be clear, we use the word ontology in a nontraditional way. In place of ontology as a stable and/or static condition, we take ontology to be fundamentally rhetorical. That is, ontology is an ongoing negotiation of being through relations among what we might, on some occasions, call human and/or nonhuman. We thus take ontology to be the pervasive *relationality* of all things—the means by which things come into relation and have effects on other things in ways that resonate strongly with existing and emerging understandings of rhetoric. Over the past several decades, it has become commonplace to discuss material rhetoric and even the rhetoric of things, but we believe the overriding interest gathering all these concerns together is a concern for rhetorical ontology.

For certain, ontology is not new to rhetoric. Even at the dawn of the tradition, rhetors wrestled with those relationships between rhetoric and reality as relationships that are not in opposition to one another. Gorgias, for instance, is reported to have discussed the nonexistence of things through (and as) rhetorical performance. In exploring the power of language and logos, Gorgias's text on the nonexistent anticipates an ontological conception of rhetoric that is fundamentally creative and formative. More recent engagements with rhetoric's ontologies can be found scattered throughout the last few decades of scholarship. Karlyn Kohrs Campbell, for instance, argues that human rhetors are guided by the ontological assumption that humans are symbol-using/signifying creatures. While not arguing for the relevance of material things in the realm of persuasion, accounts such as Campbell's open the door to further discussions of rhetorical ontologies that could also include nonhuman agents. Such a prospect is also apparent in Carol Poster's examination of pre-Socratic thought and its sense of rhetoric and natural philosophy as "aspects of unified systems of thought" (1). Poster's project, like Campbell's before, preserves the role of linguistic communication and traditional persuasion but not without gesturing toward other elements at play in rhetorical practice. Rhetoric's ontological heft becomes even more apparent in Andrew Scult's Heideggerian reading of Aristotle's *Rhetoric* as an ontological inquiry into the nature of *logos*. Rhetoric's ontological status is further strengthened by Thomas W. Benson's argument that rhetoric is a "way of being" through which speakers and listeners create one another. In each of these accounts—spanning several decades of rhetorical research—rhetoric is conceived as more than just a knowledge-making praxis; at the same time, it is thought to constitute ways of being and ways of being-with-others-in-the-world.

It is precisely because of this rich scholarly background in ontology that rhetoric is poised to productively respond to recent scholars outside of rhetoric who understand ontology as the unsettled relations between things. In a particularly evocative essay that pushes the concept of ontology beyond the dynamics of human being, philosopher and medical ethnographer Annemarie Mol proposes the idea of an "ontological politics" that highlights how our encounters with objects in a practice are often, at the same time, encounters with the "complex interferences *between* those objects" (82, emphasis added). In anthropology, a field perhaps most invested in a human-centric account of reality, Eduardo Viveiros de Castro similarly argues for "multinaturalist" accounts of objects and relationality. For Viveiros de Castro, all things share a single epistemology—drive toward food, desire to reproduce, aversion to death—but have different ontologies. What things are considered to be food/nourishment, the ways in which things reproduce, and how death is averted (including what/who is enlisted to accomplish those drives) are the ontological conditions from which each thing relates. In another important account, Andrew Pickering, a philosopher of science, foregrounds the complex relationality between things in art and cybernetics, a "mangle" he describes as performances of "ontological theatre." These theatrical occasions provide "staging and dramatizing configurations and interrelations of human and non-human agency" (7). The performances—occurring in mathematics, robotics, architecture, and design—offer a "staging in microcosm of our modern mode of being in the world. It would remind people quite forcefully . . . of the way we generally live" (9). Key to Pickering's account of ontological theater is its emphasis on engineering occasions to take part in different ontologies. The need to share, to expose, and to spread ontologies harkens to a need to participate in and be persuaded by other modes of being.

Rhetoric and writing scholars have further extended the notion of ontology as a shared rhetorical project between things and fellow interlocutors. In his aptly titled book *Writing as a Way of Being*, Robert P. Yagelski claims that the activity of writing is an "ontological act" and that the language and epistemological products known as the "writer's writing" are far less important for today than the "writer writing," the experience and the gathering together of new ways of being. Consistent with Yagelski, Ralph Cintron criticizes the social justice proponent who is "motivated by a belief in equality but never inquires ontologically into equality itself" (480). Cintron qualifies his critique by saying that in "using the terms 'ontology' and 'ontological'" he is not "saying that such critics should become philosophers inquiring into the 'beingness' of something" (480). Implicit in Cintron's critique and immediate qualification is an acknowledgement that rhetoric lacks its own vocabulary for understanding ontological encounters. Rhetoricians, much like anthropologists and social scientists before them, need to develop new ways to describe and write about ontology. The essays in this volume offer an initial foray into precisely such a project.

While the turn to ontology has intensified in related fields, we hasten to add that rhetoric is not simply playing catch-up for what, to some, is becoming one of this century's most fashionable theoretical trends. To the contrary, as many of this book's authors make clear, things and the multiple ontologies from which they emerge have a long, if oftentimes neglected, history in our field. Things have played important roles in shaping understandings of rhetoric from antiquity to the present. Recent developments in thing theory, new materialism, object-oriented ontology, and actor-network theory are thus understood in this collection as exigencies for *doing rhetoric*. The interdisciplinary turn to ontology occasions rhetoricians to undertake new research programs committed to the exploration of a distinctly rhetorical question: how to do things with things.

Plan of the Book

The essays in *Rhetoric, Through Everyday Things* explore rhetorical ontology through multiple case studies as well as historical and theoretical analyses. Rather than locate rhetorical action in human beings alone, the essays in this volume argue for an ontological approach to rhetoric that widens the circumference of rhetorical activity to include the vibrant ecology of things as occasioning possibilities for rhetoric and writing.

"Part 1: The New Ontology of Persuasion" introduces some of the theoretical and methodological questions that emerge when we adopt an ontological approach to rhetoric. In "Listening to Strange Strangers, Modifying Dreams," Marilyn M. Cooper begins by calling on rhetoric to open up its practices to the "polite modification" experienced when encountering a strange stranger. Exploring a brief encounter with a dragonfly, Cooper proposes a way of thinking and doing rhetoric that finds an active process in being persuaded by incommensurable beings. John Muckelbauer continues to engage rhetoric's orientation in "Implicit Paradigms of Rhetoric: Aristotelian, Cultural, and Heliotropic" by surveying rhetoric's paradigmatic turns and proposing another paradigm for rhetoric. By looking to heliotropism (plants turning toward the sun) as a conceptual paradigm for rhetoric, Muckelbauer problematizes our prevailing humanistic concepts of rhetoric and suggests rhetoric to be a "turning art." Christa Teston interrogates the methodological import of materiality by pursuing how and when facts are reified in scientific knowledge. In this move, Teston builds on prior reification based on epistemological frameworks and suggests that ontological frameworks might also be worth our attention. Finally, Katie Zabrowski takes up (once again) philosophy's longheld pejorative view of rhetoric as cookery by examining a single dish as an inexhaustible model for a new feminist historiography.

"Part 2: Writing Things" explores the thingness of writing as both an artifact of study and a mode of rhetorical invention. In "Writing Devices," Donnie Sackey and William Hart-Davidson draw on work in actor-network theory to examine two cases—the 1900 Lacey Act, which governs the control of non-native species, and writing devices that might be developed for diabetes health maintenance—in which writing and writing devices play active roles in bringing networks and collectives together. In "The Material Culture of Writing," Cydney Alexis introduces the concept of "writing habitats," which captures the ways writers not only live and work in material environments, but how they are also enabled and conditioned by the environs within which they write. In "The Things They Left Behind," Kevin Rutherford and Jason Palmeri extend Alexis's notion of the writing habitat to inform new understandings of rhetoric and writing's disciplinary history—what they call an "object-oriented history of composition." Returning to the debates about the writing process in the 1970s and 80s, their essay makes a compelling argument for new approaches to disciplinary history that, contra James Berlin's foundational histories of composition studies, begin from the perspective of ontology rather than epistemology. Finally, in "From Objects to Things," Scott Graham encourages rhetoricians excited about the nonhuman turn to not overlook rhetoric's long history of engaging issues of materiality. In response to the antirhetorical bent of some new materiality/object-oriented theory, Graham argues for a "Thing-Oriented Ontology" for rhetoric that precedes metaphysics and that is rooted in Heidegger's understanding of *Ding* as the gathering together of beings and ideas.

"Part 3: Seeing Things" explores how visual artifacts and technologies affect the ways we see the world and ourselves in the world. Collectively, the essays in this section argue that "seeing things" is not a passive activity but an active rhetorical event. In "Materiality's Rhetorical Work," Kristie Fleckenstein examines the nineteenth-century stereoscope as a rhetorical agent, one that persuaded into being a new way of seeing characterized by disembodiment and hyperattention. In "Circulatory Intensities," Brian McNely develops an original methodology for becoming aware of and attuned to the rhetorical importance of ontologies. Through an analysis of his local Little Free Library, where people are invited to take and donate books, he demonstrates how everyday things such as books catalyze affective intensities and visual *puncta* and in so doing disclose the world as something in which we are invested and for which we care. In "On Rhetorical Becoming," Laurie Gries articulates a notion of rhetorical becoming that, much like Fleckenstein, recognizes the ways visual artifacts change or transform over space and time, often in surprising ways that exceed the intentions of the artifacts creators. While rhetorical theorists have tended to think of images as static things, Gries demonstrates through a reading of the Obama Hope image how a new materialist approach attuned to the idea of rhetorical becoming reveals the thing power of texts and images. Finally, in "So Close, Yet So Far Away," Kim Lacey analyzes how the juxtaposition of present and past photographs in the popular *Dear Photograph* series gather new understandings—and new ontologies—of place and time, what she calls the "space of the meanwhile." In connecting the present to the past through photos taken of the same place from the same point of view, *Dear Photograph*, as Lacey shows, foregrounds the materiality of photographic representation even as it raises questions about memory and our remembrance of things past.

"Part 4: Assembling Things" brings together three sites of material suasion. First, Jodie Nicotra explores how new materialism might reframe rhetoric as "assemblage." In "Assemblage Rhetorics," Nicotra explores waste—both personal and communal—as an opportunity to approach habit formation as an assemblage of human and nonhuman, discursive and nondiscursive formations. In highlighting the materiality of habit through waste, Nicotra provides a concrete demonstration of rhetorical ontology as a critical perspective. Sara Hallenbeck's "Objects, Material Commonplaces, and the Invention of the 'New Woman'" delivers a compelling take on the capacity of traditional rhetoric to accommodate the field's turn to materiality. Hallenbeck examines the invention and subsequent innovation of bicycling for women as a material argument. In highlighting the visual and textual accounts of how the woman's bicycle evolved, the chapter shows a coincident political and gendered persuasion that occurred alongside the bicycle's innovation—an innovation that created new political positions and opportunities for women in the nineteenth century. James J. Brown Jr. and Nathaniel A. Rivers conclude the collection with "Encomium of QWERTY," a performative essay that examines the materiality of our standard keyboard and raises an important question about what it is we praise when we praise. As one of rhetoric's oldest genres, the encomium seems to us the perfect form to explore not only the thingness of QWERTY (the standard keyboard layout) but the ways in which rhetoric itself enables us to see and understand things in novel forms and configurations.

While this collection offers multiple performances of what Pickering calls "ontological theatre," we realize further shows must be staged. As is the case with any emerging and pressing topic of interest, there are many angles to take. But, as is also the case, limits on scope and size are persuadable only to a degree. We received far more excellent chapter proposals than we could include. Thus the absence of these voices may be taken as "lacks" for this current volume. Rightfully so. But with these other voices in mind, we acknowledge many more possibilities for exploring rhetorical ontologies. In particular, we recognize that digital and media technologies offer fertile ground for discussions of rhetorical ontology. On a related point, rhetorical ontologies can affect not only how we talk about politics but also how we prepare for and practice global activism, environmental politics, labor issues, race and ethnicity, and disability studies. In each of these areas, questions abound concerning how multiple and persuadable ontologies include both human and nonhuman assemblages. We hope that others will continue to extend, elaborate, complicate, and reinvent rhetorical ontologies.

Notes

1. As mentioned above, Heidegger distinguishes a thing from an object, or that which stands opposed to or against the subject. For object-oriented ontologists such as Harman, the Heideggerian distinction between thing and object is ultimately ir-

relevant since *all* entities partake in a similar relational structure defined by each being's revealing and concealing of itself. For the purposes of this introduction, we have elected to use the commonplace word "thing"; however, some of our contributors prefer "object" over thing.

2. Like Latour, Harman sees an important role for rhetoric in object-oriented ontology, in that rhetoric enables us to "expose the unstated assumptions that lie behind any surface proposition" (*Prince* 169). For a fuller and more nuanced account of rhetoric's hidden, ambient dimension, see Thomas Rickert's *Ambient Rhetoric: The Attunements of Rhetorical Being*.

3. See Latour and Harman's debate, published as *The Prince and the Wolf: Latour and Harman at the LSE*.

4. Latour's work has gained considerable traction of late in rhetorical theory. Along with the essays in this volume, see Collin Gifford Brooke, "Forgetting to Be (Post) Human"; Byron Hawk, "Reassembling Post-Process"; Carl Herndl, "Rhetoric of Science as Non-Modern Practice"; Paul Lynch, "Composition's New Thing"; Nathaniel Rivers, "Rhetorics of (Non) Symbolic Cultivation"; Jeff Rice, *Digital Detroit*; and Clay Spinuzzi, *Network*.

5. For an excellent overview of new approaches to material feminisms, see Stacy Alaimo and Susan Hekman's collection *Material Feminism*.

I

The New Ontology of Persuasion

1
Listening to Strange Strangers, Modifying Dreams

Marilyn M. Cooper

> Matter sings. In its spinning and tumbling, its locked vibrations, its transitory leaps, it sings, but we cannot hear. Behind the most placid surface ... there is a ceaseless, sibilant whispering, a kind of delicate rustling and turning, unattended sounds so profligate and spendthrift, so seductive, that if they did not lie forever beyond us, we would be held totally in their thrall.
>
> Bill Green

Timothy Morton argues that *"ecological thought* is the thinking of interconnectedness," the imagining of "a multitude of entangled strange strangers," and he asks, "What would a truly democratic encounter between truly equal beings look like, what would it be—could we even imagine it?" (7, 15; emphasis in the original). As I begin imagining the possibilities inherent in encounters among a multitude of entangled strange strangers, I put aside the questions of "truly equal beings" and "a truly democratic encounter"[1] as well as Morton's recommendation of thinking big. I turn instead to Bryan Garsten's vision of persuasion as a "practice of controversy in smaller disputes, piecemeal, as they arise in particular situations and in smaller settings" (211). Garsten argues that the project of persuasion requires that we "once again look directly at one another and speak directly to one another," that "we pay attention to our fellow citizens and to their opinions" (210). Persuasion happens when we pay attention—really listen—and not just to other humans but to all the others we share the world with. The questions I take up here are how do we listen to and be persuaded by—or, as Garsten has it, persuade ourselves in response to—encounters with these others? And what changes in our understanding of persuasion does listening to strange strangers entail? Answers to these questions involve rethinking the concepts of listening and of persuasion, and, as my answer to the first question relies on answering the second one, I will start by exploring how persuasion can be conceived of more inclusively to apply to strange strangers such as dragonflies. Then I will explore what habits of listening might enable us to hear and respond to such things as cochlear implants, hummingbirds, and the element cobalt.

My first example is of a particular encounter in a small setting between what I would call incommensurable beings. I was driving down a gravel road when something buzzed in through the open passenger side window and landed on my thigh. Glancing down, I saw a bright blue spangled dragonfly about three inches long with crawly looking legs. Fortunately, before I panicked about what to do, it buzzed out the open window on my side of the car. I was startled, and the encounter left a lasting impression. It drew me out of myself, just as Garsten says is required by the effort of persuasion (210). I was still thinking about it hours later.

Dragonflies are not entirely strange to me: I believe they won't harm me, and many are beautiful, including this one. This slight bit of familiarity accounts in part for the particular impression the dragonfly made, but the effort of paying attention has less to do with familiarity than with divergence. Isabelle Stengers, thinking with Alfred North Whitehead, observes that divergence is a more productive focus for thinking about encounters with all kinds of others. She contrasts "argumentation, interaction, and rational conversation [which] bet everything on homogeneity, that is, the possibility of putting oneself in the other's place" (514) with Whitehead's brand of speculative thought, which involves "presence rather than argument, a presence whose efficacy is to infect every justificatory argument with the adventurous questions of what is demanded by the position whose legitimacy it expresses, of what it recruits to endure or propagate, and of the ways it is liable to be affected by the encounter with another position" (512–13). Speculative thought is a polite form of persuasion: it respects the dreams of others rather than aiming at conversion or correction, but it is not a matter of toleration that simply avoids conflict. Instead, it aims to shake our certainties, thereby allowing what Whitehead calls new propositions to come into the world, new "tales that might perhaps be told" (*Process* 256). Propositions are adventures that do "not aim at awakening, leaving the cave" to dispel false illusions, to deconstruct, to engage in polemic or argument (Stengers 516). Awakening is the work of exclusion, or systematization, which Whitehead says is but one of the tasks of philosophy, one which is subordinate to the prior task of assemblage: "Philosophy can exclude nothing" (*Modes* 2). Assemblage seeks to turn what seem to be contradictions among propositions into productive adventures. It is an approach that reconceives positions as "habits of experience" (Stengers 89).

Habits of experience do not simply arise from the accumulation of experience but rather are wagers concerning the world. They are behaviors that work and thus testify to the existence of something in the world: "the existence of a mountain climber testifies to the fact that in general, the side of a mountain offers reliable footholds" (88). Habits of experience guarantee the legitimacy or endurance of certain positions. The habit of mountain climbing depends on mountains being the kind of thing that offers footholds to humans. But like adventures, habits are risky—they only hold in general. This does not mean that some habits are false, for all provide footholds whether they are judged to be good habits or bad habits. Stengers explains: "The point is not to declare war on the conventions that bind us, the habits that enable us to be characterized. Instead, it is merely to place on the same level—that is, in adventure—all of our judgments, or our 'as is well knowns,' and thus to separate them actively from what gives them the power to exclude and disqualify" (27). Instead of dismissing some habits (or positions), assemblage allows them to be placed in proximity where they can modify each other. Thus when physicists acquire the good habit of dreams that do not turn them into the thinking head of humanity they are not necessarily required to relinquish the habits that make them physicists (Stengers 516).

Garsten's concern for a kind of persuasion that makes democratic politics possible similarly relies on politeness, resuscitating its etymological link to politics. True persuasion, he says—"persuasion that lies between manipulation and pandering"—preserves the "active independence" of the listener: the orator "merely puts words into the air," and listeners engage in "an active process of evaluation and assimilation" (7). Like an infection that runs its course differently in each individual and that cannot foresee "what causes, resources, and what consequences it will invent for itself" (Stengers 515), true persuasion induces individuals "to change their own beliefs and desires *in light of what has been said*" (Garsten 7; emphasis added). Being persuaded is not something that happens to someone; it is something listeners do in response to what has been encountered, just as the physicists in Stengers's instance would do. Thus Garsten, like Stengers, observes that there is no certain outcome of persuasion: "even the most attentive and skillful efforts at persuasion often fail for reasons unconnected with the merits of the cause" (211). It is because persuasion is a response of individual listeners with their own experiences and feelings and beliefs that its success cannot be attributed solely to the intent or skill of the rhetor. Persuasion succeeds not through mastery but through polite modification of dreams and the acquisition of new habits.[2]

Garsten explains how not dismissing others' dreams that contradict our "as is well knowns" facilitates polite persuasion. He proposes that evincing respect for others' beliefs allows listeners to consider different positions by engaging their capacity for judgment:

> We judge best when we are situated within these structures of value, able to draw upon their complexity and able to feel, emotionally, the moral and practical relevance of different considerations in as subtle a way as expe-

rience has equipped us to do. And because the patterns of thought and emotion are not set in stone, because much of the art of rhetoric consists in drawing new pathways between hitherto weakly related parts of these structures, we need not view ourselves as trapped in our situation but simply grounded there. (192)

The polite introduction of a new possibility "invokes particular and personal forms of knowledge," and, juxtaposed with the structures of a listener's beliefs, the new proposition can lead to a transformation of habits (192). Whitehead attributes such a transformation to imagination, which "deliberately suspends 'what we know well'" and allows us to become aware not of its falseness, but of its partiality (Stengers 351).

My encounter with the dragonfly drew me out of myself not because it was familiar, though startling, but because it infected me with a new tale that might be told, a proposition that shook my certainties about the importance of my role and that of humans in general in saving individual animals and species. The advantage of listening to strange strangers like dragonflies is that they are strange. They have divergent interests and abilities, and their actions refuse our simple assumption that we can put ourselves in their place. Compared to other humans they can thus seem more difficult—even impossible—to listen to. But the new habits of listening we acquire by harking to them help us understand persuasion as a response arising through mutual infection, and as one that opens new possibilities for us.

Listening to strange strangers will entail transforming our habits in a way that enables us to entertain new propositions. I propose three overlapping habits as a good place to start on this adventure: believing there is someone or something to listen to; letting beings and things be in themselves in our relations to them; and finding new ways to listen. All three are ways of paying due attention to the human and nonhuman strangers we encounter and of being persuaded, just as Garsten suggests we must pay attention to our fellow citizens and to their opinions.

First, I have to believe I *can* listen to the stranger, that the stranger can communicate something to me. Whitehead argues that we can theoretically understand everything about anything we connect with: "Whatever exists, is capable of knowledge in respect to the finitude of its connections with the rest of things" (*Modes* 42). Gemma Corradi Fiumara, who like Garsten argues that listening is of equal importance to speaking in promoting thought, says that it is a mistake to think of listening as passive; instead, listening requires "laborious involvement . . . and some degree of commitment" (189–91). Rosina Lippi-Green observes that mainstream language speakers who claim they cannot understand those who speak with an accent are rejecting their "fair share of the communicative burden" (70). In the same way, humans like Wittgenstein, who avers that even if a lion could talk we could not understand him, are simply refusing to make the effort to listen (223).

Second, I have to attend to the stranger as a specific instance of a specific individual in a specific time and place. Heidegger says that when we do not let something be in itself, "the nature of a thing never comes to light, that is, it never gets a hearing" ("Thing" 168). For Heidegger, things come to presence through gathering aspects of the world "into something that stays for a while: into this thing, that thing" (172). The dragonfly, for example, gathers the currents of air produced by the car's passage, the open window, my thigh, into what Whitehead calls an actual entity, something "that 'decides for itself': thus, and not otherwise" (Stengers 263). Whitehead says: "The point to be emphasized is the insistent particularity of things experienced and of the act of experiencing. . . . *That* wolf [ate] *that* lamb at *that* spot at *that* time" (*Process* 43). Garsten similarly argues that "respect for the actual opinions of one's audience serves to acknowledge the particular features of individuals . . . a respect for what Seyla Benhabib has called 'the concrete other'" (198). I can turn to my guide to dragonflies of the north woods, as I have, and discover that the one I encountered was a blue darner, probably a Canada darner or a Lake darner, but in doing so I am not listening to that dragonfly that flew into my car on that day.

Finally, I have to find new ways of listening, ways that, as Bruno Latour and Vinciane Despret have said, allow the stranger to become interesting (Latour, "Well-Articulated"; Despret, "Sheep"). Stengers suggests that successful scientists learn "to discern what matters to what is being interrogated" (440), and Latour and Despret suggest that experimental apparatuses function as speech prostheses enabling nonhumans to participate in discussions with humans (Latour, *Politics* 67; Despret, "Becomings"). Inadvertently, my leaving the car windows open set up an experiment in which this particular blue darner could communicate something interesting about its concerns and my relation to them. Here is where turning to the scientific literature on dragonflies also becomes a speech prosthesis, for as I remembered what I had read about dragonflies—that they are fast and agile fliers due to their nearly 360-degree field of vision and ability to move their four wings independently—I realized that it did not need me to help it out of the car.

I want to develop more fully what is involved in these three habits by considering some other encounters between humans and nonhuman beings and things. But first, I need to emphasize two things I am not saying when I say that the blue darner communicated something to me. First, I am not saying that it consciously intended to do so. In arguing for a "worldly persuadability transcending human intent," Thomas Rickert proposes that intent and consciousness are not sufficient to account for rhetoric. He says, "Intent and self-consciousness no doubt matter enormously, but they no longer suffice to determine what is rhetoric and what is not" (36). I am not sure I agree that conscious intention matters "enormously" in rhetoric or communication even among humans, but I am quite sure that insisting on conscious intention in the communications of nonhumans is just another way of refusing to listen.

As Rickert acknowledges, "at any given time, we are only partially conscious of what we are doing, why we are doing it, and what will result from it" (36). I have also argued elsewhere that intent and action are largely nonconscious processes that we become aware of only after the fact ("Rhetorical Agency"). As Wittgenstein says, "the intention *with which* one acts does not 'accompany' the action any more than the thought 'accompanies' speech" (217). Intentions are enacted in speech and deed; they do not exist prior to them as causes. Listeners often do wish to understand speakers better, but, following Whitehead, I argue that when they ask "what do you mean," they are asking not "what did you intend" but "why do you say that?" Better understanding means a more complete understanding that includes an understanding of the past and present context: the connections of what the speaker said to experiences, motivations, influences, and the current topic. Listen for a moment to a very insightful teacher's comment on listening to students:

> When I'm teaching a grad seminar and a student seems to be missing the point or misrepresenting something or going in a wrong direction, I usually say: Can you say more about that? And it often turns out that they just needed more time to get to what they were trying to say or that they were actually getting at something important, but in an oblique way or in a way that listeners may not have been able to instantly recognize. My point is: rather than cutting off or jumping in (done by the professor or, more often, other grad students), listen more. Allow time. Assume intelligence. (Springsteen)

As Latour suggests in his dialog with a graduate student, "Why would you be the one doing the intelligent stuff while they would act like a bunch of morons?" (*Reassembling* 150).

In saying that the blue darner communicated something to me, I am also not saying that what it communicated is simply my interpretation of what the dragonfly did in the context of what I know about dragonflies. Oscar Wilde famously criticized Wordsworth's communion with nature, saying, "He found in stones the sermons he had already hidden there" (*Decay* 10). Whitehead, on the other hand, was inspired by Wordsworth, who, he said, "dwells on that mysterious presence of surrounding things, which imposes itself on any separate element that we set up as an individual for its own sake. He always grasps the whole of nature as involved in the tonality of the particular instance" (*Science* 83). Whitehead especially praises the first book of *The Prelude*: "it would hardly be possible to express more clearly a feeling for nature, as exhibiting entwined prehensive unities, each suffused with modal presences of others" (*Science* 84). A "prehension is a 'taking into account'"; it refers to "all situations in which something makes a difference for something else," and is not restricted only to living beings (Stengers 147). "For instance," Stengers explains, "the earth's trajectory 'takes account' of the sun." Prehensive unities are akin to what Rickert refers to as ambience and as a worldly persuadability, and what Heidegger is talking about when he says that things gather their surroundings. Though it can become a conscious action, it is not one in itself. Instead, the term refers to a general affectability—cognitive, emotional, physical. My interpretation of my encounter with the dragonfly (which is equally the dragonfly's encounter with me and my car) is not simply an interpretation of what the dragonfly did along with what I know but a part of the prehensive unity of the encounter.

The three encounters I turn to next demonstrate in more detail how the three habits of listening play out in encounters between diverse strange strangers. In each, the humans evince belief that they can listen to the specific stranger through emotional, physical, and cognitive attunement; various speech prostheses; and carefully designed and conducted experiments. The encounters also demonstrate that listening to strangers requires nonconscious attunement as much as conscious intention and that persuasion occurs through entertaining new possibilities that arise in the prehensive unity of the encounter.

First, an encounter with a thing, a technology.[3] In discussing how Michael Chorost became attuned to his cochlear implant, Glen Mazis notes that a breakthrough came when Chorost was talking on the phone to his mother, which he had been avoiding because he had not been able to understand what he was hearing. Chorost reports, "I was understanding her. Believing that I could do it seemed to be half the battle. That let me extend myself into the sound and let it sink into me" (99, qtd. in Mazis 66). Mazis attributes the change not primarily to the way Chorost's brain was restructuring itself in response to the implant but to his changed attitude: "As he started to have positive experiences with his new implant, Chorost made the call to his mother . . . believing there was something for him to hear" (66).

Mazis draws on Merleau-Ponty's ideas about attuned perception to explain Chorost's growing ability to attend to his implant. Like Fiumara, he emphasizes the active nature of human listening, but also the activity of the surround, all the other entities humans are entwined with. "When we 'pay attention' . . . we are not throwing an inert, indifferent 'searchlight' onto the scene about us. We are actively looking at something that promises to mean something for us . . . In some way, whatever we perceive 'beckons' to us and is therefore an invitation to enter a dialogue with the promise of further meaning" (64–65). The data coming from a cochlear implant are as much an invitation as a rhetor's words to which we may or may not pay attention.

But Mazis goes on to explain that fully conscious, intentful consciousness is not what is needed. Chorost discovered that while listening to the radio as he drove, he could understand what was being said only when he was not explicitly focused on trying to make sense of it. Mazis connects this phenomenon to Merleau-Ponty's concept of embodied understanding, in which the body attunes itself to its environment as a gestalt "which reflects our felt and habitual relationships" and which dissipates when it is focused on (67). He says that in addition to believing in the promise of meaning in perception, "we have to let our attention be captured, not willed. We have to open to the world as a partner in dialogue that has to be given space to form." Its meaning cannot be "wrestled into our grasp" (67). Being open to the world—or things or beings in it—as a partner in dialogue and giving that dialogue space to form meaning is part of what I am getting at in saying we need to pay attention to the specific being, letting it be in itself, as Heidegger says. Mazis alludes to Heidegger in saying "this 'letting be' of the surround is . . . a matter of modifying the will or ego" (68). It is also what the teacher I quoted earlier is doing with her students when she says to them, "Can you say more about that?" The difference lies in being open to the world, as Mazis says, rather than listening from one's own space of meaning.

Attunement produces openness to possibilities largely through emotional attachment to aspects of the environment, feelings "that make us oriented and connected to phenomena in different ways that will enable us to know them in different ways" (Mazis 68). Mazis notes that through Chorost's earlier experience with hearing aids and with the implant, he realized that "to become able to hear with the potential that the machine provide[s] him, 'I would have to become emotionally open to what I heard'" (78, qtd. in Mazis 69). Mazis comments, "To experience the way machines can open parts of the world to humanity and become more kin to us will require an emotional relatedness to things of which they can become a part" (69). But I also argue that paying attention to the machines we interact with in ways that allow us to grasp the possibilities they offer depends on our feeling a connection with them and respecting them as specific things in themselves. Chorost not only became emotionally open to the people he interacted with but also more open to the implant. His initial fear of how his body and life would be changed by the implant was replaced by a more positive attitude toward the different reality it offered (Mazis 61–62).

Donna Haraway also argues that attunement is a matter of respect and "becoming with": "To knot companion and species together in encounter, in regard and respect, is to enter the world of becoming with, where *who and what are* is precisely what is at stake" (*Species* 19). She uses the term *respecere* to convey the many aspects of this relationship, which she contrasts with the "gaze" that is the focus of much cultural theory: "to have regard for, to see differently, to esteem, to look back, to hold in regard, to hold in seeing, to be touched by another's regard, to heed, to take care of. This kind of regard aims to release and be released in oxymoronic, necessary, autonomy-in-relation" (164). Haraway notes that companion species "is a permanently undecidable category, a category-in-question that insists on the relation as the smallest unit of being and of analysis" (165). The relation, the encounter, is the focus of attention both in Haraway's notion and in Whitehead's related notion of the unity of a prehension. As Whitehead says, "our whole experience is composed out of our relationships to the rest of things, and of the formation of new relationships constitutive of things to come" (*Modes* 31).

Respect and regard are not only essential to the habit of paying attention to the specific individual but also, as Haraway argues, to how entities are changed in the unity of prehension, how they "become with," transforming and becoming persuaded in the encounter. Her example is her experience of agility training with her dog Cayenne, which she says depends on a dialogue of response between the real, specific human and the real, specific dog. As she observes, "training is for opening up what is not known to be possible, but might be for all the intra-acting partners" (223). Respect and regard open up possibilities through paying attention to the specific other emotionally and physically as well as cognitively.

Haraway says she learned about *respecere* from her relationship with her father. Not surprisingly, families are one place habits of experience are acquired, and the encounter I turn to next also begins in a daughter-father relationship. Julie Zickefoose, a bird artist and wild bird rehabilitator, acknowledges her father in the preface to *The Bluebird Effect* by remembering him encouraging her to pat a tom turkey's head: "I still remember the jolt of pure empathy that coursed through me upon laying my hand on the bird's bare head . . . The warmth of his skin awakened something deep and primal, a realization that, despite his bizarre appearance and feathered armor, there was someone in there, someone I could understand" (ix). Zickefoose's belief that she can understand birds (and other animals) underpins all her writing. Her description of raising orphaned hummingbirds illustrates multiple points of importance: the importance of the habit of believing that strangers have something to communicate; the importance of the habit of emotional connection with specific individuals; the importance of finding new ways to listen.

Presented one July day with two sets of unfledged hummingbirds whose nests had been blown down in a storm, Zickefoose quickly learned to identify each of them by their behavior and subsequently named them. "Naming them honors their distinct personalities, proclivities, and idiosyncrasies," she says (79). She is often surprised by the way their behavior contradicts her beliefs about what hummingbirds can do. When she releases them from the aviary, they return and importune her for feedings for ten days, though the literature suggests that they should be independent at this stage. She is also happily surprised that, despite her earlier fears, she does not have to climb up to their high perches to feed them. She comments, "There is so much more going on in their tiny heads than I give them credit for" (71) and concludes:

> They know me, know my voice, my names for them. They have observed that I can't fly up to them as their own mother would, and they have the sense to come down to eye level to be fed . . . They listen for my voice in the house and come to the window where they can watch me. They peep and I call back; they beg and I feed them. They regard me as their mother, a strange, huge, earthbound, flightless mother, but a source of sustenance and even comfort . . . It is knowing what they know that utterly beguiles me, that has me humming with joy along the invisible lines that connect us. (84)

How does Zickefoose understand her hummingbirds? How does she come to know what they know? She believes that understanding them is possible. She responds to them as specific individuals in a specific situation. And in addition, she also has the habit of finding ways to understand them better.

She employs a variety of "speech prostheses" that enable them to become interesting and enable her to listen to them. She reads the scientific literature about them. Instead of being blinded by her assumptions—focusing on what everyone knows hummingbirds are—she pays attention to what these particular hummingbirds are capable of, what propositions they offer. Her interactions with the hummingbirds fit with Despret's understanding of polite experiments as a practice of domestication that proposes new ways to behave that transform both entities involved. Despret notes that "An intelligent animal may provide an opportunity for the 'becoming' intelligent of the ethologist who observes it" ("Body" 132 n8). Zickefoose's joy at knowing what they know demonstrates how allowing nonhumans to become interesting leads not only to new possibilities but also to wonder. At the end of *Modes of Thought*, Whitehead says, "when philosophic thought has done its best, the wonder remains. There has been added, however, some grasp of the immensity of things, some purification of emotion by understanding" (168–69). Like Whitehead, Zickefoose believes that by due attention more can be found in nature than that which has been observed at first sight: "Whatever is going on, I know that I will never be through learning about how birds' minds work" (88).

Polite scientific experiments are one way of listening to strangers, functioning as speech prostheses enabling humans to understand others on their own terms. Latour asks, "Who is better able than scientists to make the world speak, write, hold forth?" (*Politics* 137). As he describes further skills of listening that scientists use—making it possible "to shift viewpoints constantly by means of experiments, instruments, models, and theories"; "imagining possibilities"; and composing and sheltering knowledge "in forms of life, instruments, paradigms, teachings, bodily skills, black boxes" (*Politics* 138–40)—it becomes clear that these are the skills of researchers in all disciplines. He explicitly connects them with the discipline of sociology, for instance, in *Reassembling the Social*, where he explains to a graduate student that experimental description requires "very specific texts" and "very specific protocols" (155). These ways of listening, whether in an actual laboratory, in the field, or in a written text, are also ways of engaging in persuasion.[4]

The last encounter I offer is of a geochemist who combines wonder with very specific protocols of investigation in his study of Antarctic lakes. Observations of one of the lakes presented Bill Green with a proposition: "In Vanda, something seems to be removing the metals from the oxygen-rich shallow waters and releasing them to the oxygen-poor deep waters. We're just not sure what it is yet" (150). In Lake Vanda, it was cobalt he was especially listening to. A colleague suggested collecting water samples at different depths in the lake. In the midst of describing the arduous process of acquiring, transporting, and analyzing the samples, Green tells a story of cobalt's journey into the lake:

> What sound did the loosening of cobalt make, the adsorbed ion wavering a little like a minnow at the surface of a rock, then heading off downstream? How long did it stay in the lake . . . ? . . . Then what? Perhaps an encounter with the surface of clay, glazed with a few atom-thicknesses of manganese oxide. Then capture . . . The stone sinks . . . the cobalt all the while clinging, being basketed and woven in like Moses by the manganese . . . And in the oxygen-poor waters the manganese is reduced, falls away, unravels like a thread. The cobalt is free again, waterbound. Then another encounter: Something that was once living, a few cells still clinging together drift by . . . The branches reach out, enfold it: chelation. It is on its way to the sediments. Possibly to a small eternity there . . . But even buried you can hear it, you can hear the cobalt. Like the salt plains, you can hear it sing. (159–60)[5]

Cobalt is, of course, an element, and as Whitehead says, "the inorganic . . . lacks individual expression" (*Modes* 27). Still, Green's encounter with it at that site in that lake at that time is unity of prehension. As he and his colleagues observe, other lakes in Antarctica have different chemistries and different stories.

Cobalt sings to Green through the protocols, experimental apparatuses, and texts that have allowed him to pay attention to the interactions of elements in the world. They are habits that give him footholds, that attest to the reality of the world he is listening to. His handling of the samples evinces respect for their being: he describes his obsession with the purity of the samples, his exactitude in setting up the autosampler interfaced with the computer that translates the analyses of the samples into a graph relating the depth of the water and the concentration of cobalt, his impatience as the instruments repeated the analysis of each sample in triplicate. When Latour observed soil scientists in the Amazon using a pedocomparator that sorted and arranged samples with the same respect for their individuality, he concluded that through this process, "the earth becomes a sign" (*Pandora* 49). So, too, Green's due attention to what cobalt has to say allows it to speak. When at last he looked at the graph, he found that "Point for point, the curve for cobalt analysis matched the curve for manganese . . . The story was beginning to write itself" (163).

Like Haraway and Zickefoose, Green's habit of listening to strangers was homegrown—in his case, coming from his mother who collected shells on Cape Cod. He also recognizes the import of attending to the propositions that arise. He says that his work in Antarctica "raised questions that went beyond the purview of science": "questions about the way we experience the world and respond to its physical settings; how we decide, as individuals, to do with our lives what we do with them; the sources of our wonder; the nature of science itself" (xv). Listening to strange strangers has everything to do with all of these questions.

Fiumara observes that "There must be some problem of listening if we only hear from earth when it is so seriously endangered that we cannot help paying heed" (6). Humans have for far too long assumed that nonhumans are nonconscious automatons or inert material, lacking intelligence and thus having nothing to communicate to us. Far too often we assume a similar inferiority and uncommunicativeness from other peoples and cultures. If we "listen more, allow time, and assume intelligence" we can come to understand more of what other beings in the universe are communicating to us. Paying due attention to strangers whose opinions can infect us with new propositions—this is the new ontology of persuasion.

Notes

1. Both are highly fraught and undecidable ideas when applied to strange strangers.
2. Politeness is not a characteristic of the traditional understanding of persuasion in Western rhetoric. Rickert remarks that the pursuit of an ambient rhetoric, a project with which I am deeply sympathetic, "might seem to entail abandoning the realm of symbolic action or some permutation of what we *generally* call persuasion [which] is redolent of subjectivity, epistemology, and symbolicity" (160). Like Garsten, he argues

for saving persuasion by rethinking its basis, and like Whitehead, he sees persuasion as arising prior to rhetoric in encounters in the real world: "persuasion inheres in the environment and infrastructure and not just in the attitudes of people" (265).

3. For the full account, see Chorost's *Rebuilt: How Becoming Part Computer Made Me More Human* (Boston: Houghton Mifflin, 2005).

4. Jenny Rice argues for using Latour's method of tracing networks as a more effective form of public debate: "By encouraging subjects who relate to the world through questions, wonder, inquiry, investigation, archive, we are disallowing subjects who write themselves out of the scene of rhetoric" (196). In so doing, she shifts the notion of public subjectivity toward the kind of engagement with others on their own terms that is characteristic of politeness in persuasion.

5. Green is alluding here to Pablo Neruda's "Ode to Salt."

2
Implicit Paradigms of Rhetoric
Aristotelian, Cultural, and Heliotropic

John Muckelbauer

The question of rhetoric's pervasiveness has been a recurring conundrum for scholars, some of whom believe that the study and practice of rhetoric is most productive if we locate "the rhetorical" only in particular situations where there is a recognizable instance of conscious, linguistic persuasion (such as a presidential speech). Opponents of this position see these confines as artificial, and claim that rhetoric circulates far beyond these bounds. Not only are there nonlinguistic means of persuasion but there are also numerous instances in which persuasion occurs without anyone consciously intending to persuade. From this perspective, our culture (indeed, any culture) is saturated with rhetoric whether it recognizes this rhetoric or not.

At times, this debate has become explicit—in the context of the so-called Big versus Little Rhetoric debates of the late '90s and early '00s.[1] For the most part, however, questions about the scope of rhetoric or rhetoric's proper place have remained an implicit dimension of our scholarship. That is, whether one is a rhetorical critic or theorist or historian or anything else, we all operate with some kind of more or less vague sense of what we consider to be the paradigmatic scene of rhetoric. For instance, in one of Walter Ong's famous distinctions between speech and writing, he claims that one of the major differences between the two has to do with how context operates: "Context for the spoken word is simply present, centered in the person speaking and the one or ones to whom he addresses himself . . . but the meaning caught in writing comes with no such present circumambient actuality" (10). Ignoring, for the moment, the conceptual difficulties with this declaration of "simple" presence, my point here is that Ong is implicitly relying on a paradigmatic image of speech that would involve, say, a speaker addressing an attentive group of listeners in something like a conference talk (rather than, for instance, a telephone conversation, in which the interlocutors' contexts are not simply present to one another). It seems to me that Ong's implicit scene is an extremely common one for the field. In this chapter, then, I would like to attend to some of the implications of this particular implicit paradigm (what I will call an Aristotelian paradigm), outline some challenges to it from advocates of a more "cultural" or "everyday" paradigm, and then briefly offer a heliotropic alternative to both.

The most familiar of these rhetorical paradigms is rendered explicit in Aristotle's famous division of rhetoric into the three species of deliberative, forensic, and epideictic. In Aristotle's estimation, these three species were primarily distinguished by their temporal orientation: deliberative speeches were directed toward making some decision about the future, forensic speeches focused on the past, and epideictic speeches emphasized the present. However, in addition to their temporal differences, there are other, implicit attributes that these images of rhetoric presuppose.

First, and most obviously, each of these three species largely occurs in relatively formalized social settings: courtroom trials, political speeches, and eulogies rarely happen spontaneously on street corners. Instead, they each tend to occur in very particular places, even places (such as courtrooms or legislative assemblies) that are specifically designed to host these types of events. To this extent, it makes sense to say that Aristotle's vision of rhetorical species is a formal one, by which I mean only that it focuses on acts of persuasion that occur in relatively formalized social settings.

A second attribute that is closely related to the formal quality of Aristotle's rhetoric concerns the implicit presence of well-established social institutions, particularly legal institutions. For instance, while it would be unusual to have forensic speeches without the physical existence of courtrooms, it would be impossible to have them without the prior existence not only of laws but also of the whole apparatus of a legal structure. Law, in other words, is a two-fold necessity for forensic rhetoric. It is, first of all, the basis for whatever particular legal matter is being decided: the question of whether or not the accused committed a crime would not be a question without the pre-existence of the law. But second, and more fundamentally, the existence of the legal proceeding itself is premised on the pre-existence of a law that establishes the very procedures for making such decisions. It would not be difficult to imagine that the genre of "the courtroom speech" would be quite different if, rather than a legal system organized around a trial by a jury, our system were driven by, say, trial by experts—or even no trial at all.

And this "juridical" aspect also holds for deliberative oratory, in which individuals attempt to persuade each other about the right course of action for the polis. In some exceptional cases, these exchanges are not simply about policy, but might very well be about the law itself—arguing that we should alter or supplement the law in order to address unforeseen contingencies. As we all know, a large part of what legislative assemblies do is create new laws and update existing laws (even, at times, making new laws about *how* to make laws). However, even when the matter is not explicitly a question of law, but perhaps a more general one of policy—is defense spending or health care a better investment of resources for the polis? —the conditions for this question again presume the pre-existence of a law that establishes the structure and course for posing and debating these questions.

To this extent, we can say that Aristotle's species of rhetoric are not only *formal*, but also *juridical* in that they presuppose the existence of an institutional legal structure within which bodies deliberate on particular questions of law and policy (which is why Aristotle writes that "It is more proper that Law should govern than any one of the citizens" [*Rhetoric* 1287a]).

As usual, things are a little more complicated with epideictic rhetoric, since this species does not appear to presume the pre-existence of law in the same way that the others do. While paradigmatic instances of epideictic rhetoric often include things such as weddings and funerals, and while these occasions are still most often held at formal settings intended for such events, there is certainly a great deal more variability in how and where these events occur. Nevertheless, even with greater variability, these events still maintain at least the virtual presence of some kind of religious or civic institution that validates the proceedings, and this institution represents some form of law, whether man's or God's. Funerals and weddings rarely occur without the presence of someone who has been officially sanctioned to perform either the burial or the wedding ceremony.

However, the point still holds that, unlike forensic and deliberative rhetoric, epideictic does not appear to *necessarily* presume the pre-existence of law as its condition of possibility. This may well be the reason not only why Aristotle does not pay nearly as much attention to epideictic as he does to the other species of rhetoric, but why, historically, this species has received significantly less attention than the others (and has even at times been considered a lower form, as it does not seem to have any direct practical consequences). And based on the vast majority of criticism in the field, I would argue that the paradigmatic image of rhetoric held by most scholars is rarely, if ever, epideictic. Most often, when elements of "praise and blame" are considered, they are treated largely as attributes of either forensic or deliberative speeches. This is due to the fact that this so-called rhetoric of display does not have the same immediate and obvious legal implications that Aristotle and many others implicitly believe rhetoric should have.

This point might actually have significant consequences for the question of where and how rhetoric circulates. Recent historical treatments of rhetoric have found that the rise and fall of the study of rhetoric tends to occur with the rise and fall of democratic forms of government in the West. This connection makes a great deal of sense: it seems natural that rhetoric would flourish in societies governed by the rule of law and ones that solicit the active participation of their citizens in the governing process. In such cultures, citizens will want to become versed in rhetoric, as this will be their means for engaging in such activities as representing themselves in courts or affecting policy and law.

But my point here is a different one, and it is that the historical congruence might not be a case of some fundamental link between rhetoric and democracy, but more likely a result of one's implicit paradigmatic image of rhetoric. That is, if one follows Aristotle in defining rhetoric formally and juridically, then it is not surprising to then discover its prevalence in cultures that value the rule of law and participatory democracy. The implication of this would be that a different understanding of rhetoric would likely lead to a quite different story about the history of rhetoric and about rhetoric's place in our world today.

In order to begin to pursue the implications of this different understanding, I would like to return to a third attribute of Aristotle's "species" of rhetoric—one that is likely less contentious than either its formal or juridical inclination. Simply put, it is worth noting that for Aristotle, rhetoric is primarily concerned with oratory rather than writing. The one thing that courtroom speeches, eulogies, and political speeches have in common is, simply put, that they are speeches. Of course, just as is the case today, many of these speeches were first written down before they were performed (whether by logographers or the speakers themselves). Nevertheless, the point is that the circumstances of rhetoric for each of Aristotle's species were always situations in which an individual person would address a group in speech.

Of course, there are several explanations for this emphasis. The first, and most obvious, is that in the fourth century BCE a shockingly small percentage of the population was literate—somewhere around one or two percent. Given that such a small percentage of the population could read and write, it makes practical sense that Aristotle would locate rhetoric in venues focused on public speaking, as this was quite simply the most likely way that any given Athenian would encounter public issues.

But in addition to this practical rationale, there are also some intriguing theoretical implications of this emphasis. For instance, take Jacques Derrida's famous claim that Western thought has privileged speech over writing. Turning to Plato's dialogue *The Phaedrus*, Derrida in *Dissemination* notes that the character of Socrates offers a strong condemnation of writing, claiming that writing is inferior and derivative of "living speech." For Socrates, speech offers the promise of true subjective presence—the presence of a conscious, intentional subject who can answer for his words. If you and I are speaking and I am unclear about what you are saying, I can always ask you to clarify what you have said, or to use other words in order to help me understand what you intend to say. Writing, on the other hand, is dead, mute—or, more profoundly, it is a dead form that offers the false appearance of life. For instance, if you fail to understand the words I am writing, and you pose questions to them, they will not respond as a speaking person would; they will simply continue to say the same thing over and over again.

Further, not only does writing offer the false appearance of life, but it is also surprisingly promiscuous. While speech requires the simultaneous presence of a speaker and a listener, writing can function perfectly well in the total absence of the writer. In fact, this is the very condition of its function—writing can be entirely disconnected from the physical and/or mental presence of a writer. I write this essay precisely so that these words and thoughts can be disconnected from me, and go places that I had perhaps never imagined, much less intended. To take this to its extreme, writing can be read long after its author has disappeared or died, and it can be understood or misunderstood in ways that the author could never have intended. Not only could Plato never have imagined that his writing would be discussed nearly 2,500 years after his death in a collection about rhetoric edited by some English professors in the United States, but he also had no control over *how* he would eventually be discussed. There is no way for me to know if I am being true to his intentions or distorting them without trying to. And I would have to contend with the possibility that Plato's intentions may have been exactly the opposite of what I (and other scholars) imagine them to be—keep in mind that this whole critique of writing was in fact *written* by Plato. Could it all have simply been a joke? And how would we ever know for sure?

In any case, the privileging of speech over writing in Aristotle's rhetoric is symptomatic of this commonplace privileging of intentionality and consciousness (as opposed to the supposedly mute promiscuity of writing). And this privilege becomes more pronounced when we consider the species themselves.

For instance, the circumstances of deliberative and forensic species both depict situations in which an individual employs the strategies of argument in an effort to consciously convince a larger group about some particular issue. The speaker, therefore, acts on the basis of a clear, conscious intention: to win a particular case or defeat a particular vote. And she uses various arguments in order to accomplish these things.

The listeners, however, are a more diverse group: some may be well disposed to the speaker's position while others may be deeply opposed. But regardless of their predispositions, the listeners are on the verge of being faced with some kind of recognizable decision: they will have to choose to find the defendant innocent or guilty or they will have to choose to vote either for or against the policy.

While the traditional image of epideictic rhetoric continues to rely on the importance of intentional argument, it again works a bit differently than the other species. This image still depicts a single speaker consciously attempting to influence a larger group; however, this influence does not necessarily take the form of a choice that the audience will make. That is, at the end of the funeral speech, it is not expected that the listeners will necessarily do any particular thing at all. While there is still an intention behind such speeches—the speaker wants to produce a certain kind of feeling in the listeners, whether of pride, inspiration, respect, or admiration—this affect does not necessarily terminate in any definitive kind of decision.

So in addition to offering formal, predominantly legalistic orientations through speech, Aristotle's image of rhetoric (an image, I am claiming, that remains an implicit paradigm for much current scholarship) also presumes the importance of intentional argument and, in most cases, the immediacy of a recognizable decision (on the part of those being persuaded).

Of course, each of these implicit attributes of Aristotelian rhetoric has been more or less directly challenged in the last few decades, largely as a result of the sense that they not only artificially limit the realm of rhetoric, but more profoundly because they present a dramatically oversimplified and reductive image of how persuasion actually happens in the world.[2] In other words, the issue is not whether or not forensic, deliberative, and epideictic are really rhetorical species, but whether or not these species cover all (or even most of) the spectrum of rhetorical action. For many of us working in the field today, the answer to this would be a resounding "no." And yet it is unclear to me if the implicit paradigms that govern our thinking about rhetoric are really as distinct from Aristotle's as we might claim.

First and least controversially, rhetoric scholars challenge the formal quality of Aristotle's species. While this is clearly the emphasis of Aristotle's work, it is certainly mistaken to imply that deliberative rhetoric is necessarily confined to situations of organized legal decision-making. There are undoubtedly many kinds of deliberative bodies—from faculty meetings to corporate boardrooms—in which groups of people gather together in order to make decisions about their future course of action. Most would agree that in these scenarios, rhetoric continues to play a crucial role.

Things become a bit more contentious when we reduce the size of the group: am I practicing rhetoric when I try to persuade my friend over lunch to support gay marriage in an upcoming referendum? Well, yes. Even on Aristotle's terms. After all, we have most of the telltale signs: an overtly democratic issue, an impending political decision, the presence of subjective intention, and an emphasis on argumentation. All that has really changed is that the setting is less formal—not only less formal than the meeting of a legislative body, but even less so than that of a faculty meeting.

Now, what if, instead of trying to persuade my friend to support an issue via an upcoming vote, I am simply trying to persuade her to pay for our lunch? In this scenario, we are no longer dealing with an overtly democratic issue or an impending *political* decision. But of course there is still a decision—she will either agree to pay or not—and there is still the presence of a subjective intention, and still an emphasis on argumentation.

This is the first of what I believe are two crucial hinges for thinking about the prevalence of rhetoric, because if one accepts that this scenario is rhetorical, the scope of rhetoric expands significantly (and expands much further than even many advocates of this image are willing to pursue). Rhetoric now moves not only out of its relatively formalized institutional space, but it also now treats any content whatsoever. As a result, the everyday conversations in which we try to persuade others to go to the movies, or pick up some food for dinner, or help us with a task—all these become rhetorical moments. But why stop there? Why not include those moments when we attempt to persuade ourselves to, for example, go to the gym or finish reading this chapter? Would we not also consider these instances of rhetoric? Indeed, rather than solely remaining an art confined to courtrooms and wedding chapels, rhetoric would become a practice in which everyone is engaged all the time.

One crucial consequence of this shift is that one must fundamentally reorient one's conception of rhetoric. Instead of seeing "everyday" rhetoric as banal or idiosyncratic instances of the formalized, institutional art of Aristotle, we would have to completely reverse this perspective. That is, perhaps our paradigmatic image of rhetoric would become such everyday instances of persuasion, and Aristotle's forensic, deliberative, and epideictic species might just be highly specialized and idealized instances of this commonplace practice.

If we are able to shift this perspective, then a great many other things will follow. First, let us consider the privilege accorded to argument (and thereby to language). If we take everyday persuasion as our (admittedly vague) paradigm case, it quickly becomes apparent that people are frequently persuaded by things that most of us would not readily call arguments (and that certainly are not primarily linguistic). For instance, we are often persuaded by images, or sounds, or even by physical structures.

I am thinking here of Bruno Latour's famous speed bump example, in which a mass of concrete functions to persuade drivers to slow down.[3] Of course, one might justifiably say that the only reason a speed bump is effective is because drivers will extrapolate an argument from it: "If I do not slow down, I will damage my car." Nevertheless, a speed bump is not in itself an argument—it is merely a mass of concrete. But that does not make it any less persuasive—if anything, it makes it *more* persuasive. The point here is that everyday physical structures may not exactly be arguments (and they are certainly not primarily linguistic—though they are surely integrated with language), but they are undoubtedly persuasive. As a result, it is important to consider these types of objects as crucial components of rhetoric.

But this very same logic would apply to many other physical structures: not just the exceptional speed bump, but the everyday physical existence of roads themselves. Simply put, roads are rhetorical in that they persuade drivers to go some places rather than others. Anyone who has lived in a small town that was circumvented by some kind of highway bypass can attest to the significant economic and cultural consequences of these rhetorical artifacts. They are indeed highly persuasive objects, encouraging certain types of behavior and discouraging others. Of course, as is the case with all persuasion, roads do not simply *determine* people's actions—not only is it possible for a person to get off the highway and visit the small town, but more simply, one can always go off road. There may be consequences to ignoring roads, but this simply indicates the complexity of any rhetorical situation.

The larger theoretical point is that if we take everyday rhetoric as our paradigmatic instance (rather than as a particular occurrence of an Aristotelian paradigm), our view of rhetoric starts to change. We begin to see that arguments—and even language—may not be the fundamental grounds of persuasion. Indeed, even if we return to Aristotle's formal, juridical species, it is questionable as to whether argument alone is sufficient to understand the actual practice of persuasion *even in those settings*. Consider the image of lawmakers arguing about a policy decision. Is it really the case that "arguments" made in these venues are the primary determiners of the decision? Certainly there are all kinds of persuasive variables that go into any such decision, some of which may have nothing to do with the issue at hand—maybe I am hungry and want to leave to get some food, maybe the person trying to persuade me reminds me of a childhood enemy, maybe I am leveraging this issue for some future interest, etc. One could extend this list indefinitely. And indeed, I may not even be consciously aware of all or even any of these other forces. I might believe, for instance, that I am cautiously and attentively listening to the argument and weighing the policy implications in a reasonable manner. But most of us now believe that the human psyche is not simply reducible to my conscious awareness—whether or not I am aware of the multiple persuasive forces acting on me would not simply determine their effectiveness. So while I might likely never be fully aware of all the multiple forces that constitute the rhetorical dimensions of a situation, this does not mean they are irrelevant or that rhetoricians can simply continue to ignore them in favor of focusing on the recognizable argument.

But for the sake of provocation, I would be inclined to go a step further and say that, despite the emphasis of our field for over two millennia, it is actually extremely rare for one person to persuade another solely with an argument, regardless of whether the argumentative paradigm comes from Aristotle, Rogers, Toulmin, or any other. Even though we continue to teach, research, and act as if linguistic argument is or should be a crucial hinge of all decision-making, it seems to me that intra-human persuasion only very rarely happens so immediately, clearly, and instrumentally as our focus on argumentation implies. Is it possible, then, for the field to take such complexity into account?

Consider another historical example of a rhetorical moment that further amplifies the unconscious and unintentional aspect of much persuasion. The first color image of the earth taken from space was printed in 1967 (while the more famous "blue marble" image dates from 1972). This image is so ubiquitous to us now that it is hard to imagine a world in which it did not exist. Nevertheless, prior to 1967 almost no humans had actually seen this sight. Shortly after this image was released, the modern environmentalist movement in the United States began (usually dated around 1970 with the first Earth Day). This likely was not a mere coincidence. As a result of the distribution of this image, a great many more people began to think of the earth as a living thing and even potentially as fragile and in need of care. Obviously, this image was used in the context of arguments advocating environmentalism, but the first point here is that, like the case of the speed bump, the image of the earth is not in itself an argument. And yet, nevertheless, it clearly had a persuasive impact on people—perhaps simply by making them more susceptible to listening to arguments advocating environmentalism. The second point, however, is that this persuasive effect was not the intention of the NASA technicians that outfitted a satellite with color photography. But even if it had been, this image produced persuasive effects (even if only a slight change in perception or attitude) without an argument and without the necessity of a conscious intention.

The point, for me, is that if we can break out of the implicit paradigmatic commitments of Aristotelian rhetoric, the line of thought that follows from this break will lead to an image of rhetoric that does not require a formal setting, a legalistic orientation, an argument, language, or even the presence of an intending subject. If rhetoric is not only at play in all our casual conversations, but is also circulating through speed bumps, roads, and pictures, would this not effectively mean that everything in our culture is rhetorical?

And this is the point at which many cultural approaches to rhetoric today arrive. Having freed themselves of the constraints of Aristotle's implicit paradigms, they offer instead an image of cultural rhetoric that begins with everyday acts of persuasion and necessarily includes the multiple (nonlinguistic, unintentional, and nonhuman) variables that are part of such persuasion.

But again, why stop there? Why limit ourselves to "cultural" instances of rhetoric? Why not consider that there may be "natural" instances of rhetoric as well. To my mind, this is the second significant hinge for thinking about the scope of rhetoric (and the most important one today)—the possibility that "the rhetorical" might move beyond not only the formal, juridical image of Aristotle's, but also beyond "the cultural" image of everyday rhetoric and its anthropocentric emphasis.

For instance, in the last few years, scholars have begun to explore the rhetorical quality of animal activity.[4] While animals may not use language, they certainly exhibit all kinds of persuasive behavior. As George Kennedy points out, the qualities of courtship and sexual selection among animals indicate a wide variety of persuasive behavior—ones that could potentially teach us a great deal about how persuasion actually happens. As a field, however, we have largely ignored such instances of persuasion because they do not cohere with the implicit Aristotelian paradigm.

So I would like to close by offering a different paradigmatic image of rhetoric—one that (I hope) is distinct not only from the formal, legalistic, argumentative qualities of Aristotle's species, but also from the broader, cultural image of "everyday" rhetoric. To my mind, the implicit paradigmatic image of rhetorical studies today should be the event of heliotropism, or the movement of plants toward the sun. I recognize that this image will not be easily accepted, precisely because it seems to deal with the domain of nature rather than culture—in other words, there is nothing whatsoever human about a plant turning toward the sun. And that, to me, is its advantage—allowing for the possibility of flattening out the nature-culture distinction that is absolutely fundamental to the field. This distinction is made explicit in something like Burke's action-motion distinction, but it is implicit in virtually all rhetoric scholarship. (To be clear, by "flattening out" this distinction, I do not mean "erasing." I am not interested in rendering culture indistinguishable from nature, but simply in interrupting the desire to treat them as fundamentally different kinds of things [a difference usually premised on the distinctiveness of consciousness]).

In any case, rhetoric and heliotropism are not entirely unrelated phenomena. After all, the word itself derives from *tropos*, which of course is also the etymological basis for the tropes or figures that were historically seen as the very element of rhetoric. And there are also some further hints of precedent for this connection. Not only did Aristotle disparagingly refer to the Sophists as "being like plants" (*Metaphysics* IV 1008b), but Kennedy also, in his consideration of animal rhetoric, points to the persuasiveness of plants. He writes, "Since the activity of insects and birds is essential to disseminating pollen and thus to the survival of the plant's species, by coloration and sweetness even plants can be said to practice a rudimentary form of rhetoric" (*Comparative* 24).[5] Of course, whether or not color and taste are "rudimentary" (and not rather "fundamental") is a question I will leave open for now.

But there are also conceptual justifications for this image. As Michael Naas has shown in his analysis of Homeric rhetoric (a book that deserves more attention from our field), this sense of simply "turning" is a more adequate rendering of an earlier, pre-Platonic sense of persuasion, one that only mutated into the consciousness-driven sense through Aristotle and his teacher. In other words, rather than indicating two different kinds of things, *perhaps figures of speech are simply very determined, linguistic instances of a larger rhetorical tropology of persuasive turning.* That is, plants turning toward the sun and audiences accepting an argument might well involve the same kind of action/motion. As a result, as rhetoric scholars, we would have a lot to learn from plants (and from the botanists who study them) *about persuasion itself.* By this I mean that the goal would not be to show the rhetorical quality of botanical discourse, but to *learn about persuasion from plants*—or any number of other so-called natural and artificial phenomenon. And I would argue that this style of promiscuous interdisciplinarity is crucial if we are to begin to take seriously how persuasion actually happens in the world.

The objection will be raised, of course, that this is simply an argument for an even bigger sense of big rhetoric. Perhaps. Yet for me this is not at all the claim that everything is rhetoric, but rather that everything is rhetorical. The debates about the size of rhetoric were always too concerned with hypostasizing rhetoric as a noun and as a domain. Instead, we might consider "rhetoric" primarily as an adjective, or better yet, an adverb—that which modifies or qualifies actions in some way. That is, everything is necessarily immersed in (and constituted by) multiple persuasive (turning) forces. And as such, everything is . . . rhetorically. However, a crucial element of the claim that "everything is rhetorical" is that this claim should come at the beginning of an inquiry rather than as a conclusion. In other words, when one knows that something (such as a speed bump) is rhetorical, that does not mean that it is the same as a courtroom speech; quite the opposite. In fact what it means is that one must rigorously attend to the different rhetorical forces in these different settings. Claiming that "everything is rhetorical"—rather than indicating some fundamental similarity—means precisely that things are immersed in (and constituted by) differential forces of turning. The task of rhetorical scholarship (and frankly any research whatsoever) would be to attend to these differential tropological fields. And to paraphrase Aristotle, the task of rhetorical training would be similar: to affect a turning whereby the rhetorical tropology of things—both human and nonhuman—becomes visible.

Notes

1. See, for instance, Gross and Keith for a collection of essays dedicated to this question.

2. Here I would point to any number of recent books that advance challenges to the so-called humanist paradigm in rhetorical studies. See, for example: Davis, *In-*

essential Solidarity; Muckelbauer, *The Future of Invention*; Rickert, *Ambient Rhetoric*; and Vivian, *Being Made Strange*.

3. I take this example from Latour's *Pandora's Hope* (186).

4. See, for example, Hawhee; Davis, "Creaturely"; Muckelbauer, "Domesticating."

5. Thanks to the anonymous reviewers of the essay for calling my attention to these two plant-onic moments in rhetorical history.

3
Rendering and Reifying Brain Sex Science

Christa Teston

In spite of scientific advancements, concussions and other brain-related debilitating diseases such as Parkinson's disease, Alzheimer's disease, and posttraumatic disorder baffle us. Anecdotes, lore, and pseudoscience abound. In April 2013, Barack Obama initiated an investment of $100 million of federal support in an initiative called the Brain Research through Advancing Innovative Neurotechnologies (BRAIN) project. Controversy surrounding the BRAIN project illustrates our fraught relationship not only with the materiality of the human brain, but also with methods for how the brain should be studied, and the public policy decisions that result from those studies. Meanwhile, scholars in rhetorical studies caution against using the prefix "neuro" as a value-free, objective qualifier for claims about human behavior, cognition, and differences between men and women (see Jack and Appelbaum; Pruchnic; Gruber et al.). In light of rhetorical scholars' neuro-critiques and in anticipation of results from various BRAIN studies, in this chapter I explore the rhetorical ontologies from which claims about brains can be made. I extend the work of Celeste Condit, who in 1996 asserted that "bad science stays that way" because scientists are sometimes unreflective about ideologies that inform their scientific inquiries, hypotheses, methodologies, and findings. The bad science that Condit and I take to task is brain sex science, or science that postulates differences between sexes based on visually and statistically rendered differences in human brains.[1]

Anne Fausto-Sterling argues that the brain is "a perfect medium on which to project, even unwittingly, assumptions about gender" (118). Perhaps the BRAIN project will help make definitive claims about whether or not sex differences in the brain truly exist. Perhaps this project will put to rest arguments in favor of same-sex educational policies (referred to by Halpern et al. as pseudoscience). Perhaps linkages between brain scan images and women's capacity for caregiving—linkages that yield arguments about women being "hardwired" for parenting (Medical Xpress)—will temper.

Rather than make assertions about how scientists use the brain as a sounding board for hegemonic assertions about the differences between men and women, in this chapter I explore one way in which facts about brain sex science are rendered and reified by and through partnerships between human and nonhuman agents—in particular, null hypothesis significance testing (NHST). This chapter is divided into four sections. In the first section, I provide more detail about Condit's critique of bad brain sex science. I set out to extend Condit's critique through an analysis of how brain sex science is accommodated (Fahnestock) for popular audiences. The results of this analysis are reported in the second section. After finding results from this analysis to have limited explanatory power for how bad science stays that way, I trace arguments about brains and sex differences to their source. I then ask how inferences about difference and similarity among male and female populations are made. In the third section, therefore, I detail a theoretical framework for understanding inference-making as rhetorical and ontological. Finally, I report on NHST as a rhetorical ontology that disciplines scientists to see difference and significance in particular ways. I explore the nature and propagation of so-called bad science by characterizing scientific methods (e.g., NHST) for enacting phenomena (e.g., inferring difference or similarity) as rhetorical ontologies. That is, methods such as neuroimaging and statistical analysis, due in part to their disciplining materiality, exert suasive force.

Condit's Critique

Nearly two decades ago, Celeste Condit engaged in a contentious debate with authors of an article published in *Science*. These were researchers who, like other brain sex scientists at the time, hypothesized that "men and women's brains are significantly different" ("Bad Science" 88; see Gur et al. for the original *Science* articles about which she writes). Rubin Gur et al. infer, based on their study, that differences between men and women with respect to cognitive and emotional processing "have biological substrates" (528). Condit's fundamental critique of Gur's hypothesis is that it assumes only dimorphic differences between men and women's brains. Such a hypothesis, according to Condit, renders possible only certain ways of knowing about difference, specifically that "any minor locatable difference counts as substantive and important" and "*averages* are taken as signifying *essential* differences" (Condit 96). Condit concludes as a result of this debate that "bad science stays that way" because scientists are sometimes unreflective about ideologies that inform their scientific inquiries, hypotheses, methodologies, and findings.

To clarify, according to Condit, "bad science" is not necessarily science that makes "errant contact with material reality" (100). Rather, bad science is that which "produces results that are far less rich than they should be, given the available scientific tools and linguistic structure, as well as the reasonable possibility that human biological sex features diversity" (100). Condit's critique is rooted in feminist epistemologies proposed by scholars, such as Sandra Harding, who suggest that "the selection of hypotheses and research tools both constitute major loci where biases can be introduced into science."

In order to extend Condit's research into how bad science stays that way, I offer an analysis of brain sex science articles that have been accommodated (Fahnestock) for popular audiences. This analysis only shifts the blame for bad science away from scientists' misguided hypotheses (per Condit) and toward popular science writers who failed to account linguistically for the intricacies of scientists' approaches and findings. In either case, the faulty mechanism lies in the lap of language's epistemological limitations. I conclude this analysis by suggesting that methodological materialities with which scientists partner when constructing claims about the human brain—materialities that exist well prior to the accommodating move—are overlooked as key contributors to how bad science is both rendered and reified.

Brain Sex Science, Accommodated

Hypothesizing that bad science stays that way in part because of what happens to it once it enters the public domain, I examined scientific articles that had undergone what Fahnestock refers to as accommodation. "Scientific accommodations emphasize the uniqueness, rarity, originality of observations, removing hedges and qualifications and thus conferring greater certainty on the reported facts" (275). Rather than examining shifts in genre, as Fahnestock did, I investigated how popular scientific writers warrant neuroscientific claims about sex differences in the human brain. Article titles alone illustrate how popular science publications sensationalize and reify hegemonic, cultural and social behaviors based in presumed sex differences.

Consider Eiman Azim et al.'s article, "Sex Differences in Brain Activation Elicited by Humor," which was published in the *Proceedings of the National Academy of Sciences of the United States of America*, and its accommodated counterpart published in *Discover Magazine*. While the original scientific article is entitled "Sex Differences in Brain Activation Elicited by Humor," the accommodated version is entitled "Women Don't Understand." Condit's argument that scientists too often assume that human brains are dimorphic is supported by article titles in *Scientific American* such as "X and Y Brains" (Weber), "Sex Differences in the Brain" (Kimura), and "His Brain, Her Brain" (Cahill).

Assumptions in article titles were reflected in their content as well. All articles included in this small-scale study are accommodated, popular science articles published after Condit's 1996 article. Guided by popular science magazine rankings, I limited my analysis to articles in *Discover Magazine, Nature Magazine, Newsweek, Psychology Today*, and *Scientific American*. I mapped accommodated popular science articles about brain sex science onto actual scientific articles that inspired them. However, original scientific articles drew on several previous studies and articles, either to ground their deployment of a previous study's methodological approach or to build on previously published data. To mitigate the unwieldiness associated with tracing claims and their corresponding data, I constructed Toulminian traces for each accommodation instance. Below I describe a representative sample from this analysis. This includes a Toulminian trace of data, claims, warrants, and backing between and among Azim et al.'s "Sex Differences in Brain Activation Elicited by Humor" and its accommodated counterpart (Casselman's "Women Don't Understand). Findings from this small-scale analysis suggest that, once accommodated, sex differences are gendered. In other words, rather than enrich our understanding of brain-based sex differences, these accommodations describe sex-based brain differences.

I mobilized Toulmin's (2003) model for argumentation to trace how the accommodated publication (Casselman et al.'s [2006] "Women Don't Understand") came to be. The scientific studies and methods that back and warrant respectively in a Toulminian sense Casselman et al.'s (2006) argument includes Azim et al.'s (2005) findings in "Sex Differences in Brain Activation Elicited by Humor" and statistical analyses of 20 fMRIs. Azim et al.'s (2005) study asked participants to subjectively rate 70 verbal and nonverbal cartoons as funny or unfunny. Azim et al. (2005) analyzed their data by comparing blood oxygenation-level-dependent signals during funny and unfunny stimuli. The researchers found that females activate their left prefrontal cortex more than males, which suggests a greater degree of executive processing and language-based decoding. Azim et al. (2005) argue that their results point to the presence of sex-specific differences in neural responses to humor. They infer that such a finding has implications for sex-based disparities in cognition and emotion. When providing specifics about their methodological approach, Azim et al. (2005) cite Reiss (2003). Such methodological specifics embody Toulminian warrants and backing for their key claim. Reiss (2003) published an article entitled "Humor Modulates the Mesolimbic Reward Centers" motivated by the following research question: What are the subcortical correlates of the most fundamental feature of humor—reward? Reiss's (2003) methods section provides highly technical descriptions of the fMRI techniques and statistical tactics employed in the study. Reiss (2003) describes how findings were rendered in the laboratory right down to how voxels were activated and analyzed using multiple univariate regression analysis. These details back Reiss's (2003) findings, which go on to warrant Azim et al.'s (2005) arguments.

Unearthing the nested nature of Reiss's (2003) research within Azim et al.'s research (2005)—findings from which are nested within claims that Casselman et al. (2006) leverage in their accommodated publication—provides a bit more detail about accommodated arguments' parts of speech. There are myriad contributors to the construction of scientific fact in this and each of the articles I analyzed. What each Toulminian trace affords a clearer picture of, however, and what is most significant for the purposes of this chapter, is the provenance of particular claims. That is, on what material and methodological conditions are claims about the brain made? This analysis suggests that functional magnetic resonance imaging (fMRI) and NHST were two of the most frequently deployed methods of data collection and analysis across all scientific publications. Moreover, once scientific facts are accommodated for popular audiences, details pertaining to fMRIs and statistical analyses are rendered invisible, if not lost. Rhetoricians of science and medicine understand that these details are important because they are not neutral tools that humans use to construct knowledge about other objects. These objects have a history. They exert agency. They are apparatuses in which human and nonhuman actors are ensconced and enmeshed.

It is true, as Condit argues, that scientists' ideological positions shape the kinds of research questions they ask and influence their methodological dispositions and findings. It is also true, based on a Toulminian trace of a representative sample of scientific publications, that there are preaccommodating, nontextual contributors to final claims. I hypothesize that these preaccommodating, nontextual factors "back" in a Toulminian sense the ideologies Condit critiques. Functional magnetic resonance imaging renders brain activity visible with voxels, computer programming, and colorful imagery. Scientists pair fMRI and NHST to make inferences about differences and similarities based on those renderings. In the next section, I describe a theoretical framework for reconsidering bad science not just as a problem of ideologies, but also a problem of rhetorical ontologies.

Rhetorical Ontologies in Science

Scholars in rhetoric of science have long been concerned with the problem of extratextual fact-constructing agents in the laboratory. Chad Wickman, for example, addresses materialities of scientific knowledge-making. He does so instrumentally, however. In other words, Wickman attends to materialities of scientific knowledge-making with the fundamental assumption that those materials are tools used by humans in some goal-directed activity. For Wickman and others, inquiries proceed with questions about how those materials are used toward a particular end, or how they are wielded by the scientist toward some final, epistemological goal. However, what if we take our inquiry further? What if we ask about not just what these instruments do *for* scientists, but also how they do this work in relationship to one another? What do they do to or *with* scientists? What are these objects' potentialities? Their agencies?

Most readers are likely familiar with Bruno Latour and Steve Woolgar's work wherein they demarcate facts from artifacts (236). Latour and Woolgar insist on "the importance of the material elements of the laboratory in the production of facts" (238). They clarify, "*our argument is not just that facts are socially constructed. We also wish to show that the process of construction involves the use of certain devices whereby all traces of production are made extremely difficult to detect*" (176, emphasis in original). Motivated by Latour and Woolgar's desire to unveil "traces of production" made invisible by discursive representations and accommodations, in the next section I explore how NHST exerts ontological suasiveness.

In his examination of brain scans and ontologies of fibromyalgia, Scott Graham argues that material objects exert suasive influence, and that rhetorical agency comes from a "material-semiotic network" ("Agency" 400). The relationship between materials and semiotics is fraught with ambiguity, however. Consider the following positions:

> Position A: "Values and interests cannot be inactive in the search for understanding, because they are inherent to the materiality of language in which knowledge must be constructed. They are not 'froth' or 'mist' with no discernible weight on matter. They have material effects on any search for understanding, knowledge, or truth. Only by recognizing this materiality can a scientist—or humanist—correct for the biases languages introduce." (Condit "Race" 403)
>
> Position B: "Discourse is not what is said; it is that which constrains and enables what can be said. . . . [D]iscursive practices produce, rather than merely describe, the subjects and objects of knowledge practices. . . . [T]he basic idea is to understand that it is not merely the case that human concepts are embodied in apparatuses, but rather that apparatuses *are* discursive practices." (Barad Meeting 146–148, emphasis in original)

In Position A, Condit draws attention to language's suasive capacity during conversations among geneticists about causal relationships between genes and race. In Position B, Karen Barad sees such a material-semiotic relationship as overly representationalist. Barad asks readers to consider ways things or objects afford and constrain human concepts—not just that we linguistically describe things or objects and thereby exert ontological power over them through language. Moreover, Barad asserts that matter and meaning are "iteratively reconfigured through each intra-action" (Meeting ix), where "intra-action" is "the mutual constitution of entangled agencies" (33). Lamenting our representationalist imperative, Barad claims that "the only thing that doesn't seem to matter anymore is matter" (132). Similarly, Richard Cherwitz and Thomas Darwin argue that "this tendency to approach meaning as a function of *either* objects or language use leads to an inability to account for the simultaneous capacity of language to be constrained by *and* shape objects" (17).

The problem of "bad science" is greater than ideological constructions of what counts as fact or sensationalized accommodations of scientific facts to lay audiences. The problem of bad science is as much ontological as it is ideological or epistemological. It is as much material as it is linguistic. Michael Callon, Pierre Lascoumes, and Yannick Barthe argue that "what human beings can say and write, what they can assert and object to, cannot be dissociated from the obscure work of the instruments and disciplined bodies that cooperate and participate in their own right in the elaboration of knowledge" (57). The authors are careful to qualify the work of instruments and disciplined bodies as participating *in their own right*. Callon et al. describe Edwin Hutchins's *Cognition in the Wild* as illustrative of the ways in which instruments and artifacts play a critical role in ship navigation. In what follows, I build from Callon et al.'s "in their own right" qualification to explore assemblages of both human and nonhuman objects when making inferences about differences and similarities (among brains).

To provide a robust account of how bad science stays that way, we must attend to the rhetorical ontologies that afford, constrain, and fortify scientific facts. In what follows I proceed with an inquiry into how bad science stays that way based on the fundamental assumption that ideologies are *enacted or practiced* (see Annemarie Mol's *The Body Multiple* for a detailed investigation and explanation of ways realities are enacted). Said enactments involve complex assemblages of both human and nonhuman objects. They involve, for example, not just scientists and statisticians, but also medical imaging devices and NHST. Scholars in rhetoric of science often describe materials and methods as the means by which science is legitimated by scientists. In what follows I seek to shed assumptions about methodological materialities as mere means. I seek to trace our entanglement with NHST as a rhetorical ontology that participates "in its own right" in the enactment of sex differences in brain function.

Mathematics and Null Hypothesis Significance Testing (NHST) as Rhetorical Ontologies

Borrowing Barad's refusal of a "representationalist fixation on words and things," I define rhetorical ontologies as entanglements of devices, disciplined bodies, and discursive practices that co-construct phenomena. Rhetorical ontologies undergird scientific hypotheses, motivate methodologies, and fortify findings. I invite readers to resist the temptation to limit critiques of bad science to scientists' assumedly faulty (and in some cases hegemonic) epistemologies or ideologies represented by their linguistic hypotheses (and popular science writers' accommodations). Rather, I encourage readers to consider the relationality between devices, disciplined bodies that "participate in their own right" (Callon, Lascoumes, and Barthe 57), and scientists' discursive practices. Specifically, I invite readers to consider the ways NHST disciplines scientists to see in certain ways—ways that might, indeed, be ideologically charged and socially or culturally insensitive.

Very few scholars have attended to the ways mathematics is more than an invisibilized form of writing. And yet mathematics is bound by time and space. To illustrate this, Brian Rotman in *Mathematics as Sign: Writing, Imagining, Counting* proposes a semiotic account of mathematics, and reminds readers that chaos theory and fractal geometry exist precisely because of computer-generated images (67). He argues, "mathematical objects, by being constructed inside a computer, reveal themselves as materially presented and embodied" (69). For Rotman, then, mathematics is a "technosemiotic apparatus" (106) that includes ideograms, diagrams, tools for reasoning, thinking, predicting, and imagining, as well as a system for writing and manipulating actual, material symbols. Motivated by Barad, Cherwitz and Darwin, and Rotman's theories, I revisit Condit's critiques of bad brain sex science and attend explicitly to how facts are fortified epistemologically and ontologically—through both objects and language. Inferential statistical analyses such as NHST have a history. They discipline. They devise. How? And what might it mean for scientists who rely on, for example, analysis of variance (ANOVA) to render findings about differences in the human brain? How might ANOVA discipline scientists' final claims—final claims that, after they are accommodated and popularized for public audiences, shape how we think about who we are and ought to be (e.g., good versus bad mothers; better versus worse at math)?

One might question the efficacy of a mathematics-as-rhetoric characterization (i.e., "isn't math what Aristotle would call an inartistic proof?"). Mitchell Reyes, however, has challenged Aristotelian assumptions that mathematics is arhetorical. For Reyes, mathematics is "something other than pure logic" (163). In order to make this argument, Reyes examines Newton's and Leibniz's idea of the "infinitesimal"—a "rhetorically constituted" construct that ultimately had major implications for practice both within and outside the mathematical discipline (167). Similarly, James Wynn argues that Charles Darwin's use of mathematics to make arguments about the origin of species helps us think of how mathematics, and quantitative comparisons in particular, can be used rhetorically. "With evidence from calculated averages, precise numerical comparison and argumentation from the commonplace of the *more and the less*, [Darwin] reasons that patterns of correlation exist between the size of populations and the development of variation within related subpopulations" (87, emphasis in original). According to Wynn, Darwin spoke into existence correlations and variations by using mathematics. Instead of calculating averages, Darwin used "ratios of varieties to species" in order to understand species variation. Moreover, Wynn argues that were it not for Darwin's "overt quantitative comparisons and behind the scenes mathematical operations," his claims about natural selection "would have been purely speculative. But by using precise data and mathematical comparison and a quantitatively informed commonplace, Darwin hopes to establish for his argument an *ethos of precision and rigor*" (87, emphasis in original). This "ethos of precision and rigor" is never more apparent than in scientific publications akin to the ones Condit critiques. Note, however, that even in the two examples of mathematics-as-rhetoric above, suasiveness is limited to humans who merely deploy the mathematical system instrumentally (Newton, Leibniz, Darwin). Let us also consider how the mathematical system is more than mere tool. Let us consider how the mathematical system "participates in its own right" in the construction of scientific fact, specifically as can be observed in the enactment of inferences.

Null hypothesis significance testing (NHST) is but one locus of human-nonhuman partnership in the construction of scientific fact. Such testing is a method of data analysis that affords inferences about group differences. However, NHST affords inferences about group differences that, although significant statistically, may in fact be quite small. In many cases, the overlap among groups is far greater than differences between them. When such is the case, small group differences become reified and magnified, especially once those small group differences move into the popular press. Even prior to accommodation, however, small group differences are, quite often, transformed erroneously into nominal categories. Here, unwittingly, NHST does its thing. Good science is sure to confess such reifications and magnifications through articulations of effect size, even if it means the strength of the resultant claims is diminished. In what follows, I attend to several additional ways NHST exerts suasiveness that may or may not yield bad science. The only way for me to see NHST's suasiveness is by examining entanglements between human and nonhuman objects when enacting inferences. Below are some of the moments at which human and nonhuman objects co-construct phenomena from which inferences can be enacted.

Null

Nickerson concedes that "null" is intended to "represent the hypothesis of 'no difference' between two sets of data with respect to some parameter, usually their means, or of 'no effect' of an experimental manipulation on the dependent variable of interest" (242). Herein lies the first potentially problematic suasive contributor: are the results of NHST indicative of *no difference* or *no effect*? Ultimately, when a researcher rejects the null hypothesis, such a result is typically thought to mean that their alternative hypothesis is *right*. This is not always the case, however. Joseph Berkson illustrates this through an example that could be characterized as an unwarranted syllogism. "Consider [the argument] in syllogistic form. It says 'If A is true, B will happen sometimes; therefore if B has been found to happen, A can be considered disproved.' There is no logical warrant for considering an event known to occur in a given hypothesis, even if infrequently, as disproving the hypothesis" (qtd. in Nickerson 267).

Group Means

Difference or similarity is detected by assembling two or more groups. Generalized knowledge about those groups is rendered through group means. Already the mathematical mechanism exerts suasive power by summarizing or distilling whole populations into a group mean. Dissenters to NHST might suggest that these group means are a kind of logical fallacy—a constructed strawperson, composition, or hasty generalization fallacy. The same can be said for the ways in which "mean differences" are constructed. Those who deploy NHST are now required to report effect size, which is believed to guard against fallacious logical inferences.

Difference

Many have noted spurious ways in which differences between sexes are discerned in the first place. For instance, Cordelia Fine describes how if twenty researchers test for sex differences, even if there is not an actual difference between the populations, one researcher will find a statistically significant difference. She argues, "given [that] the publication process is geared toward emphasizing difference rather than similarity, this 1-in-20 finding of difference will be reported while the 19 failures to find a difference will not" (281).

Significance

The ways in which statistical significance in NHST is determined can be problematic as well. For instance, Joachim Krueger reminds readers that Karl Pearson, the mathematician who is credited with establishing statistics as a discipline, "could not reject the hypothesis that his coin was fair after 24,000 flips and 12,012 heads" (18). Steven Goodman argues that the emergence of significance only occurs because "whatever effect we are measuring, the best-supported hypothesis is always that the unknown true effect is equal to the observed effect" (1007). In other words, small effects, even when significant, can evade "significance" as an inference.

Each of the above examples demonstrates how NHST "in its own right" can produce fallacious or misleading findings. There is a good deal of internal dissent among researchers about how scientists hide behind NHST's "ethos of precision and rigor," effectively taking advantage of a method that may produce fallacious or misleading findings. In a scathing critique of NHST, Raymond Nickerson summarizes some of this dissent. In these critiques, we hear echoes of Condit's critique about the lack of richness in scientific findings. Imre Lakatos wonders "whether the function of statistical techniques in the social sciences is not primarily to provide a machinery for producing phony corroborations and thereby a semblance of 'scientific progress' where, in fact, there is nothing but an increase in pseudo-intellectual garbage" (88). Gerd Gigerenzer claims that NHST is "surely the most bone-headedly misguided procedure ever institutionalized in the rote training of science students" (335). William Rozeboom argues, "NHST provides researchers with no incentive to specify either their own research hypotheses or competing hypotheses. The ritual is to test one's unspecified hypothesis against 'chance,' that is, against the null hypothesis that postulates 'no difference between the means of the two populations' or 'zero correlation'" (200). James Shaver claims that NHST is dysfunctional "because such tests do not provide the information that many researchers assume they do"; he additionally claims that it "diverts attention and energy from more appropriate strategies, such as replication and consideration of the practice or theoretical significance of results" (294). Frank Schmidt and John Hunter argue that, logically and conceptually, "the use of statistical significance testing in the analysis of research data has been thoroughly discredited," adding that "statistical significance testing retards the growth of scientific knowledge; it never makes a positive contribution" (37).

Among the dissenters, Rozeboom actually sympathizes with researchers who deploy NHST; he claims that researchers simply do not know how to discipline that which disciplines. He argues that it is understandable that the scientist unquestioningly applies NHST. Specifically, Rozeboom says that the research scientist should not "be held responsible for the principles of the computers, signal generators, timers, and other complex modern instruments to which he may have recourse during an experiment" (416). Rozeboom seems to understand the ways in which NHST exerts suasive force well enough on its own, even prior to ideologically misguided motivations. Rozeboom concludes that NHST is used inappropriately when what is rendered as a result is "a *decision* rather than a *cognitive* evaluation of propositions" (428). Rozeboom is keenly aware of the ways in which NHST disciplines scientists to see certain things and not others, in turn making it possible for some inferences to be at once mathematically viable, statistically significant, and also socially irresponsible.

Conclusion

What I have tried to do in this chapter is call attention to rhetorical ontologies that render and reify ideologically charged claims about difference and similarity with respect to sexes and human brains. I have extended Condit's criticism that scientists sometimes produce "results that are far less rich than they should be" beyond considerations of ideological or epistemological concerns and into material, rhetorical ontologies. The above analyses confirm Condit's claims that "any minor locatable difference counts as substantive and important" and "*averages* are taken as signifying *essential* differences" (96). Attention to NHST as a suasive contributor to the enactment of differences and similarities affords another explanation for how it came to be that minor differences become nominal and averages become essential. The lack of richness Condit identifies, therefore, is rooted in more than ideological error or linguistic failure.

I have also demonstrated that textual analyses of accommodated science can only provide us with a one-dimensional understanding of how scientific facts are rendered or reified. Had I concluded this inquiry with the Fahnestock-Toulmian analysis described in the second section, I would have "produced results that are far less rich than they should be" (Condit 100). Accounting for how methodological materialities render and reify difference and significance captures some of the complexity associated with how scientific facts are enacted. Furthermore, representing for readers the internal strife among scientists with regard to their perception of NHST's shortcomings provides nonscientists a fuller understanding of how publication does not always suggest scientific consensus. As a related aside, in an informal conversation about this chapter with a clinical psychologist who uses both fMRI and NHST in his own research, I asked why, given the ways these methods limit his work, he still defers to them as a way to construct scientific facts. He replied somewhat exhaustively: "This is what we have." Mindfulness that there is not always consensus about certain methodological paradigms in a particular discipline might mean we take more time to understand scientific disciplines' histories, theories, and debates—debates that are often had not in plain sight, but behind ideologically charged, popular-science publication curtains. (As another related aside, this meant I had to go clear back to Fisher's "Studies in Crop Variation" in order to understand the very economic and material origins of inferential statistics.) I hope this chapter encourages us to consider how our own instruments and disciplined bodies exert suasive power as we go about our work (e.g., the ways in which Toulmin's model for argumentation disciplined this chapter's earlier analysis of accommodated popular scientific articles). Future studies might carefully consider the role of fMRI and its constitutive rendering properties (e.g., magnets, radio waves, bloodflow, computers, screens, voxels, etc.). Additional investigations into alternative statistical techniques for enacting difference and similarity (e.g., taxometric and Bayesian methods) would help to further our understanding of how methodological materialities exert suasive power in science.

Note

1. Regarding so-called sex differences, Eagly and Wood reiterate that "sex" is defined by the Oxford English Dictionary as categories "into which humans and most other living things are divided on the basis of their reproductive functions" (10). However, "observed differences between women and men are termed *sex differences*, regardless of their causes. The term *gender* is then free to refer to the meanings that individuals and societies ascribe to males and females" (10, emphasis in original).

4
Alinea Phenomenology

Cookery as Flat Ontography

Katie Zabrowski

> An ontology is flat if it makes no distinction between the types of things that exist but treats all equally. . . . In a flat ontology, the bubbling skin of the capsaicin pepper holds just as much interest as the culinary history of the enchilada it is destined to top.
>
> Ian Bogost, Alien Phenomenology

Alinea, Grant Achatz's famed Chicago eatery, serves a single course of lamb consisting of 86 individual components. Plated together on a single sheet of glass, garnishments for the lamb (itself served separately as a kind of blank canvas) range from variations on ingredients such as blueberry, fava bean, black licorice, couscous, coffee, and smoke. During its preparation chefs place a labeled grid beneath the glass to aid them in arranging elements according to an organizational scheme. Diners, however, receive the dish without the help of explanatory labels. Lacking any more knowledge of the identity of the ingredients than speculation provides, diners must first taste them to determine what it is they are ingesting. Upping the stakes for accurate identification is the fact that these ingredients are intended to be combined both with other ingredients and the lamb they are meant to garnish. The dish, named Lamb 86, does not arrive at the table preformed as if to impose a particular combination of ingredients, but instead invites diners to join in its becoming.

Not simply an innovative take on plating, Lamb 86 is also an ontograph. In *Alien Phenomenology*, Ian Bogost describes an ontograph as "a record of things juxtaposed to demonstrate their overlap and imply interaction through collocation" (38). As an ontograph, Lamb 86 lays bare its parts, tuning diners to its diversity of ingredients and their potential for combination. By separating and collocating ingredients that might ordinarily remain unaccounted for in combination with others, the dish makes pronounced the complexity of a whole by complicating its parts and placing them together on a grid. For Bogost, and for this chapter, attending to distinct units challenges our assumptions about how individual units might be combined. In this flurry of assuming, we are likely to overlook or wrongly classify units that exert rhetorical force among other units. Ontography commits to the work of engaging with distinct units as they are unto themselves, and it does so by tracing—but not imposing or assuming ahead of time—individual units' potential for relationship with other units.

Cookery that functions in this deliberative way is quite distinct from Plato's denigration of rhetoric to cookery based on the fact that it is "evildoing, deceitful, ignoble, and unfree, deceiving with shapes, colors, smoothness" (*Gorgias* 465b). Plato's pejorative use of cookery situates some rhetorical elements as additives rather than agents fundamental to the coordination—or, to use Margaret Syverson's language, co-construction[1]—of rhetorical situation. Anyone who has added a pinch more salt and a sprinkle less sugar to a cake batter knows that every granular element matters for all the others, and therefore likely sees the error in Plato's understanding of cooking. No ingredient is, for cooking or for rhetoric, *mere* garnishment. In Plato's ontology, however, ornamentation (rhetoric) does not play a co-constructive function but rather serves as deceptive flattery, distracting from the "real" or "true" construction. Frosting as flattery, then, would be said to distract us from the real taste of the cake, without itself being a constructive element. It is, however, an element no less real than the others; after all, frosting makes the cake.

In addition to overlooking the efficaciousness of all rhetorical elements, Plato allies flattery and ornamentation with the feminine, noting how *she* "pretends to be this that it has slipped in under, and gives no heed to the best but hunts after folly with what is ever most pleasant" (464d). With this contention he reveals he is mistaken about more than cookery. He—as an early, chauvinist correlationist[2]—insults the feminine by aligning it with what he deems ignoble in addition to refusing to acknowledge the complexly vital nature of each and every rhetorical element. The unfortunate consequence of this move has been a reluctance to see just how generative the analogizing of rhetoric with cookery can be for rhetoric's ontological turn. This turn, a relatively recent—or recently popular—move for rhetorical studies, is steered by increasing scholarly interest in nonhuman actors. Attunement to the material suasion of nonhuman objects and processes has precipitated a change in the field's persisting epistemic methods. The move away from epistemology calls for an expansion of rhetorical inquiry beyond human-centered approaches. Thinking rhetoric ontologically evades and counters a correlationist privileging of human perception as the condition for nonhuman existence by attending more to a nonhierarchical understanding of existence. In doing so, rhetoric recognizes the materially suasive nature of objects as independent from human use of, or assumptions about, them.

Plato's worry about cookery is that it mixes together the "good" with the "bad" or the "true" with the "false," thereby diminishing the dividing line between a whole host of other contentious binaries. Ontography *is* still "mixing it up;" however it does so in the way cookery mixes together equally existing ingredients. Ontography—and, in particular, *flat ontography*—helps us record all elements as equally existing and therefore equally rhetorical. By placing ingredients together on a flat grid equidistant from one another, Lamb 86 is a flattened ontograph that refuses to establish a hierarchical order among individual ingredients. The flatness of ontology is made particularly apparent by cookery, as there is no cooking without some intra-action of elements that all share the capacity to affect and be affected by the others. As in the case of the cake, the frosting needs the sugar just as much as it needs the salt in order to be palatable.

Cookery understood as flat ontology exemplifies a strategy important for revitalizing inquiry into all rhetorical elements, and the material realm in particular. Reclaiming the cookery analogy helps us to see how rhetoric functions ontologically without the Platonic pitfall of using a gendered, uneven ontology. In other words, cookery helps us see rhetoric as flat ontology. Under Bogost's definition, it is clear to see how Alinea, and cookery more generally, could be said to perform flat ontology. In the case of Lamb 86, the course's name is not a label or definition so much as it is ontography—a sort of list or litany that maintains its components' distinctness by way of an organizational grid yet hints at their interobjectivity by placing them side by side, readied for combination.

In order to reclaim the cookery analogy we must contend with Plato's two missteps in regard to the material and feminine spheres. I propose reimagining cookery as flat ontology as a strategy for revitalizing inquiry into the ontology of all rhetorical elements and the material realm in particular. I contend that a revitalized inquiry of this manner helps us reconsider rhetoric as deeply material and principally concerned with the complicated material relations circulating among the humans and nonhumans that assemble our worlds. Revisiting the valuation of rhetoric as cookery ultimately reveals that the analogy is an especially apt one for seeing rhetoric's generative activity within the complex of human and nonhuman relations. A revised conception of cookery invites us to see in Alinea's Lamb 86 an occasion of rhetorical cookery functioning in the way it always already has been—as flat ontology.

Cookery: Rhetoric :: Ontography: Ontology

Plato's evaluation of rhetoric describes it as distracting us from the objectivity of the objects that generate its influence. For Plato this distraction is of the kind that steals away our ability to recognize distinction, which is, apparently, the way we come to *know* things. He writes in the *Gorgias*, for instance, that with rhetoric "all matters would be mixed up together in the same place, with the things of medicine, health, and cookery indistinguishable" (465d). Unable to tell the difference, we are served deceit and yet still taste truth. Put another way: we naively and passively ingest what rhetors and rhetoric prepare for us.

Alinea's Lamb 86 reveals a different kind of cookery, one more closely aligned with the kind of ontological interest characteristic of rhetoric's present moment, which sees the vast nature of existence. Whereas the dish's emphasis on garnishments might seem to echo Plato's criticism of rhetoric as cookery—that is, being all embellishment with little meat behind it—we might instead take the dish as uncovering the primacy of *all* objects for rhetoric.

In many ways, Lamb 86 exemplifies the ontographical method of the litany. With its 86 individual elements it is, likely to Plato's chagrin, an explosion of the category of things "mixed up together," and yet it is still an analogy better equipped than his to signal the nuances of cookery as a rhetorical ontology. Bogost points to the presence of lists in the work of both Bruno Latour and Graham Harman. According to Bogost, lists of objects constitute an ontographical method. He calls Latour's lists "litanies," and Harman has followed suit. The purpose and benefit of litanies, says Bogost, are "their real purpose: disjunction instead of flow. Lists remind us that no matter how fluidly a system may operate, its members nevertheless remain utterly isolated, mutual aliens" (40). The litany saves us from privileging humans, imposing a narrative structure fraught with anthropocentric and patriarchal biases.

Bogost's appraisal of lists shares this chapter's understanding of their facility in maintaining flat ontology, where humans are not placed above the material in such a way as to assert that humans exist more or more significantly than things. The litany is one way to take note of complex and complicated relations among individual units without inscribing an uneven or hierarchical ontology. The door his account opens for rhetoric stands at the threshold of becoming. Bogost presents lists as "an antidote to the obsession with Deleuzian becoming, a preference for continuity and smoothness instead of sequentiality and fitfulness" (40). His alien phenomenology, he writes, is not about the compatibility and relations between things, but about their incompatibility. Bogost ties this emphasis on alienness to object-oriented ontology (OOO), the widely discussed philosophical movement with which his text can be aligned. He writes that "the inherent partition between things is a premise of OOO, and lists help underscore those separations, turning the flowing legato of a literary account into the jarring staccato of real being" (40). He takes issue with literature here for its traditional narrative structure that puts things together in a way that disguises their disjunctiveness. Lists, upon reading, are jarring. The literal flow of our reading is disrupted as we traverse the commas between words in a list both visually and with our breathing. This jarring is productive, attuning us to the distinctions between objects. What Bogost and OOO do differently than rhetorical ontography is rest with a notion of objects as complicated aliens without probing the complexity of their intra-action. Rhetoric's explicit focus on relations calls us to affirm the difference between OOO and rhetorical ontology as another instance of the historical and ongoing philosophy versus rhetoric debate.

This chapter is concerned explicitly with the possibility of relationships between individual rhetorical elements. So how can ontography qua Bogost contribute to a rhetorical understanding of ontology if it assumes the opposite? The partial answer is that Bogost's focus on distinction and disjunction is not, in fact, diametrically opposed to rhetorical ontology. Rhetoric, after all, accepts disjunction; only it understands it as disjunction of an affirmative flavor. That is, even the lack of connection among things is a kind of relationship. The rest of the answer to the question of ontography's contribution to a rhetorical understanding of ontology can be pieced together through this chapter's engagement with Lamb 86. Because ontography works to reveal the material and nonhuman realms as "placed on the same ontological footing, with no privilege granted to the humans in this armada of entities" (Harman "Latour Litanies"), we can treat Lamb 86 as a rhetorical litany and thereby articulate differently the nature of rhetorical relationships between things.

Ontography is not arbitrarily jumbling things together; rather, functioning in a way similar to Latour's litanies, it "involves the revelation of object relationships without necessarily offering clarification or description of any kind" (Bogost 38). We can see the parallel here to Alinea's label-lacking lamb course and its seemingly endless possibilities for object relations. Clarifying Lamb 86 with explanatory labels would unflatten the dish and the ontography, in the way that clarifying butter ostensibly removes its impurities but actually results in a substance other than butter. Clarifying—in both the sense of a cooking method and an explanation of object relationships—constitutes the separation of individual components for the purpose of preserving the better ones, unencumbered by those lesser. Clarified butter privileges milk fat, separating it from the water in butter in order to produce a purer (fattier) butter product. Ontography wishes not to clarify for the purposes of reducing and separating components in order to achieve something singular, but rather to reveal the assembled nature of complex systems. This is precisely what Lamb 86 does by exploding and laying bare the number and collocation of garnishments.

The distinction between clarification and revelation is central to ontography's project. As Bogost explains, ontography involves noting relations between things, recognizing that things "exist not just *for us* but also *for themselves* and *for one another*, in ways that might surprise and dismay us" (50–51, emphasis in the original). To further his articulation of ontography, Bogost draws a comparison between ontographs and the information design technique of exploded view diagrams. These diagrams, he explains, are drawings similar to assembly instructions—

showing in great detail how individual parts relate and work together. He identifies in these diagrams the capacity to reveal the "unfamiliar repleteness" (52) of complex systems, a richness of "countless things that litter our world unseen" that we often take for granted and to which ontography strives to draw our attention. We can learn from these diagrams and enjoy them as aesthetic pieces; we can also learn about how a complex system operates as well as how "to fathom a small aspect of its murky otherworldliness" (52). We can, in other words, witness the alienness and effectiveness of all things, particularly those that persist most often beyond our perception.

Rhetoric thought ontologically extends its inquiry into the murky otherworldliness of objects that assemble the objects we *do* notice. Cookery, at its most basic, is a kind of assembling. We might consider recipes a sort of exploded view, the ingredients an ontographic cataloguing of objects irreducible to but constitutive of the final meal. Lamb 86 bears a striking resemblance to the exploded view diagrams Bogost presents in his book in that the sheer number of ingredients and their possible permutations inspire the diner to account for all of the elements. Should the dish arrive at the table already prepared, with 86 ingredients combined instead of separated onto a grid, the diner would have no opportunity to bask in the murkiness of cookery's own "unfamiliar repleteness." The dish succeeds as flat ontography because the fava bean, couscous, smoke, and 83 other ingredients stand on ontological footing as flat as the plate of glass on which they are served.

Cookery read as flat rhetorical ontography reveals *all* ingredients as equally playing a role in the emergence of a meal and likewise sees all things as equally existing for rhetoric. Further, cookery's status as a generative, performative activity centered on objects and *making things* by way of their combination—their being assembled with other things—situates it as capable of what Bogost calls "philosophical creativity" (93). Working with Harman's notion of carpentry, Bogost describes philosophical creativity as the activity of "making things that explain how things make their world" (93). Making is the important term here, as it signals our doing something with things rather than merely talking about those things. Only in this way does our speculating about their natures evade the anthropocentric underpinnings of correlationism. The cook, and by way of analogy the rhetor, must, as Bogost explains the carpenter does, "contend with the material resistance of his or her chosen form, making the object itself become the philosophy" (93). Cookery and rhetoric, then, are not meant to explain things—as rhetoric's epistemic tradition strives to do—but rather to see their natures emerge in the process of making something with other things and with us. Our participation in this emergence is not dominating or directorial, but rather marked by a sincere investment in the abilities of all actors in a system to affect and be affected by all the others that are a part of their world.

Much of this making consists of exploring relations between things in such a way that reveals their alienness by seeing the kinds of distinction uncovered in relation. It is not a distinction that serves to divide, but rather to uncover sites of relation. It is by making that we come to know, rather than coming to know what has already been made. Knowing the latter is impossible, especially if we accept vitalist principles that assert the dynamic, always-emerging nature of being. Rhetoric understood as generative, as ontography, is of the kind best suited for philosophical sincerity toward all objects in light of their continual emergence. For cookery none of the ingredients are mere garnishments. Similarly for rhetoric: everything matters.

Framing rhetoric with a more generous reading of cookery is one way to investigate the intricacies of the kinds of material suasion so apropos in rhetoric today, opening it to realms beyond Platonic, discursive rhetoric. In jumbling things together, rhetoric, like cookery, measures all elements and accounts for their influence. In this way, cookery is far from the mere ornamentation that Plato described. It is instead a fundamental methodology that requires of us, and of all implicated objects among which we dwell, an active participation marked by the two-sided coin of the abilities to affect and to be affected. We can look again to the cake batter as an example. The salt affects the sugar by enhancing its sweetness, and the salt is affected by the sugar working to ensure the salt does its work while passing across the tongue undetected. It is upon this axis of affecting and being affected that we see how objects can equally exist without always existing equally, as Bogost suggests (11). That is, the sugar and salt are both elements vital for the recipe. Even though sweetness appears the dominant taste, it is because of the configuration of sugar and salt together that the cake emerges as the sweet thing it is. In this way, salt's savory existence is not, and cannot be, diminished.

An exploded view of rhetoric, something cookery helps us to conceive, must account for more things than the discipline's history has traditionally. Like Bogost's assembly instructions and Lamb 86's organizational grid, ontography in rhetoric works to account for its own repleteness, tracing more components and recognizing the ways those exist for one another and not just for us.

Alinea Phenomenology: Revisioning Material Rhetoricity

Plato's division between the masculine and feminine sphere, aligning the feminine with values he deemed less worthy than those aligned with the masculine, places units of an ontology on different planes. This kind of distinction ignores the interobjectivity of those units, as well as the role each plays as co-constructor of the ontology. Whereas Plato deployed cookery as a description of an immoral and unproductive thing, cookery as we deploy the term prepares us to ingest the ethical and generative dimensions of rhetoric being made more pronounced in the discipline's ontological turn. Rhetorical ontography helps us understand differently Plato's appraisal of rhetoric as unsavory, and by doing so we can answer calls in rhetoric for alternative, material accounts of its methodologies.

Contemporary examples of supposedly unsavory cookery—and also particularly effective rhetoric—are the techniques and attitudes of the contentiously named *molecular gastronomy*. Many chefs feel relegated to this sector of cuisine—described as molecular because of its use of unconventional cooking techniques and technologies that work upon the foundational elements of ingredients. These chefs who employ liquid nitrogen, spherification, deconstruction, sous vide, and many more advanced techniques dislike the term "molecular gastronomy" as an explanation of their craft because of its tendency to reduce their art to science. In this rejection of the terminology we see a parallel to our rereading of cookery. These chefs—Grant Achatz, Ferran Adrià, Jose Andrés, Heston Blumenthal, and Thomas Keller among the most well known—contend with the valuation of their cookery as "molecular," and the pejorative scientific connotations that follow, in much the same way rhetoric scholars take issue with Plato's aligning of rhetoric with a negative reading of cookery. Of course, one obvious objection to the term is that cooking has always been "molecular." To label what these chefs do as molecular gastronomy is at best redundant and at worst an insult that reveals an abiding ignorance about what cooking is and always has been. That is, cookery is a deliberative, transformative, and generative process rather than a reductive breaking down of complex wholes. So too is rhetoric.

These so-called molecular gastronomists feel so strongly about being properly understood, in fact, that Adrià, Blumenthal, Keller, and food science writer Harold McGee teamed up in the British newspaper *The Observer* to release a "Statement on the 'New Cookery.'" The statement consists of four principles that describe the work of the new approach to cooking of which they consider themselves to be a part. Most pertinent for us is their description of the statement's exigency. Its authors believe their cookery is misunderstood, and in particular that "certain aspects of it are overemphasized and sensationalized, while others are ignored." They address the term *molecular gastronomy*, calling it "fashionable" and contextualizing its advent in 1992 "to name a particular academic workshop for scientists and chefs on the basic food chemistry of traditional dishes." Pointing to this workshop and the term associated with it is not an attempt to resist the work of the collaboration between science and cooking. In fact, they admit "the disciplines of food chemistry and food technology are valuable sources of information and ideas for all cooks." The desire to resist *molecular gastronomy* as a label for their work comes instead from the term not being comprehensive enough. Their collaboration extends beyond a relationship with science, reaching out to "artisans and artists (from all walks of the performing arts), architects, designers, industrial engineers." Science, we can deduce, is one of those aspects of their cooking they believe to have become overemphasized and sensationalized. Self-conscious of being labeled reductionist, so-called molecular gastronomists appear to dance a tango similar to the one that philosophers and rhetoricians dance together, tiptoeing along the line between idealism (privileging human perception) and realism.

Chefs such as Achatz and the authors of the new cookery perform work populated by relations between objects that often play out beyond the realm of human perception. This is what makes Lamb 86 unique; it unapologetically draws diners' attention to the relations between individual ingredients that they do not normally encounter. Decentering humans, these chefs dip their toes in both idealism and realism with their concern for object relations. Their reaction against *molecular gastronomy* is not unlike the accusations of reductionism that have been hurled at both realism and idealism. In his book's introductory section, titled "The State of Things," Bogost reflects, "culture, cuisine, experience, expression, politics, polemic: all existence is drawn through the sieve of humanity, the rich world of things discarded like chaff so thoroughly, so immediately, so efficiently that we don't even notice." He wonders further, "how did it come to this, an era in which 'things' means ideas so often, and stuff so seldom" (3). He points to philosophical history for a clue, noting especially idealism for making so much of "being" dependent on human perception of existence. The new cookery, relational and rhetorical as it is, is neither reductive realism nor idealism; it is ontographical.

Alinea's Grant Achatz in particular seems to have anticipated charges instituted by critics against his cuisine with a preemptive strike at naming, thereby defining his restaurant in terms more precisely reflective of its rhetorical action. The name Alinea is one shared with the symbol used in writing and editing to signal a new paragraph and therefore a new idea—otherwise known as a pilcrow—and is intended to call attention to the generative nature of the cuisine. The case of Alinea is a helpful one for our discussion because its rhetoric recognizes the power within its techniques and attitudes—its cookery—to affect and generate a complex dining system that acknowledges the roles its diners, ingredients, techniques, objects, atmosphere, and more play in the emergence of meals. The *newness* of "the new cookery," and Alinea in particular, is akin to that of a "new" rhetoric; it is, in the words of the authors of the "Statement on the New Cookery,'" a move that "values tradition, builds on it, and along with the tradition is part of the ongoing evolution of our craft." New cookery's "evolution" is similar to the new orientation within rhetoric that this chapter suggests. Neither endeavors to overturn tradition—I agree with Plato after all that rhetoric is cookery—or even to be tradition's additive. Instead, each understands innovation as a deployment of traditional materials and processes in ways that make different features of those more pronounced.

The cuisine's methodology is object- and ingredient-centered, and it is insistent upon the relations that occur when those objects and processes come together. It is so object-centered, in fact, that these relations are what constitute the cuisine. Breaking traditional ingredients and techniques down to their elemental parts and calling attention to those miniscule pieces—as Lamb 86 does by positioning them on a complex grid—is an occasion of gastronomy reseeing its past. In this way, the cuisine as a whole is a kind of flat ontology.

The mathematical formula for determining the number of possible permutations of Alinea's garnished lamb, 86! (factorial), yields a truly colossal number of flavor combinations: 24,227,095,383,672,732,381,765,523,203,441,259,715,284, 870,552,429,381,750,838,764,496,720,162,249,742,450,276,789,464,634,901, 319,465,571,660,595,200,000,000,000,000,000,000 to be precise. Diners are invited into this collection of sensuous qualities as it requires their participation in order for the dish—as a complex, self-organizing system of which diners are a part—to emerge as a meal. "Lamb 86" is a description of the relational possibilities that inhere in the course as a system of potentially relating objects. The distinction between definition and description is an especially important one given rhetoric's current ontological focus. As Bogost explains, defining elements would work as a "correlationist amplifier" (40). Correlationism maintains human perception as a necessary component of the existence of things. It is, in that way, anthropocentric. Alinea's litany of ingredients does the philosophical work of what Bogost describes as "hon[ing] a virtue: the abandonment of anthropocentric narrative coherence in favor of worldly detail" (42), but it does so rhetorically. Lamb 86 centers itself upon the rhetorical vitality of things and their propensity for relating to other things, and therefore does not arrive at the table with a sort of narrative structure already imposed. The relating has yet to be done. Out of our own way we can then embark upon the philosophical work of knowing objects *as they are* rather than *as we assume they are*.

From the perspective of object-oriented ontology, Lamb 86 constitutes an occasion of what Harman and Bogost term *carpentry*. Diners encounter the dish—come to *know* it, we might say, as witnesses to the potential relations between its ingredients. The meal emerges from the complex system of which the 86 ingredients, the lamb, the diner, the diner's ability to discern the identity of the ingredients and further combine them according to his or her taste preferences, the diner's skill with a fork and knife, the physical space of the restaurant and its ambiance, the chefs, the servers, the kitchen tools, and many more elements—material and immaterial—are a vital part. None of these elements are to be privileged over any other. Each holds the same kind of capacity to affect and be affected; each share equal ontological footing.

Given the extraordinary number of possible relations between the course's elements, the dish and its constitutive objects necessarily and unceasingly withdraw from a diner's firm grasp of them. At a practical level, there is no way for a single diner to exhaust and enjoy all of the possible permutations the dish's ingredients could yield.[3] In addition, it is unlikely that any two diners will enjoy the same combination or sequence of ingredients. In much the same sincere spirit with which rhetoricians approach rhetorical ontologies, diners, too, participate in the emergence of the course understanding that an enormous number of flavor relations will necessarily elude them. They can never taste and know the course's full potentiality; they can never grasp the extent of relations that inhere in this complex system of which they too are a part. This should in no way diminish our resolve to continue cooking, making, and eating. Instead, it reveals our responsibility to "interrogate, test, and unfold" (Glenn 15) the materials we encounter.

Diners at Alinea are, as Harman reflects he is, "condemned by [their] own inherent limits to choose from a restricted range of possibilities for exploring the vastness of the universe" (Guerrilla Metaphysics 49). In spite of this limit, diners still implicate themselves in this system of relationality by building multi-ingredient bites with their forks and knives. Just as diners accept the impossibility of tasting all of the potential combinations among the dish's 86 garnishments, so too must we submit to the fact that full knowledge of complex systems always evades our grasp. Still, we cannot be dissuaded from digging in. Instead, a flat ontology, along with all of its elements, invokes our participation always. By admitting our lack of knowledge, "honing a philosophical virtue," we become all the wiser. Honing a rhetorical virtue, we become material. With this admission we also open rhetoric to the elements we have failed to invite to our consciousness but whose existence prevails nonetheless. For some time, materiality has been the element most strikingly undervalued in rhetorical accounts. We have a responsibility to ourselves and to all objects with which we share our worlds to continue this work.

In enjoying a number of flavor combinations before the lamb runs out, diners do their best to make sense of the individual objects placed before them. Although they cannot exhaust their knowledge of the system, diners do play a hand in making one possible meal emerge. They do so in precisely the same kind of capacity as all the other objects involved. Acting almost as catalysts, diners set in motion relations between objects whose prior rhetoricity—a function of both their being plated together as well as their having chemical structures whose combinations yield palate-pleasing results—is itself a glimpse of objects making their world. Influencing the meal in the way any element in a complex system makes its significance known, diners are "making things that explain how things make their world" (Bogost 93). Making things in this way, in a manner that attends to how each of these elements makes others and determines others' roles in a system of relationality, constitutes participation concerned with more than gustatory pleasure. Alinea's open, deliberative cookery is akin to the material methodologies rhetoric is left wanting in its current ontological moment. Jumbled together among the complex of humans and nonhumans, flat ontography guides our treatment of all individual units as the rhetorically efficacious materials they are even long before we decide to understand them as such.

Notes

1. In her *Wealth of Reality* Margaret Syverson writes composition as ecology. An ecology, she suggests, "is a set of interrelated and interdependent complex systems." We can see rhetorical situations as such a system. As she explains, "in a complex system, a network of independent agents—people, atoms, neurons, or molecules, for instance—act and interact in parallel with each other, simultaneously reacting to and co-constructing their own environment" (3).

2. Correlationism is philosopher Quentin Meillassoux's term for the prevailing logic in post-Kantian philosophy that assumes that reality can only be known in terms of its significance for human beings. Correlationism, Meillassoux writes, is "the idea according to which we only ever have access to the correlation between thinking and being, and never to either term considered apart from the other" (5). The term correlationism has since gained traction in the works of speculative realists and object-oriented ontologists, including Ian Bogost and Graham Harman, who argue that for philosophy to properly understand the ontology of things it must first come to terms with its correlationist past.

3. For an in-depth discussion of Lamb 86 and its connection to categorization and human cognition, see Ryan Dewey, "Human Cognition and Lamb 86 at Alinea—An Encounter with Basic Human Categorization."

II

Writing Things

5
Writing Devices

Donnie Johnson Sackey and William Hart-Davidson

Michel Callon presents writing devices as critical in assembling organizations, "constructing and objectifying services, their consumers, and, more broadly, the collective actions that make it possible to deliver services" (199). In short, he provides an approach to ontology wherein writing devices lie at the "center" as integral components of how and when infrastructures assemble. While human actors are often credited with inoculating these devices with their own ideologies and purposes, these nonhuman actors assume lives of their own. We use two cases drawn from our own ongoing research as a space for analysis. Our aim is less to investigate each case in depth than to open a scholarly conversation on what it means to build, maintain, and live with nonhuman writers in our human worlds. The first case explores the dynamics of a set of durable (one-hundred year old and older) human and nonhuman actors with a focus on the rhetorical ecologies that grow up among the management of biological systems. The second case is a brief look at a project to construct and introduce a writing device. The functional goal of this device is to close a feedback loop between patients and primary care providers in an attempt to address systemic inequality in the quality of care for cardiovascular disease in the United States. We see the ability to *trace and analyze* the workings of writing devices as well as the effort of *creating and maintaining* them to be increasingly important (though currently not well understood) rhetorical work in the coming years and decades.

Concerning Nonhuman Subjectivity and Place Matters

For Michel Callon and John Law, the ideas of human and nonhuman agency exist as a contradiction, playing into a Cartesian paradigm that separates the cultural from the natural and limits possibilities for agentive action from nonspeaking subjects. The hunt for agency often centers upon agents who perform themselves and those agents' intentions as subjects through the manipulation of linguistic systems. Nevertheless, these performances cannot happen without the existence of other networked entities whose presence makes activity happen and carries meaning. For example, texts can do specific organizing work just as they can create discretionary spaces for activity among a variety of actors. Texts carry their own "logics of action" and enroll other subjects into their fold long after their authors have died (see also Callon and Vignolle; Derrida Writing; Foucault; Winner). Callon and Law introduce the idea of *collectif*, differentiated from *collective*, as a means of rethinking agency. *Collectif* places emphasis on relations and actors' heterogeneity, which make up a network and create positions from which an actor or many actors can perform. This portends agency as an emergent property of relationships rather than one contained within speaking subjects. This understanding of subjectivity collapses scale so that a subject is always individual and network simultaneously; thus, it makes a case for considering any actor's identity within networked space as perpetually unstable. In fact, Law's reconception of network-space positions nonhuman actors as topologically multiple, as they are the intersections/interferences between different topoi (networks and regions) and shifting reconfigurations of relations (see also Law's *Aircraft Stories* for his understanding of multiplicity). This holds that their identities are never stable; in fact, they are fluid or variable, as they exist across spaces. While an actor might retain the same form or shape to the naked eye, as space shifts from one region to another the actor becomes something else. For example, a Haitian composting toilet can be defined as a mechanism for sewage removal, a community-building tool, or a resource for local farmers, depending upon its network topology. Here we raise the idea that in attending to artifacts' conduct of politics, "what matters is not technology itself, but the social or economic systems in which it is embedded" (Winner 25).

Our cases below illustrate ways to investigate the networked performances of nonhuman actors in the creation and preservation of spaces that advance particular interests. Central to our work with these cases is the tracing and analyzing of existing systems and their evolution over time with a more critical focus on how we can build and introduce better writing devices to work within human systems. Several scholars inform our approach to human and nonhuman spatial relations. Latour finds much interest in networks because their "simple properties" allow us to "get rid of the tyranny of distance" (proximity), "dissolve micro-macro distinction[s]" (size/scale), and, following Gilles Deleuze, force us to see that "a network is all boundary" as it lacks the spatial distinction of interiority or exteriority (inside/outside) ("On Actor-Network Theory" 4). Theodore Schatzki theorizes sites as occurrences created via event relations, which appear as agents' activities assemble in a "cluster." Seeing sites as layered in this manner is a way of understanding how "a social site is not roped off, but rather that it inhabits a 'neighbourhood' (sic) of practices, events and orders that are folded variously into other unfolding sites" (Marston, Jones, and Woodward 426; see also Delanda). The following cases emphasize how a turn toward ontology affords rhetoricians the opportunity to not only understand issues with greater complexity but also places us in the position to engage with others and act as advocates in the creation of writing devices and space. If writing performs reality, then it also can adjust the relations that produce reality. Here we actively advocate considering ways in which acting rhetorically can make and remake the physical world.

Case 1: Illegal Acts: Performing Bighead Carp

Invasive species are made in a variety of ways (Lien and Law; see also Mol and Law for a similar take on sheep and Thompson on elephants). One route is the result of legislative processes that involve the synchronized mobilization of political entities, which exist on federal, regional, state, and local levels. In fact, most activity has occurred on the federal level through Congress, the US Fish and Wildlife Service (Service), the Army Corps of Engineers, the president, and the Supreme Court. Federal actors pass legislation and coordinate activities between local, regional, and state governments. Political entities acting within and beyond the federal level are governmental or nongovernmental organizations. These include regulatory agencies such as states' departments of natural resources, attorneys general, legislative assemblies, and governors that exist within the US (primarily the upper-Midwest) and the Canadian provinces bordering the Great Lakes. Nongovernmental organizations include the Alliance for the Great Lakes, American Rivers, Natural Resource Defense Council, Illinois Black Chamber of Commerce, Missouri Dairy Association, and American Water Operators.

At a smaller level of granularity, rulemaking is one of several avenues for constructing species as ontologically invasive. Rulemaking is an assemblage of many activities, people, documents, laboratory procedures, and events scattered across multiple locations. Its primary purpose is regulatory. Rulemaking makes regulations, *not* laws (5 USC 553, 2000). A regulation is a requirement or set of requirements established by federal agencies. A regulation is intended to have the effect of law, but it is not law. Congress passes legislation that authorizes regulations, and the president signs regulations *into* law. On a daily basis the Office of the Federal Register (housed within the National Archives and Records Administration) publishes regulations in a running document called the *Federal Register* (*FR*). *FR* is the federal government's official journal. Annually, all the regulations are codified in the *Code of Federal Regulations* (*CFR*). The following is an excerpt from *CFR*:

The U.S. Fish and Wildlife Service (Service) adds the bighead carp (*Hypophthalmichthys nobilis*), a large fish native to eastern Asia, to the list of injurious fish, mollusks, and crustaceans. The importation into the United States and interstate transportation between States, the District of Columbia, the Commonwealth of Puerto Rico, or any territory or possession of the United States of all forms of live bighead carp, gametes, viable eggs, and hybrids thereof is prohibited, except by permit for zoological, education, medical, or scientific purposes (in accordance with permit regulation at 50 CFR 16.22) or by Federal agencies without a permit solely for their own use. ("Injurious Wildlife Species")

This abstracted architectonic statement does several things. It lists important actors; it names spaces; and it dis/connects spaces and actors. If we want to know how bighead carp became legally invasive, we have to move backward from this statement (from the document) and trace the long line of assemblages that authorize its existence. This necessitates locating the source(s)—the entities responsible for publication *and* authorization.

Tracing bighead carp's emergent invasibility begins with the Service, which is the body responsible for publishing notices regarding invasives in *FR*. Rulemaking involves a series of notices—notices of inquiry, notices of proposed rules, and notices of final rules. Additional writing devices, mostly letters but also statistical analyses, news releases, bibliographies, and scholarly publications, follow each published notice. To understand the process, Donnie conducted an interview with an official from the Service named "MH." The purpose was to understand rulemaking with respect to types of solicited information and how the Service uses information during deliberations. MH noted that the Service seeks "more science-based/technical-based information" that helps them evaluate issues such as ecological separation and the impact of bighead carp on the Great Lakes or Mississippi River Basin. Clear throughout the interview was that the Service neither actively sought economic data nor went out of its way to consult businesses. In fact, part of their conversation centered on the 2003 Aquatic Invasive Species Summit Proceedings Conference that the Service sponsored together with other entities. These entities included representatives from the State of Illinois, the Army Corps of Engineers, and the City of Chicago. In addition, members of the United States and international scientific communities were in attendance. The Illinois Chamber of Commerce, however, was not invited.

"We were looking for science-based input at arriving at solutions to the issue of exchange of invasive species between the Great Lakes and Mississippi Basin," MH said when I inquired why the meeting excluded economic interests. This statement, which helped to define the Service's reality of invasive species, conflicted with MH's oft-stated position that the issue of invasive species is one of complexity and requires a robust set of solutions to mitigate negative effects. The summit produced four recommended action items that were supposed to "deal with the intricacies" of the Chicago Waterway System. All of these solutions were science-based interventions. Here a world emerges from the standpoint of the Service. Scientific units materialize as authorities in defining and determining how to deal with invasive actors. Economic analyses are appreciated, but factor little. The chief rhetorical constraints in assembling and maintaining spaces of dependence (locations that actors depend upon to preserve their essential self-interests) are rhetorical constructions of a public that the Service is answerable to. According to MH, the Service understands the public as "stakeholders that are interested in technical problems that can be fixed via technical solutions." Their primary concerns, according to MH, regard the dual questions: "are we doing enough and are we doing it fast enough?"

Time matters a great deal. While the Service operates from a scientific sphere, it is also nested within the space of the federal government, whose bureaucracy (e.g. paperwork, statutes, review processes, etc.) limits its level of engagement with local, state, and regional entities outside the federal government. The relationship between space and time presents the question of whether federal intervention through rulemaking is an effective solution or whether states should have the sole power to make invasive species. Here the guiding document that governs the Service's activities is the Lacey Act. "Our Lacey Act is cumbersome and slow," MH noted with much frustration. "Our process for listing injurious wildlife under the Lacey Act takes years." This was a trend that Donnie noticed across several interviews. Each interviewee in some form raised the Lacey Act and its rulemaking process as a matter of concern. These concerns differed among stakeholders with respect to how the document functioned in relation to the actions and actors it authorizes.

Performing Bighead Carp in Aquaculture

How do fish farmers understand bighead carp? How is this represented in the networks they construct? What writing actors disrupt and destabilize fish farmers' understanding of bighead carp? Consider the following statements: "The negative economic impact of listing the bighead carp as injurious is enormous and will not prevent a single bighead carp from swimming up the Mississippi River through the man-made Chicago ship canal and into the Great Lakes," and, "If bighead carp were listed as injurious, will a commercial fisherman be allowed to harvest bighead carp on the Iowa side of the Mississippi River and transport these live fish to the Illinois side of the river? Can bighead carp harvested in one state be transported live to a processing facility in another state?" These statements come from Mike, a fish farmer. They best represent the complexity of the argument that originates from the space of aquaculture in terms

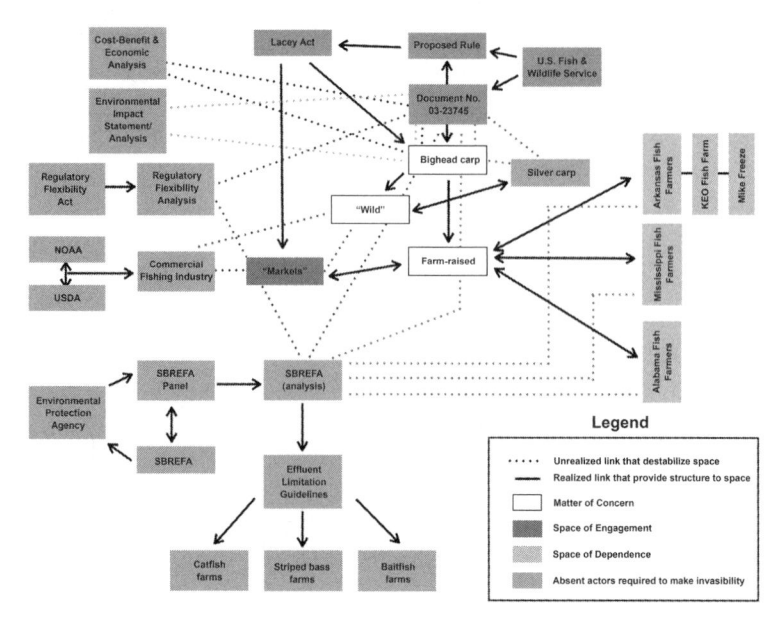

Figure 5.1. A network map of how Mike realizes bighead carp's non/invasive identity.

of how we should understand bighead carp's ontological making. Like most aquaculturists, Mike frames bighead carp's identity solely within the purview of economics. Bighead carp are not a problem for him. The real problem regards regulatory procedures. Of concern are the ways bureaucratic actors link to fish farmers' spaces of dependence and the many levels at which they fail to make connections. To bolster the case of why bighead carp is not an invader, Mike assembles a network that features writing actors such as the Lacey Act and "Review of Information Concerning Bighead Carp (*Hypophthalmichthys nobilis*)" (Document No. 03–23745) (fig. 5.1). This is a fiscal ontology built from legal frameworks that denote why bighead carp are not invasive and why actions to label them as invasive are problematic.

Start from the position of Mike's reality. This means acknowledging the links that stabilize carp as noninvasive. Although he does not state this directly, Mike distinguishes between *wild* and *farm-raised* carp. The distinction between the two is important and gets to the heart of the aquaculture industry's concern with listing. *Farm-raised* carp exist within containers. Bighead carp are a helper species used to control the taste of catfish bound for markets. They are also sold as food in the United States and abroad. If there is legitimate risk regarding invasion of the Great Lakes, it is not from these actors. They do not exist within the main waterway networks that connect to the Great Lakes. The spaces of dependence for actors who use the Lacey Act to frame these carp as invaders lie between markets and farms. Trucks, roads, boats, and other vessels located near bodies of water become an unnecessary risk. Disrupt these networks and you suspend the invasion. Still, what does this do for *wild* bighead carp, which are also fished for sale at markets? *Wild* carp have freely roamed waters below the Great Lakes for decades. While listing would most definitely stop the unlikely transit from the aquaculture industry, it is not as if *wild* carp will automatically become regulation-abiding entities. They remain free to travel. Disrupting transportation also entails the consequence of making a legal business practice (constitutionally protected through interstate commerce law) illegal by issuing a final rule.

At this point, statements become critical with respect to how the Service will write the final rule on bighead carp. Both the Lacey Act and Document No. 03–23745 take center stage for Mike and other fish farmers. Earlier we wrote about the significance of the distinction between *wild* and *farm-raised*; however, *alive* and *dead* add a new layer of regulatory complexity. This is best illustrated in Mike's second statement. Most fishing boats in the Mississippi River Basin are not factory ships. Instead, commercial fishers are largely dependent on kill facilities. Yet, a condemned Illinoisan fish traveling the last mile to a death chamber in Missouri is a serious matter of concern. The problem here is not transporting the fish from water to land where it may potentially find uninvaded spaces. It is actually transporting the fish across the invisible boundary that Missouri and Illinois share along the Mississippi River. Any bighead carp caught in Illinois must be dead before it arrives in Missouri; otherwise a fisherman has committed a misdemeanor or felony. This may sound highly unlikely; however, it represents a legitimate concern, especially when penalties for violating the Lacey Act can amount to a felony conviction with a possible prison sentence of up to five years and/or a $250,000 fine per individual.

Additional language from the Lacey Act affects how fishermen perform their identities and bighead carp. The difference between a misdemeanor and a felony hinges upon three words—*knowingly* and *should know*. When Congress amended the Lacey Act in 1969 to broaden its scope, liability covered violations committed *knowingly* and *willfully*. In 1981, Congress removed *willfully* when it joined the Black Bass Act of 1926 with the Lacey Act. The change in language occurred to ease prosecutorial efforts (R. Anderson). After amending the act in 1988 and 2003, Congress amended it again in 2008 to address the mislabeling of protected plants. Part of this amendment involved a minor tweaking of language: "knowingly engages in conduct prohibited by any provision of this chapter . . . *and in the exercise of due care should know* that the fish or wildlife or plants were taken, possessed, transported, or sold in violation of, or in a manner unlawful under, any underlying law, treaty or regulation." According to Mike, the Service and Congress made this change without alerting the aquaculture industry. "One of the things that we'd like to get changed back is the language that said that the perpetrator who was doing this [transporting banned species] had to *knowingly* violate the law [inaudible] and now it says *should have known* that he was violating the law," Mike said. "That's a huge legal difference, because what we used to tell people in the '80s and '90s . . . is that ignorance was excused." Prior to the 2008 amendment, if a catfish farmer had a bighead carp in her truck and she was unaware of it before officials had discovered it, then the burden of proof would be on the official to prove that the farmer knew she was in violation. What seems like a minor change in language switches the burden on to the farmer. Fishing bighead carp and farming catfish through catfish-bighead polyculture become very difficult. Here an actor's statement composed to regulate the spaces of the logging industry inadvertently enrolled aquaculture (and other spaces), transforming farmers into potential criminals. For aquaculturists, the stability of their spaces of dependence hinges largely on key terms within the Lacey Act, and these terms also serve as spaces of dependence for actors wanting to list bighead carp as an invasive species.

So far we have focused on actors that are present and actively *writing* to affect realities. There are others who have not been enrolled into networks that denote bighead carp's invasibility. For aquaculturists, if these network elements are not enrolled then the species is not legally invasive. In his letter, Mike lists four technical objects that are necessary in bringing together the heterogeneous networks that form an invasive identity: 1) an environmental impact assessment; 2) a cost-benefit and economic analysis; 3) an analysis as dictated by the Small Business Regulatory Enforcement Fairness Act (SBREFA); and, 4) a regulatory flexibility analysis as defined under the Regulatory Flexibility Act. We will not go into a long explanation of what each of these actants do. Each works independently to modify our understanding of bighead carp; however, it is necessary for the Service to join them into a single network through Document No. 03–23745. This is mandated by the rulemaking procedure. Yet, the Service issued the notice of inquiry without these nonhumans. "Is the addition of a species to the injurious list without a formal risk assessment going to become a 'normal procedure' for the [Service]?" Mike asked. "This rule will have a significant economic effect on a substantial number of small entities." Through his network building, Mike illustrated that in rulemaking the Service broke its own rules and that this put fish farmers at a disadvantage.

Entr'act: Writing [New] Ways of Doing

If asked to sum up the conflict between fish farmers and the US Fish and Wildlife Service in a phrase, we might say that Mike and his fellow fisherman "do" carp differently than the US government rules allow. It is not simply that there is a gap in knowledge among the various players about carp—the varieties of them or their habits. So "knowing" carp is not the problem. Neither is a carp "being" a carp, by itself, a trigger for the problem state, which is the declaration of the fish as an invader and the subsequent actions of humans in response to this declaration. The same carp seen as an invader, depending on the time and place, is a helper. What our foregoing analysis shows is just how carp came to be performed in such ways as to cause conflict via writing. If writing can influence the way we do carp such that it causes conflict, can it also offer the means to resolve conflict by providing ways to refigure relationships among the actors? Mike's strategy appears to move in this direction. In our second case, we take up this possibility of writing new ways of doing, of building "writing devices" that intervene in strategic ways to reconfigure relationships so as to produce beneficial outcomes rather than conflict.

Case 2: Learning to Build Writing Devices that Help Patients "Do Bodies"

> We all have and are a body. But there is a way out of this dichotomous twosome. As part of our daily practices, we also do (our) bodies. In practice we enact them. If the body we have is the one known by pathologists after our death, while the body we are is the one we know ourselves by being self-aware, then what about the body we do? What can be found out and said about it? Is it possible to inquire into the body we do? And what are the consequences if action is privileged over knowledge?
>
> Annemarie Mol and John Law

Over the last few years, the Writing in Digital Environments (WIDE) research center at Michigan State University has undertaken efforts not only to study writing devices, but also to create them. Working in a range of specific domains that include formal and informal education (e.g., schools and museums) as well as health care, our demonstration projects have shown that it is possible to make writing devices that interact with human participants to produce desirable benefits such as learning, cultivating stronger relationships, etc. Recent projects in WIDE have explored the use of a web services platform and mobile devices to create feedback loops that positively influence healthy decision-making for activities with hundreds or even thousands of participants. We were inspired to do this work by Mol and Law's aforementioned quote. We see the opportunity to make writing devices that intervene in health problems by helping people to "do" heart disease or diabetes differently and, in so doing, to move beyond "having" these diseases. But can they work this way?

To investigate, we have sought to take part in studies that determine if writing devices can influence behaviors shown to have measurable benefits, such as decreased morbidity rates from chronic disease. In demonstration projects, we have created services that vary the type of feedback participants may seek, including everything from precision analytical data to participant-created narratives and photos. We can also vary the conditions under which information is received, basing responses from the service on variables that include individual and group activity, and environmental data such as time, date, and weather. In these projects, we have worked with colleagues from human medicine, epidemiology, land use and policy, and outreach and extension. We also work from the general premise that in day-to-day practice outcomes of individual decisions may be too remote for individuals to know how they will affect progress toward individual and large-scale public health goals. By increasing situational awareness among a social group's members, we may also be able to motivate positive behavioral changes that address these large-scale challenges in a measurable way.

As reported by Albert Bandura and Edwin Locke, significant evidence exists to support the idea that self-efficacy—the belief that one can act in ways that produce desired outcomes—is a causal determinant of motivation and performance across a wide variety of activity domains, including health functioning. Gathering results from nine meta-analyses, Bandura and Locke note that changes in self-efficacy have been repeatedly shown to strongly predict behavioral functions in individuals over time, as well as between individuals. The strength of this evidence allows for a simple but compelling portrait of human nature to emerge: "People are not only agents of actions, they are self-examiners of their own functioning. They reflect on their efficacy, the soundness of their thoughts and actions, the meaning of their pursuits, and make corrective adjustments if necessary" (Bandura and Locke 97).

If writing devices assist human agents in this process of self-examination and course correction, what meditational functions of writing devices might work best? In collaboration with colleagues from the College of Human Medicine at Michigan State University, William is working on a community clinical trial designed, in part, to address these broader questions. These questions are shared by health professionals concerned with implementation of secondary (i.e., informational and behavioral) therapies designed to enhance patient self-management (e.g., Koh et al.; Wagner; Renders et al. propose this Health Literacy Care Model). We present the details of the study here to show where our disciplinary interest in understanding the range and effectiveness of writing devices in the physical world meets the disciplinary interests of others, creating an opportunity to advance our understanding of human-machine ontologies with potentially powerful effects.

Study Background: For some patients, the supposed gold standard of medical care for cardiovascular disease simply does not work as well. And we do not know why.

Nearly 26 million Americans have diabetes. Most of these patients face life-shortening risks related to cardiovascular disease. Low-income and minority patients bear a greater percentage of this risk due to a variety of barriers to accessing care. In particular, lifestyle-related prevention and secondary therapies proven to be effective can be difficult to implement because they require reliable contact with caregivers. Additionally, low-income patients are more likely to have interruptions in taking their medications on time.

Our project evaluates the use of two secondary therapies that may better reach low-income and minority patients: introductory group visits that focus on evidence-based therapies and encourage patient investment in their own care, and the use of mobile phone messaging (SMS) as reinforcement during care. Together, these patient activation and reinforcement methods can help to improve patient-caregiver communication, leading to better decisions by both patients and doctors. Better decisions may lead to better health outcomes, including reduced cardiac risk, better blood sugar control, and longer life.

The patient activation and reinforcement programs had been shown to work in an earlier pilot study (see Olomu). But there have been no studies that systematically evaluate these secondary therapies. So we do not know much about why they work when they do work. To find out, we plan to conduct a randomized community trial in a network of Federally Qualified Health Centers (FQHCs) in Michigan. We plan to enroll approximately 600 patients in twelve clinics around the state. Each patient will receive standard care and medication for diabetes and cardiovascular disease. Four clinics will be randomly chosen to continue with standard care as a control. Four clinics will be randomly assigned to use our patient activation approach either alone or in combination with an SMS service in which patients interact with care providers. Two additional clinics will use the phone service without the activation protocol in combination with standard care. The SMS service sends several kinds of messages, including reminders (about medication and upcoming appointments) and prompts to patients to enter information. All of the messages reinforce evidence-based care strategies. Our aim in this project is to evaluate how well those patients who work with the writing device do in comparison to those who do not. We are most interested in whether the feedback protocol can work in real clinical settings to reach and improve treatment outcomes for a group of people who are underserved in the current US health care environment. We also hope to positively impact caregivers at FQHCs by helping them to more consistently use evidence-based treatments and communicate with patients about these in more consistent and coherent ways.

Secondary Therapies as Writing Devices: How Do They Function in Care Relationships?

Why do we think that information and feedback given to patients can be good medicine? We believe that, taken together, the secondary therapies might work as *writing devices*. Written messages distributed at group meetings, interactive

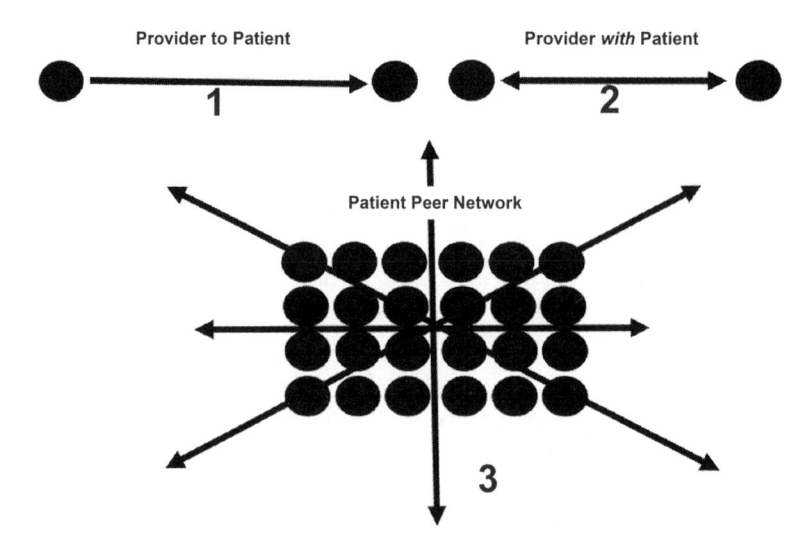

Figure 5.2. Three patterns of information flow among patients and care providers.

websites, or SMSs are a few of the forms these take. Multiple genres and media are typically used in a single therapy program, making the problem of isolating the mechanism as a function of medium (e.g., brochures versus SMSs) difficult and pragmatically undesirable. Instead, we seek to differentiate between the flow and use of information rather than medium or genre. When we take this perspective, we can see the three plausible mechanisms operating in distinct ways as writing devices in use in clinical settings.

Mechanism one is caregiver-to-patient interaction, and it proceeds from a presumption that the patient suffers from an information deficit that can be overcome with information delivered in a helpful way. This has been the basis for many self-management education programs, publications, and other materials recommended or prescribed for newly diagnosed type 2 diabetes patients (American Diabetes Association). Mechanism two involves two-way interaction between caregivers and patients, and it operates on the idea that interaction and engagement with one's care providers fosters greater accountability, while the feedback received leads to greater self-efficacy. Mechanism three involves peer interactions such as those experienced in expert-led group information sessions. This approach proceeds from the assumption that peer interactions permit enhanced situational awareness and patient identification with others who share their challenges and goals. Figure 5.2 illustrates the differences in information flow the three mechanisms represent.

We designed our study to answer the following question that will guide the functioning of a writing device: "which of the three mechanisms best accounts for any positive outcomes related to cardiac risk in type 2 diabetes patients who receive decision-making support as a part of routine primary care?" Each mechanism implies different levels of patient engagement and activity. And as the variety of digital and mobile technology options for implementing these kinds of programs expands, care providers need to be able to advise patients about the relative benefits they can expect from using one or more of the above interaction types.

A meta-analysis by Norris et al. has shown that self-management education, alone, reliably leads to moderate improvement in glycemic control in type 2 diabetes patients but that these gains do not persist after three months. As a result, the long-term value of mechanism one programs for controlling life-threatening symptoms of chronic disease is not known. Ellis et al. reach similar conclusions and, using regression analysis, note that face-to-face delivery methods consistent with mechanism two were one of very few factors that predicted better patient outcomes. The amount of the information or length of the education program ("the dose") were not predictive factors. These results suggest to us that mechanism two may produce better results than mechanism one. However, gains from group interaction *may* also be explained by the ability of individuals to identify with peers who share their situation and share their goals consistent with mechanism three.

In Law and Mol's terms, these three mechanisms represent different ways to "do diabetes" so as to manage cardiac risk factors. Our three trial arms separate these in order to measure which of the three approaches is more likely to lead to sustained positive benefits for patients. The results may help to guide the building of writing devices that more reliably work to help patients do diabetes and cardiovascular disease differently so that they avoid these diseases' negative effects. The results also provide some guidance for those interested in tracing change attributable to the introduction of writing devices into existing human systems.

Conclusion

As we stated in the beginning, our aim is less to investigate each case in depth than to open a scholarly conversation on what it means to build, maintain, and live with nonhuman writers in our human worlds. The central idea that connects these cases regards the need to think about what it means to design writing devices to perform complex activities. Donnie's trace of the Lacey Acts' effects on Asian carp's ontological status illustrates the unintended consequences that emerge from our failure to consider how writing devices perform in ways that their designers never intended. Yet, William's turn toward writing devices in a clinical setting attends to the ways in which we might build sustainable rhetorical writing devices that work better within dynamic and complex human systems. Thus, we offer these cases as a way to sketch a possible research path for those interested in writing devices and their networked effects.

6
The Material Culture of Writing

Objects, Habitats, and Identities in Practice

Cydney Alexis

> We have things to study, and we must record them dutifully and examine them lovingly if the abstraction called culture is to be compassed, if the striving of the human actor is to be met with fellow feeling.
>
> Henry Glassie

> Too seldom do we try to read objects as we read books—to understand the people and times that created them, used them, and discarded them.
>
> Lubar and Kingery

Picture yourself as you sit down to write. Like Laura Ingalls Wilder, you might write using a lap desk given to you by your husband. Perhaps you write in bed, as did Proust and Twain. Like scholar Claudia Mon Pere, a working mother, you may have developed "a pretty good sense of what can and cannot be accomplished in a moving vehicle" (166). No matter what environment you typically write in, one thing is fairly certain: you have developed preferences around it, you have populated it with objects, and your behavior within it follows some sort of routine. In this chapter, I develop the concept of the *writing habitat* to theorize writers' relationships with the material goods and rituals that support their work. I suggest that *things* matter to our writing practices, and by *things* I mean simple, ordinary objects such as pens, notebooks, and desks. As we use these objects, we inscribe them with histories, memories, and practices—and we attach[1] to them. For as much as writing is a product of the mind, it is also an act of dwelling. Virginia Woolf voiced this explicitly in 1929 when she stated that "a woman must have money and a room of her own if she is to write" (4). Her words point to the economic and material exigencies that confront, support, and—at times—bear down on writers.

Despite the elaborate and intimate relationship to objects, place, environment, and rituals that writers form, qualitative ethnographic research in writing studies has largely ignored the topic, with objects generally being peripheral, rather than fundamental, to research studies.[2] As Sherry Turkle asserts, "We find it familiar to consider objects as useful or aesthetic, as necessities or vain indulgences. We are on less familiar ground when we consider objects as companions to our emotional lives or as provocations to thought" (5). We have seen objects of literacy illustrated in many of our field's texts: Lynn's thinking aloud with writing tools (Emig); the Spanish magazines and computers that fostered the development of Dora and Ray's literacy (Brandt, *Literacy*); and a card table a writer uses as a barrier to hold herself hostage while writing (Prior and Shipka, "Chronotopic"). A picture of object dependency is created by all of these texts. And indeed, many others explicitly call for attention to the materiality of writing (Barron; Brandt and Clinton; Cooper; Gere; Reynolds; Selzer and Crowley). Yet while these texts and their references to materiality are compelling, as a field, rhetoric and writing studies still do not know enough about the materials that support writing practice and what these materials tell us about how we come to identify as writers, develop a writing identity, articulate it for others, and negotiate it with objects.[3]

Material culture scholars labored successfully, throughout the 1970s and '80s, to demonstrate that objects are indispensable in the study of culture and humanity.[4] In this chapter, I rely on seminal work in this field as a means of directing rhetoric and writing studies scholars' attentions toward this body of scholarship that will help us conduct grounded studies of what I hope our field comes to think of as the material culture of writing.[5] As art historian Jules David Prown writes, "human-made objects reflect, consciously or unconsciously, directly or indirectly, the beliefs of the individuals who commissioned, fabricated, purchased, or used them and, by extension, the beliefs of the larger society to which these individuals belonged" (11). Hence this text takes as its focus the inner workings of writers' object-populated writing environments, or *writing habitats*, as I think of them. I have adopted this term in order to describe the rich, constructed environments that writers create to work in. The term responds to calls within rhetoric, writing studies, and literature to take a geographic and ecological approach to the study of writing (Barton; Cooper; Dobrin and Keller; Reynolds). Thinking of our writing environments as habitats allows for the discursive construction of the "scene of writing" as a complex system and environment in which writers work in varying degrees of harmony (Brodkey).

The habitat, as I conceive of it, is comprised of the place in which a writer chooses to write and the objects that populate that place. It can be private or public. Movement between such spaces is important—writers shift between different habitats as they hit different developmental stages, in order to inspire writing in different genres, or to control for what they see as their most essential writing conditions. Thinking of our writing spaces as habitats changes our perception of their ecologies and encourages us to create environments that enrich—instead of inhibit—our creative practices. These habitats are constructed *for us* when we are young, and then—through our varied experiences—we construct our own spaces in which to work that often echo the spaces of our early learning.

Qualitative and quantitative studies of writing materials and their impact on our writing practice and writing identity could reveal beliefs about writing and writing culture. By "writing identity," I suggest that people who write develop an identity around writing, one that manifests and is expressed largely through material objects. How does such an identity emerge? What fosters its growth? How does a positive identity around writing impact writing success? How are material objects working in the production of writing selves?

In these pages, I sketch answers to these questions using data culled from my ongoing life story interviews with about thirty individuals who at the time of their interviews were engaging in a daily writing practice of some kind. Not everyone who writes daily identifies as a "writer." I use the term *writing identity* to mark the shifting, contested, and sometimes rejected positionality of those who write, whether they currently identify with the term or not, and I highlight how objects participate in this identification. In this chapter, I draw on seminal texts in material culture studies and related fields, primarily consumer research and social psychology. These texts predate most work in rhetoric and writing studies on objects. My hope is that this research proves helpful to those who are trying to understand material dependencies and affordances in rich ways and who are trying to further our field's understanding of the material culture of writing.

In the next section, I present small excerpts from my interviews, read through interdisciplinary research on things.

A Brief Introduction to the Material Culture of Writing

> Material culture is usually considered to be roughly synonymous with artifacts, the vast universe of objects used by humankind to cope with the physical world, to facilitate social intercourse, and to benefit our state of mind. A somewhat broader definition of material culture is useful in emphasizing how profoundly our world is the product of our thoughts, as that sector of our physical environment that we modify through culturally determined behavior.
>
> James Deetz

Natalie, a government historian, remembers the production made over the purchase of her first writing desk. Her father—who kept his bold and heavy work desk after he retired as a symbol of his working self—championed the idea that if one wants to be a student, one needs a desk. Natalie's father and mother supported her scholastic identity—which emerged early—by providing her with material resources. In this way, Natalie's family members *passed down* rituals and values to their children, who in turn internalized them.

Similarly David, a writing center administrator, describes how he used the purchase of a writing desk to demarcate space in the room he shared with his musician brother. By having a desk he claimed a writing identity; by placing that desk in his room, he simultaneously gained space and marked a boundary between himself and his brother. Fiona, a graduate student in English, argued as an adolescent for her own room—with its own desk—by articulating to her parents that because she was a writer, she needed space to write. She was the only one of four siblings to win this privacy. These examples illustrate that buying and having a desk is often less about working at it than the way in which it is perceived and used as a symbol of entry into a new identity or practice.

The desk also "extends" the self. In his essay "Possessions and the Extended Self," Russell Belk charts, from Henry James to Sartre to his own work, how possessions are intertwined with self-concept. His notion of "self-extension" explains how humans not only attach to possessions, but also begin to see them as comprising a fundamental part of their self-concept (139). In some ways, possessions physically extend the self—by using a certain instrument, we are capable of performing an otherwise impossible action. Extension is also metaphorical. When asked to rate the "me-ness" of varied possessions, respondents across a range of studies rate certain objects as being nearly as much a part of their selves as body parts (141; cf. Kleine, Kleine, and Allen). In Belk's words, "The more we believe we possess or are possessed by an object, the more a part of self it becomes . . . Apparently, in claiming that something is 'mine,' we also come to believe that the object is 'me'" (141). Belk demonstrates how individuals define themselves through possessions that reflect their ideal senses of self and the identities of groups to which they belong (143–54). This sentiment is echoed in various studies that demonstrate how possessions intersect with identities in practice. Kleine, Kleine, and Allen find that possessions, as "artifacts of the self," "place identity in its sociohistorical context" and "are used in the processes of *becoming* by signaling that a desired identity is developing" (328). Relatedly, Kleine, Kleine, and Kernan find that an identity's "salience," the "relative importance of a given identity in an individual's self-structure," results from a person's identification with the identity, positive feedback received for it, "media connections" that teach people how to enact it, and "identity-relevant" possessions used to perform it (224–26).

The writers mentioned above—Natalie, David, and Fiona—each referenced the writing desk as central to his or her developing identity as a self who writes, and this identity was negotiated in the presence of others who supported this emergence, often by providing the goods that became the tableau for this identity work. David, for example, uses the desk to extend his physical and figurative space in a shared room—and the desk, like philosophy's notoriously theorized table, takes on an agentic function as its presence communicates David's identity to those who see it, regardless of his absence in the room and the absence of work performed on it (Ahmed, "Orientations"; Arendt; Banfield; Heidegger, *Being*; Harman, "Technology"; Latour, "Interobjectivity"). Fiona's private room similarly helps her family to read her as a person who writes. As a part of the extended writing self, the desk presents a literal stage on which to conduct work, but also a figurative stage for identity performance. It is no accident that Natalie remembers staging schooling scenes with her brother at her desk, though he disliked school. In acting out these scenes, she experiences the "meness" of schooling while simultaneously noticing the otherness of schooling for her sibling, against which her self-concept is constructed.

Some social psychologists use the concept of *possible selves* to explain the dynamic reality of selfhood and the link between one's ability to imagine oneself in a role and actual achievement of it (Oyserman et al.; Markus and Nurius). The self-concept is constantly evolving. Incorporated into this concept is a fluid amalgam of who we have been in the past, how we envision ourselves now, and what our future hopes are. Markus and Nurius explain possible selves as "The essential link between the self-concept and motivation. . . . What others are now, I could become. . . . [T]he pool of possible selves derives from the categories made salient by the individual's particular sociocultural and historical context and from the models, images, and symbols provided by the media and by the individual's immediate social experiences" (954). Context and environment, then, affect one's ability to project oneself into, and then inhabit, a certain identity. Oyserman et al. demonstrate the connection between academic outcomes and the ability to imagine possible selves. "Our results demonstrate the real-world power of a social psychological conceptualization of the self as a motivational resource," they conclude ("Possible Selves" 201).

An inference could be drawn, then, that how one envisions what is possible is likely directly tied to the goods one uses to perform and enact those possibilities. For those who write, everyday objects that populate their habitats tell a story about their values, histories, identities, practices, and imagined futures. I turn, now, to two case studies that exemplify these ideas.

Desk and Table as Sites of Becoming, Identity Articulation, and Mobile Writing Practices

Diana, a Midwestern school administrator, has a habitat comprised of the two writing spaces pictured in figure 6.1 and 6.2. Diana is keenly aware of the impact of physical settings on her writing process, as well as the role that objects play. Her practice is mobile. She shifts between the two different rooms pictured here: her kitchen table is her primary writing site; she situates her desktop computer in the living room.

As is the case for most of my study participants, Diana's early experiences with reading and writing took place in the gendered space of the kitchen. A chalkboard situated in the kitchen was a site not only of play with her brother, but also written communication with her mother. The chalkboard signifies Diana's developing, parent- and self-sponsored literacy tasks, but also the negotiation of her own identity as a learner against her brother's, whom she always considered a more able student. The chalkboard is an object marker inscribed with key memories of comfort, kinship, and competition that Diana associates with learning.[6] As was also the case for most of my study participants, adolescence marked an inward turn—she moved from the common space of the kitchen to a bedroom in order to write. Yet she says: "But if we were having troubles, we always came to the kitchen to kind of talk about it. And if you couldn't write, then you sat there and mom would be cooking or baking and she'd, you know, 'Well, think about this,' or 'How about if you wrote it this way?' It helped to talk. She was always there." Diana's mother supported her early literacy by teaching her how to read and write before she entered school. Her mother was a constant presence in the kitchen, making that a key learning site. She says, "This is why I feel the most comfortable in the kitchen." She adds, "I always do my best work, whether it's correcting papers or just doing the grocery list, it's at the kitchen table. And if I'm really stuck, I'll come at the kitchen table and then go on the computer and write." The kitchen table is a central site of Diana's writing, a space she returns to whenever she is blocked, after which she exits again to compose at the computer. It is significant that she comes back to a nostalgic site for help with unblocking, since this was also her childhood practice. In one instance, her mother is the person who helps her find her words; later, the kitchen table, as if invested with human power, triggers Diana's writing. About the table, she says, "You know how you just feel right, it's like a glove? You just sit in that kind of chair and just—I guess it gets things flowing and going." As noted earlier, this observation accords with cross-disciplinary scholarship that acknowledges objects' agency; they stay present as we move, providing a stable point of reference for our work that exists in our absence. Their existence in human conception is a reflection of all of our tacit and latent experiences of them, which might explain the special power that gathers around them and that they occupy in our writing practice, often as writing spurs (Brandt and Clinton; Heidegger, *Being*; Harman, "Technology"; Latour, "Interobjectivity"). In Diana's case, the kitchen table carries a legacy beyond that of which she is consciously aware throughout the writing process.

Diana's movement to the living room is also a function of task: since that is where her computer resides, that is where she completes the work she finds

Figure 6.1. Diana's primary writing site (kitchen). Photograph by author.

Figure 6.2. Diana's alternative writing site (library/living room). Photograph by author.

most taxing. Her choice to place the computer in the living room is significant. Beyond providing light, the windows afford her a feeling of connectedness during the less-preferred task of typing up ideas and allow her to "be in the world" while writing. When asked about her identity as a writer, Diana did not identify in that way and instead repeatedly cited a colleague she perceived as more talented. This comparative move echoes her early understanding of her brother (but not herself) as a scholar, despite her persistent writing and professional success, success that hinges upon the space and time she dedicates. She finds a place in her home for her two writing surfaces, and she interacts in relative harmony within her habitat, shifting between writing spaces as a means of projecting herself into a writing task. Diana's desk attachment and mobile writing practice are not singular, though they contrast with the next case study of an assistant professor named Teo, who also owns two desks and who has much more trouble finding space for them and for writing in his life.

A writing desk gifted to Teo by his uncle plays a large role in his imagination, if not his practice. Teo describes the process of reintegrating this desk into his writing life: "I finally got my desk into my office. It was at my ex-girlfriend's place. This is a desk that I have had since I was in college. One of my uncles gave it to me. I've written many a paper on that desk. I wrote my [thesis] on that desk. I'm finishing my dissertation on that damn desk. I swear it felt like some—like we were reunited." This desk was Teo's cousin's desk. It became even more weighted in his imagination after his cousin died. You can hear this extra something in his personification of the desk, in his view of it as something with which he was "reunited" after parting. Teo buys a second writing desk while shopping with a friend:

> It was one of those old style and it was literally a writing desk—you know roll the top up and inside they have the sections for envelopes, clips and pens. And you can't fit a computer on it. It is a writing, like, longhand pen—something that you would use to write letters to somebody. It was just—*it was riveting. It was this feeling* like, I still handwrite a lot. I still write poems on occasion—*and I finish and I polish on my cousin's desk.*

Teo here connects a writing object with a writing task or genre. This is a common shift: an object is selected for its ability to help a writer channel a specific form. And to be a writer, he feels as if he must have the right tools. We can see the concept of possible selves at work here as well. Teo buys this desk, and imagines using it, as a means of embodying a writerly identity. Of particular interest is Teo's description of the desk as "riveting," as a "feeling"—the desk is turned from a physical object into a sensation, highlighting how much aesthetic experience writers achieve through physical objects while writing (a sensory, material experience that deserves more theoretical attention).[7] Teo also describes a mobile writing practice similar to Diana's: he begins writing on one desk and revises on the other.

Going deeper into Teo's practice illustrates how out of early habitat and object attachment emerges a materially and spatially dependent writing practice. I would describe his as exceptionally mobile and destabilized. I read this partly as a manifestation of his interior struggle with academic labor. Teo was raised by his parents, factory workers who moved to the United States from Puerto Rico. Teo describes his family as working poor. He grew up in a six-family tenement house in Brooklyn in close proximity to relatives who contributed greatly to his literacy development. Although he did not attend kindergarten, his family members taught him how to read and write, and by first grade he was labeled gifted. Despite this early success, test scores later denied him entry into the four elite Manhattan public schools. This and other events triggered a tension in regard to higher education that Teo negotiated throughout his schooling.

Teo was one of two siblings to first attend college and pursue an advanced degree. His family expected him to use his high school as a means of "going to work." Teo struggled with conceptualizing his academic work as "labor" and was only able to get through graduate school by working in a kitchen and other jobs that provided a feeling of being engaged in manual labor, the kind his family expected of him. He says about his schooling identity: "I remember my adviser asking me, 'so does your mother rent or own?' I nearly laughed in my . . . it was just so telling of how little they knew about me and why, for instance, this is so important and yet it takes me so long to do . . . I could never be just a student. That was never my reality, never at any point. And it's because we were and still are working poor." Embedded in this statement is an awareness of how student identity is tied up not only in materials of literacy but also in material dwelling. He feels he does not fit in, as is evidenced by his lack of identification with his adviser. And it is almost as if he never seems to fit perfectly into a writing habitat, either.

Teo has had a mobile sense of the writing habitat since childhood. At home, he did not have private space to write. In consequence, much of his work was performed either in the kitchen or on the living room floor. A substantial part of his work was also completed in nearby cousins' apartments. A strong parallel is evident in the nature of Teo's shifting writing and learning habitats as a child and adolescent and his decentered practices as a graduate student. If he were not so frustrated by his own process, I would present his movement between habitats and his desire to find the perfect writing setting as somewhat humorous. For instance, he gives his girlfriend his cousin's writing desk that is critical to his process, saying that he wanted *her* to have it so *she* could write. In public, he shifts between three different cafes, including the one most commonly cited by my study participants as having the most conducive layout and space required for academic work. At all three of these sites, if one or two particular tables were not available, he would leave. The common denominator of this movement: space. Teo gravitates toward working in an expansive space that echoes not only the room he had working as a child on the living room floor but his travel between different spaces.

Teo, like Diana, has practices that emerged out of the context of his early writing and learning habitats. Teo had a tactile experience with tools and with space as a child. He spread out on the floor and was conscious not only of the aesthetic dimension of his own writing utensils but also those of siblings and cousins who mattered. This aesthetic dimension followed him into adulthood, as he tries to enter the writing life through the pleasure an object affords, as well as its signification both of important relations (such as his kinship with his cousin) and important work (how the rolltop desk signals being a writer).

Teo's narrative also signals an intuitive understanding that we turn to materials not only as tools for thinking, in Turkle's words, but also as tools for becoming. I observed this not only in Teo's attachment to the desk but to other materials of learning as well, attachments that were also dependent on childhood ritual:

> My mother, with the little that she had, she would buy me—she saw that I liked writing—she bought me Little Golden Books. She bought me books that I could trace over. She bought me a lot of pens, pencils—and my aunt taught me how to write my name. And I would practice—it was always about my experimenting and perfecting letters—in the third grade when I was learning longhand script, which also coincided with my affinity for pens.

Note that Teo here discusses not only learning materials but also kin who fostered his literate development. Teo contrasts his interests to those of his graffiti artist brother: "I wouldn't write graffiti letters. I would write *letters*." Similar to David's understanding of the desk and its importance as an identity marker that distinguished him from his musician brother, Teo acknowledges an early awareness of his literacy in relation to his brother's. Teo was provided with the tools necessary to being a writer. However, he did not have the toys that other children possessed; his mother made critical decisions about which types of objects to provide to assist in his development.[8] So while Teo had pens, he did not know what Legos were until he encountered them in a doctor's office in middle school. Teo here also signals how affirmative feelings toward objects are connected to early experiences around learning to write.

Through Diana's and Teo's examples, I have tried to show how writers use objects in becoming a desired self; how material attachment begins young and helps adolescents to define themselves in relation to important others; how adult writing and material practice echo young writing and material practice[9]; and how objects embody human relationships and subsequently play complex roles in writers' lives.

Conclusion

By taking a material perspective on literacy development, identity articulation and negotiation, and the expression and maintenance of adult writing practices, we can learn much about what it means to be one who writes. The everyday objects that people use to embody the role of writer tell us what writing means to our culture and about cultural expectations for writing performance. Having the money to purchase a writing desk, for example, is a way that families can signal their awareness of writing tropes, of material writing necessities, and of cultural values around writing. Buying a writing desk is also a way that families pass down ideas about writing and schooling that were passed down by their own families—thus preserving family traditions through this ritual act.

Through Teo's narrative, I have preliminarily sketched how issues of access impact object use, attachment, and identity. More work is necessary on the effect that access to literacy's materials have on writing identity and practice. Teo's mother was crafty in her procurement of the materials of writing—not all parents have the ability to provide in this way. On a broad scale, we do not know the import of material goods in schools and the role they are playing in what students perceive as possible for themselves as adults.

Within rhetoric and writing studies, objects are an understudied player in writers' early and adult imaginings of what it means to be a writer, though these objects make strong guest appearances in our field's key texts. When a writer picks up a particular object, this is in part a matter of aesthetic-sensory preference; it is also a response to sociocultural scripting of idealized notions of what it means to write. Buying a fountain pen might be a first step toward embodying the role of writer as buying running gear is the first step in becoming a runner. The best way for us to understand the roles these objects are playing is by digging into the varied writing habitats in which and around which writers are working. As Prior and Shipka illustrate, writers are continually structuring and restructuring their habitats in a complex web of activity that is as much a part of the writing process as the moment of putting fingers to keyboard. And if we wish to understand these practices, we have to trace them back to their roots—to the early habitat and object attachments out of which grow particularized, spatial, and material learning and writing practices that are a part of the senses of self we develop in adolescence, the implications of which ricochet throughout our adult lives.

Notes

1. In multidisciplinary research on possessions, the emotional investment displayed by people in objects is referred to as "attachment" (Kleine and Baker; Passman; Wallendorf and Arnould).

2. A notable exception is Susan Wyche's work on ritual, which is a precursor to, and resonant with, the ideas expressed in Prior and Shipka's "Chronotopic Lamination."

3. Most of the identity work in and around rhetoric and writing studies focuses on academic identities, teaching identities, writing from liminal positions, or writing as it intersects with identity categories such as race, ethnicity, and gender (Ivanic; Finders; Mahiri and Godley; Villanueva). In this chapter, I conceptualize identity through the fields of psychology and consumer research, which understand the self as a construction that develops in stages and that individuals maintain through a variety of outlets, including their arsenal of possessions (cf. Belk; Kleine, Kleine, and Kernan). In line with McCarthey and Moje, I see identity as both unconsciously and consciously performed (233).

4. Beyond the works and individuals referenced in the body of this text, Csikzentmihalyi (also with Rochberg-Halton), Richins, Schlereth, *Winterthur Portfolio*, and the *Journal of Consumer Research* are good starting points for those interested in material culture studies.

5. Material culture studies gathers scholars in diverse disciplines in the study of everyday objects. Over the past ten years, I have been asked repeatedly to share my material culture bibliographies; this chapter provides some foundation. I am struck by moments when writers articulate a need for texts that help them to theorize materiality. Consider two statements from *Rhetorical Bodies*, perhaps our field's most compelling collection on materiality: Blair writes that "[she] cannot pretend to advance any declarations or fully developed theories about the material character of rhetoric" (17), and Selzer claims that "Even though rhetoric has long been concerned with the situatedness of literate acts . . . the relationship of rhetorical events to the material world that sustains and produces them has not often enough been fully elaborated" (9). However, scholars outside of rhetoric and writing studies have been considering these relationships for decades (cf. Butler; Deetz; Epp and Price; Glassie; Miller).

6. This memory of the chalkboard and the many memories of learning to write with family members I have collected seem to contradict Brandt's finding in "Remembering Writing, Remembering Reading" that while memories of learning to read with family members abound, they are scarce when it comes to writing.

7. Cf. Diana Fuss and Alice Glarden Brand, though Brand's focus is not on materiality per se.

8. It was the case for my study participants that being poor had little impact on parents' ability to procure material goods for schooling. However, most of the indi-

viduals I interviewed were in some way success stories, as they had made it into college, graduate school, or the professional world. Issues of access and materiality are subjects of research I am conducting on the back-to-school shopping process and its impact on literacy development.

9. This observation is supported by research, including that of Kleine, Kleine, and Kernan.

7
The Things They Left Behind
Toward an Object-Oriented History of Composition
Kevin Rutherford and Jason Palmeri

Recently, composition and rhetoric scholars have argued for an ontological turn in the field (Barnett; Hawk, "Reassembling"; Reid; Rivers, "Some Assembly Required"), placing engagement with everyday things to the fore of our attention. This engagement with object-oriented ontology (Bogost, *Alien Phenomenology*; Bryant; Harman, *Guerrilla Metaphysics*) has been productive; however, rhetoricians have not yet explored how the ontological turn might be informed by composition history, tending to accede to James Berlin's contention that composition has historically been centered on questions of epistemology. In contrast, we turn to object-oriented ontology (OOO) as a methodology for reseeing composition studies—a move in sympathy with Byron Hawk's vitalist "counter-history" of the field.

In this chapter, we contend that a close re-examination of composing process scholarship in the 1970s and '80s reveals a rich tradition of composition pedagogies and theories that centered on the ontological investigation of the inter-relations among nonhuman and human objects. In recovering the ontological thinking of such foundational composition theorists as Ann Berthoff, Richard Young, Alton Becker, and Kenneth Pike, we demonstrate that compositionists have long recognized the agency of everyday things in the act of composing. By placing composing process theories in dialogue with object-oriented ontology, we ultimately seek to articulate composition history as a productive resource for developing rhetorical theories and practical pedagogical heuristics for engaging with questions of ontology in our writing classrooms.

Although we seek to recover the ontological history of the process movement, we acknowledge the validity of Berlin's claim that Berthoff as well as Young, Becker, and Pike were invested in a social-epistemic worldview (Berlin 170–73, 176). Nevertheless, we contend that Berlin's epistemological reading of the process era is not the only story that can be told. As object-oriented theorists, we recognize that any assemblage of objects (Berlin's or our own) is partial and incomplete. By looking at the field through an ontological lens, we seek to add complexity to our history by revealing glimpses of the nonhuman objects that have always already been shaping our field's pedagogies.

OOO as Rhetorical Methodology

In this chapter, we turn to the philosophical movement of object-oriented ontology as a methodology for revisionist historiography. OOO theorists attempt to move philosophy away from a single-minded focus on epistemology by expanding the philosophical conversation to include not only questions of *how we know* the world but also questions of *what the world is*. Arguing that ontology is "first philosophy" (Bryant 51), object-oriented ontologists refocus the philosophical enterprise to engage a variety of human and nonhuman objects on equal ontological grounds. In this way, OOO enables theorists to ask more complex and difficult questions about ontology by repositioning humans as one kind of object among many rather than as the ultimate arbiters of reality. This decentering of the human perspective, argues OOO theorist Levi Bryant, pushes us toward "what anti-humanism and post-humanism ought to be" (22–23). We assert that composition history—particularly the work of Berthoff as well as Young, Becker, and Pike—contains glimpses of just this kind of shift.

OOO is a complex field, so it would be impossible for us to treat it in depth here; instead, we rely on a few key concepts that are shared among various object-oriented philosophers. Specifically, we draw on three key elements of OOO that we see at work in Berthoff and Young, Becker, and Pike: 1) the concept of a flat ontology; 2) the understanding of objects as complex assemblages with their own agency; and 3) the recognition of the "inherent withdrawal" (Harman, *Guerrilla Metaphysics* 76) (or unknowability) of objects and the necessity of metaphor as a vehicle of translation among them.

The term "object" is a complicated one, carrying a variety of meanings dependent on discipline. For instance, computer programmers might see objects as one kind of programming paradigm, whereas humanists may see the term as oppositional to a human subject. In OOO, "object" can refer to any *thing*. The grade school concept of a noun as a person, place, thing, or idea applies, but objects in OOO can also refer to properties of things as well as the relationships between them. In short, the "object" in OOO can refer to anything that exists: symbols, systems, people, material things, fictional characters, and daydreams can all be viewed as equally real objects in an ontological sense.

Bryant refers to this capacious understanding of objects as a "flat ontology" in which: 1) no object (or type of object) should be granted special status as the origin of all other objects; 2) there is no single world but rather a multiplicity of objects and object relations; 3) no kind of relation should be inherently privileged over another; and 4) all beings are equally real, though not necessarily of equal importance in their local networks. For Bryant (and, as we shall soon see, for Berthoff), there is no fundamental difference between "subjects, groups, fictions, technologies, institutions . . . quarks, planets, trees, and tardigrades" (32).

While OOO theorists reject any fundamental difference among types of objects, they also recognize that all objects exert autonomous agency. Graham Harman argues that an object must "have a sort of independence from whatever it is not. An object stands apart—not just from its manifestation to humans but possibly even from its own accidents, relations, qualities, moments, or pieces" (*Prince of Networks* 152). Perhaps the most familiar treatment of objects as autonomous agents is in Bruno Latour's actor-network theory, and appropriately, Harman argues that Latour is effectively (if not expressly) an object-oriented ontologist (*Prince of Networks* 16). For both Latour and Harman, objects are separate, autonomous, and unified, but are also composed of an infinite number of other objects in infinite regression. In this chapter, we contend that OOO's emphasis on the recursivity of object assemblage bears a striking resemblance to Young, Becker, and Pike's articulation of the "particle-wave-field" heuristic for composing.

Although OOO theorists recognize the autonomous agency of objects, they also argue that all objects are inherently withdrawn—that the essences of objects only (partially) emerge in their *relations* with other things. Latour's actor-network theory is a structure designed to engage with and trace such relations (although Latour is disinclined to believe that objects essentially exist apart from their relations; on this point Harman disagrees). In contrast to Latour, Harman describes the relations between objects as "vicarious causation"—they do not directly interact but require some intermediation (*Guerrilla Metaphysics* 48). Relying on Harman, Ian Bogost develops the concept of metaphor to describe this process of vicarious causation. For Bogost, humans and other objects "never understand the alien experience, we only ever reach for it metaphorically" (*Alien Phenomenology* 66). Metaphorism is a method by which humans might begin to understand other objects on their own terms, recognizing that such understanding will always be incomplete. (Similarly, the experience of the object apprehending the human will also necessarily be metaphorical and hence partial.) Metaphorism relies on seeing things *as if* they were understandable, while simultaneously realizing that the essences of objects—all objects—are unknowable. As we seek to consider ways of teaching students to employ metaphor as a tool of ontological investigation, we suggest that recovering Berthoff's pedagogical uses of metaphor will be helpful.

"Related Everything": Berthoff's Rhetorical Ontology

Undoubtedly, Berthoff is a humanist in the sense that she believes in the primacy of human linguistic thought in constructing the "reality" of the world, emphasizing "thinking about thinking" and "interpreting interpretations." Yet, Berthoff's work is also notoriously complex, and we highlight here numerous moments in which she appears to belie or exceed the epistemological frame in which her work has thus far been contained. Although Berthoff is well known for her trenchant critique of positivism (Berlin), she nevertheless is also deeply interested in the ontological investigation of the natural world.

Resisting the common binary between scientific and humanistic ways of knowing, Berthoff powerfully asserts in her 1981 *The Making of Meaning* that "observation is central to all disciplines" and thus "what the biologist does is comparable to what the poet does" (116). By articulating observation as an act of composing, Berthoff seeks to bridge the divide between rhetoric and science—repositioning the composition class as a place where students employ language in creative, metaphorical ways to arrive at probable truths about the ontological existence of objects in the natural world.

Challenging the common notion that composition should focus on the epistemic power of words alone, Berthoff argues that "making sense of the world is composing. It includes being puzzled, being mistaken, and then suddenly seeing things for what they probably are. . . . [W]riting is like the composing we do all the time when we make sense of the world" (*Making* 11). Rejecting both a positivist epistemology that suggests that language transparently describes reality *and* a radical social constructionist epistemology that suggests that language *completely* constructs reality, Berthoff instead foregrounds a *rhetorical ontology* that views language as a dialogic tool that can be employed reflectively to discover what things "probably are."

Positioning composing as an ontological activity, Berthoff begins her textbook *Forming Thinking Writing* by engaging students in close observation of and dialogue with a natural object—a milkweed pod, a crab leg, a walnut husk—over a week's time. Specifically, Berthoff instructs students to "address yourself to the object; ask it questions; let it answer back; write down the dialogue. Record your observations and observe your observations" (*Forming* 13). For Berthoff, the natural object is not mere lifeless matter wholly constructed by the linguistic and ideological frames that students bring to it; rather, the object is an active participant in the students' composing processes. By asking students to attribute agency to the object, Berthoff challenges them to push beyond common linguistic ways of characterizing objects by attempting to understand and empathize with the object from its own point of view.

As an example of how observation exercises can help students develop complex and empathetic understandings of objects, Berthoff includes in her textbook a journal excerpt in which a student named Emily describes her observation of how a walnut husk changed over a week. As Emily records the changing shape of the husk and the diverse objects that are assembled within it, she metaphorically empathizes with the husk—imagining it alternately as struggling to give birth, to confront the challenges of aging, and to fend off attack (*Forming* 16–18). As Emily engages in dialogue with the walnut husk as an object to which she grants agency, she even begins to consider her ethical relation to the husk by asking if she should feel guilt about how she has contributed to its destruction by carelessly carrying it in her backpack (18). At the end of the week's observation exercise, Emily has not only developed a more complex understanding of how she uses language to construct the reality of the walnut husk, but has also arrived at a more ethically and ontologically complex vision of the reality of the husk and her own relation to it. Although Emily's ethical reflection about her relation to the walnut husk may strike some readers as insignificant, we would note that humans' ethical relations to natural and material objects are a truly pressing concern in our current moment of ongoing ecological crisis (Morton, *The Ecological Thought*). As a result, Berthoff's pedagogical emphasis on dialogic observation and empathy with nonhuman objects can be seen as offering a powerful ontological basis for contemporary critical pedagogy.

Although Berthoff emphasizes teaching students to empathize with objects, she also recognizes that it is impossible for Emily to fully experience the world as a walnut husk or any other object does. Berthoff (like Harman and Bogost) asserts that we can only understand objects, both human and nonhuman, *metaphorically* in relation to other objects. Highlighting the powerful role of metaphor as a tool of ontological investigation, Berthoff asserts that "the way we make sense of the world is to see something *with respect to, in terms of, in relation to something else*. We can't make sense of one thing in itself; it must be seen as being *like* another thing" (*Forming* 44). In addition to showing students ways that nonhuman objects may be metaphorically viewed in terms of human experience, Berthoff also importantly encourages students to consider the relations that nonhuman objects have with each other. For example, Berthoff asks students to explore bird feathers in relation to train tracks (*Forming* 68–69) and snowshoes in relation to rug beaters (72). In Berthoff's view, students can gain a more complex understanding of objects if they resist relying solely on clichéd anthropocentric metaphors and instead explore a wide variety of possible *relations* among objects.

In seeking to teach students to explore unexpected relations among objects at varying levels of scale, Berthoff turns to the insights of science. For example, Berthoff asks students to observe a table both with their human eyes and through the lens of a physicist's laboratory equipment: "You look in front of you and see a solid object—say a table, which is usually the philosopher's favorite example. Modern physics tells us that this table is really an event, but we don't see the electrons moving in that frenzy of activity that makes the table an event. We do not have eyes that can take in that scene" (*Forming* 44). In addition to helping students understand the ways in which language and social context influence our perception of the table, Berthoff also wishes to challenge students to understand the ontological reality of the table from the nonanthropocentric point of view—to consider what the table might look like from the perspective of electrons interacting with one another viewed through an electron microscope. In this way, Berthoff suggests that empirical scientific technologies can offer us useful ways of apprehending the ontological reality of complex assemblages of objects—that humanistic metaphor and scientific study can complement one another. For Berthoff (as for OOO theorists), the table is "real" and the electrons are "real" and the challenge of the rhetorical ontologist is to attempt to develop as complex a vision of these realities as possible.

In addition to attending closely to individual objects such as tables and walnut husks, Berthoff also encourages students to generate complex assemblages of objects in relation to one another as a strategy of invention. In describing the art of composition as assemblage to students, Berthoff asserts that "a composition is a bundle of parts: you get the parts by generating a chaos of names and you bundle them as you identify the relationships among them" (*Forming* 72). Encouraging students to resist common taxonomies for organizing objects, Berthoff asks students to generate associative lists and then experiment with different ways of categorizing them. For example, she demonstrates how a student could generate a "chaos" of objects in relation to a snowshoe, including "foot, protection, Massachusetts . . . an old trapper, L. L. Bean, old fashioned rug beater, bear paw" (72) and many more. Importantly, Berthoff asks students to consider humans, animals, material objects, and ideas as equally real objects that can be assembled in various ways, foregrounding a flat ontology in which "entities at all levels of scale, whether natural or cultural, physical or artificial, material or semiotic are on equal ontological footing" (Bryant 279).

By encouraging students to create object assemblages within a flat ontology, Berthoff seeks to help them avoid reductive, clichéd thinking. For example, when Berthoff asks students to generate lists of animal names and then place them in unfamiliar taxonomies—such as "tails/no tails" or "salads/not salads" (Berthoff and Stephens 107)—she is asking writers to overturn the notion that objects inherently spring from some originary source and naturally follow a preexisting categorization scheme. Berthoff's quixotic lists of objects are reminiscent in both form and function of what Bogost has called "Latour litanies." While Berthoff asks students to contemplate possible relations among "rolling pins, baseballs, UFOs, Superman, as well as herons and plovers" (*Forming* 96), Latour asks scholars to trace the associations among "black holes, rivers, transgenic soy beans, farmers, the climate, human embryos, and humanized pigs" (*Politics of Nature* 151). In both cases, the lists of seemingly unrelated objects provide moments to produce and examine new taxonomies with the eventual goal of creating new perspectives and connections.

For Berthoff, assemblage is a method for ontological investigation of objects in the world as well as a powerful approach for inventively composing with words, sentences, and paragraphs. Specifically, Berthoff's textbook asks students to compose assemblages of linguistic objects at differing levels of scale: "A composition is a bundle of parts in which each element is both a part and a bundle; a sentence is both a bundle of grammatical parts and a part of the rhetorical bundle called a paragraph; a paragraph is both a bundle of sentences and a part of the whole composition" (*Forming* 156). Rather than encourage students to proceed deductively from outline to sentences, Berthoff instead asks students to begin with lists of words and sentences and then explore multiple ways of reassembling them.

Using a strikingly material (yet still anthropocentric) metaphor for arrangement, Berthoff tells students that the "paragraph gathers like a hand" and that "the kind of gathering a paragraph makes is thus dependent on both the kind of elements and the way in which they have been gathered" (*Forming* 158). After students have gathered a variety of words and sentences in a paragraph, Berthoff then challenges them to compose a brief gloss as a way of "stabilizing a cluster of sentences so that [they] can consider them collectively as well as individually" (162). By conceptualizing paragraph composition as a method of reassembling objects (akin to methods for engaging material objects in the world), Berthoff demonstrates the usefulness of grounding writing pedagogy in ontology. As she argues, a pedagogy of composition should not be limited *solely* to engaging the epistemic power of language; rather, a truly ontological approach to composition must recognize that "everything leads to everything else. A good course in composition could be entitled, 'Related Everything'" (63). In this way, Berthoff outlines a truly capacious vision of composition as a discipline—one that disrupts the conventional binaries between the epistemological and the ontological, the humanistic and scientific, the linguistic and the material.

Readers Are Like Houses: Young, Becker, and Pike's Ontological Heuristics

While Berthoff elucidates the associative generation of chaos as the most useful method of ontological investigation, Young, Becker, and Pike offer more formalized heuristics as the primary means for discovering probable truths about the existence of things. Despite their disagreements about strategies of invention,

Berthoff as well as Young, Becker, and Pike are aligned in their attempts to position rhetoric as an ontological (as well as epistemic) discipline. In the preface to their famous textbook *Rhetoric: Discovery and Change*, Young, Becker, and Pike draw on Augustine to define rhetoric as first and foremost an ontological art: "The most succinct summary of our concept of rhetoric is the one St. Augustine made of his own rhetoric over 1500 years ago. 'There are two things necessary . . . a way of discovering those things which are to be understood, and a way of teaching what we have learned.' Despite significant differences between our concept of rhetoric and Augustine's, we share his views that the process of discovering knowledge must be yoked to the process of communicating it and that, of the two, the first demands greater attention" (xiv). Young, Becker, and Pike contend that discovering knowledge about objects should be the primary concern of rhetorical pedagogy. Like object-oriented ontologists, they assert that the first concern of rhetoric is about being (an ontological concern), rather than being *for us* (an epistemological one).

In their attempt to refocus rhetoric on ontology, Young, Becker, and Pike turn to heuristics as a key method of ontological investigation that can bridge the gap between humanistic and scientific ways of apprehending objects. Noting that heuristic procedures played a key role in both rhetoric and science in the classical and Renaissance eras, Young, Becker, and Pike assert that "although the sciences today employ a well developed heuristic procedure, the scientific method, rhetoric seldom makes use of one. The art of inquiry in rhetoric has declined; the need for it, however, has not" (120). In outlining rhetorical heuristics for discovering knowledge about objects in the world, Young, Becker, and Pike place special emphasis on ontological investigation of what they term "units of experience." Articulating a capacious flat ontology for rhetorical study, the authors define "unit of experience" in broadly inclusive terms: a unit might be an oak tree, a house, a human reader, a sentence, or an abstract concept such as democracy. By demonstrating how houses, oak trees, and words can be investigated via similar heuristic procedures, Young, Becker, and Pike disrupt the conventional binary between the scientific investigation of *objects* and the rhetorical investigation of *language*.

To help students investigate the complex networks of relations among diverse units in a flat ontology, Young, Becker, and Pike suggest that "a unit of experience can be viewed as a particle, as a wave, or as a field. That is, the writer can choose to view any element of his experience as if it were static, or as if it were dynamic, or as if it were a network of relationships or part of a larger network" (122). Significantly, Young, Becker, and Pike first explicate this particle-wave-field heuristic by applying it to objects, specifically a house and an oak tree. According to the authors, an oak tree can be broken down into smaller "particle" units (branches, roots, cells, etc.); it can be viewed as a dynamic wave changing over time (growth, decay); and it can be viewed as a field by seeing it as an agent interacting in a broader ecological network (128–29).

In their example of applying the particle-wave-field heuristic to the oak tree, Young, Becker, and Pike powerfully assert that viewing units from different perspectives and levels of scale is key for ensuring a complex and nuanced ontological view of objects and their relationships to one another:

> The perspectives in the chart supplement each other; each reveals a partial truth about the unit being investigated. Approaching a unit from different perspectives gives us some assurance that we are thinking well, that we have not overlooked important data. Finally, notice that the procedure is infinitely recursive. Any feature of the tree (one of its components, a system of which it is part, a particular stage in its development and so on) can itself be a new unit of investigation. (130)

By emphasizing the importance of recursively investigating units at multiple levels of scale, Young, Becker, and Pike encourage students to resist the stereotypical assumptions they may have about objects (whether they are oak trees or abstract concepts such as "civil disobedience"). Instead of focusing on asking simply "what is the object in itself?" or "what is this object for me?," Young, Becker, and Pike provoke students to recursively investigate the question "how does this object relate to other objects in a network over time?" In this way, they position the rhetoric classroom as a space in which students can employ heuristics as a method for developing more nuanced and complex understandings of the existence of things in the world.

Like Byron Hawk, we see Young, Becker, and Pike's heuristic as a potentially useful method to help students "tackle complexity" (*A Counter-History* 38) by bridging the gap between scientific and humanistic forms of knowledge-making; however, we also agree with Hawk's critique that the heuristic is "too rigid and attempts to control and direct the invention process too much" (38). Hawk notes that Young, Becker, and Pike's investment in offering a teachable, scientific method of invention causes them to unduly privilege the role of human perception—precluding a more complex understanding of the emergent agency of nonhuman objects in making meaning. Like Hawk, we too are concerned that Young, Becker, and Pike problematically tend to figure objects as "out there" waiting for humans to come along and inscribe them in some symbol system. For example, in the authors' analysis of Pike's house, the house merely exists, waiting for a human perceiver to approach and to apprehend it in his (sadly, always his, not her) perception. Indeed, Young, Becker, and Pike explicitly argue that it makes no sense to speak of "a unit without some formulation of it in a mind" (122). However, the particle-wave-field heuristic itself *need not* be this exclusionary. We might imagine applying the heuristic from multiple perspectives, some of which are perspectives outside the mind of the human interpreter: how is the human observer figured from the perspective of the house? How might exploring the house's perspective cause the human observer to see it in a new way? How does a digital camera apprehend the house at a particle, wave, and field level? By expanding the particle-wave-field heuristic to explore how nonhuman objects perceive other objects, we could add even more ontological complexity to students' investigations of object relations in the composition classroom.

In addition to applying their flat ontological heuristic toward an analysis of nonhuman objects and linguistic concepts, Young, Becker, and Pike also demonstrate how their heuristic can be employed as a tool for investigating the ontological reality of particular audiences. Moving beyond simplistic understandings of audience, Young, Becker, and Pike assert that:

> A reader, like an oak tree or a house, has contrastive features that separate him from other people, features that identify him. He also varies over time. . . . By encouraging the writer to note a number of the reader's contrastive features, to observe the way he actually changes over a period of time, and to examine the various contexts in which he acts and is acted upon, the heuristic procedure tends to correct the writer's stereotypes. (179)

Paradoxically, Young, Becker, and Pike suggest that we might be able to develop a more complex understanding of human audiences if we viewed them not as stable human agents but rather as complex assemblages of objects situated in time and space. By looking at human readers *as if* they were houses or oak trees, we can challenge ourselves to push beyond stereotypical frames for audience analysis—to consider the ways in which our readers can best be apprehended by exploring their relations with multiple objects (including material places, ideological concepts, social organizations, and so forth).

In asking students to investigate human readers as complex assemblages of objects rather than as stable subjects, Young, Becker, and Pike seek to help students discover more points of connection or identification with audiences who are different from themselves. Seeking to explain the process by which people can be persuaded to see the world differently, the authors assert that "change between units can occur only over a bridge of shared features" (172). Significantly, Young, Becker, and Pike articulate the process of Rogerian negotiation in strikingly material terms. Powerfully demonstrating how paying close attention to nonhuman objects can help us develop more ethically responsive ways of practicing rhetoric, Young, Becker, and Pike assert that "the characteristics of an actual bridge over a river can give us insights into a rhetorical bridge. We can travel over an actual bridge in two directions; because traffic seldom moves in one direction only, changes may occur at either end of the bridge" (177). By using a material bridge as a metaphor for theorizing rhetorical interaction, Young, Becker, and Pike encourage students to resist conceptualizing persuasion as a unidirectional process of one stable human subject changing the mind of another stable human subject. Instead, by articulating both the writer and the reader as complex, shifting assemblages of objects interacting with one another, Young, Becker, and Pike challenge students to engage in ethically responsive dialogue with those whom they perceive as different and to recognize that this dialogue must necessarily change them as well as their readers.

Although we think that Young, Becker, and Pike's bridge heuristic offers a useful starting place for an ethically responsive, object-oriented pedagogy, we think it important to note that they problematically elide considerations of how embodied positionalities (Haraway, *Simians*) influence the interactions among objects. Young, Becker, and Pike almost always implicitly position the human ontological investigator as a white, middle class, cisgender, able bodied *man*—without considering how race, class, gender, sexuality, and ability are themselves objects that exert force in rhetorical situations (Ahmed, *Queer Phenomenology*). In order for an object-oriented rhetoric to truly help students build bridges across differences, we believe that it must account for and challenge structures of privilege and domination (Ratcliffe).

Composition History as Object Assemblage

This essay has deliberately placed past composing process theories in conversation with contemporary articulations of object-oriented ontology. Taking cues from Bruno Latour, we have forged an alliance of actants by tracing associations (*Reassembling* 5). Like all assembled alliances, we acknowledge that these connections are incomplete, partial, and contingent, and that they require work to maintain. However, we see these connections as generative and ultimately productive. We believe that attending more directly to the role of nonhuman agents in composition's history allows us to better situate our current practices and to re-see the necessary work of the field in the future. Essentially, we contend that composition historians and instructors need to generate their own "chaoses"—to create new multivalent taxonomies that account for the messy and complex distribution of our work through and with different kinds of objects inclusive of humans and nonhumans alike.

We reassembled this history by paying close attention to the nonhuman objects lurking in plain sight in the work of Berthoff as well as Young, Becker, and Pike. But there is much more work to be done toward an object-oriented history of composition. We ask: what would the history of the field look like if we began not by starting with epistemology but rather by looking first at James Berlin's writing desk, at Linda Flower's tape recorder, at the Los Angeles freeways that surrounded the 1963 CCCC meeting, at the pay stubs of TAs and contingent faculty at Harvard, at the flying brick that inspired Williamson's infamous call for filmmaking as composition?

And, as we begin to recover the nonhuman objects that have shaped our past, we can also be inspired to engage in more complex and empathetic dialogue with the everyday things acting within and around our contemporary writing classrooms. For example, we might ask students not only to analyze the language of the lab report genre, but also to look and look again at the objects the report describes—to use rhetorical heuristics to discover knowledge about the material world (not just to analyze how that knowledge is made). We might not only engage students in writing with computers, but also ask them to explore how the material structure of the keyboard influences their thinking, to consider how a search engine might perceive their writing differently from a human reader, to feel empathy for the dead computers they have consigned to the scrap heap. Just as our understanding of our field's history can be enriched by forging new alliances with a more diverse range of objects, so too can our students' composing be enhanced when they come to understand themselves as assemblers of things and not just as writers of words.

8
Object-Oriented Ontology's Binary Duplication and the Promise of Thing-Oriented Ontologies

S. Scott Graham

Recent scholarship across humanistic and social scientific disciplines has enthusiastically embraced a (re)new(ed) turn toward ontological inquiry. A few prominent examples include Annemarie Mol's multiple ontologies, Graham Harman's object-oriented metaphysics, Hans-Jörg Reinberger's epistemology of the concrete, Diana Coole and Samantha Frost's new materialisms, Andrew Pickering's nonmodern ontology, Jane Bennett's vibrant materialism, and Ian Bogost's alien phenomenology. As this collection of neologisms suggests, new materialisms (Coole and Frost's umbrella term) are marked by a strong interest in objects, ontologies, reality, and the concrete. However, turning toward is also turning away—even in the case of this metaphorical turn (Keeling and Kim). Each of the scholars above includes in his or her justification for renewed attention to brute reality an explicit rejection of academe's last turn: the linguistic/semiotic/rhetorical. In short, new materialisms enjoin researchers to confine their inquiry to the analysis of discrete objects and their processes of coordination and articulation with other discrete objects.

Given that the turn to new materialisms is often grounded in a rejection of the rhetorical, it is a bit odd that rhetoricians would so enthusiastically embrace this new theoretical agenda. Nevertheless, scholars of rhetoric are increasingly endorsing new materialisms and a renewed engagement with objects (Graham, "Agency"; Graham and Herndl; Gruber; Herndl; P. Lynch; Morton, "Sublime Objects"; Murdy; Ploeger; Rickert; Scott; Shea). Certainly, the power and pervasiveness of the new materialisms turn require that it not go unaddressed. At the same time, however, it is incumbent upon rhetoricians to develop a theoretical relationship with new materialisms that does not undermine (at best) or completely reject (at worst) two and a half millennia of scholarly development.

The primary aim of this essay, therefore, is to sketch out one possible horizon of inquiry that grounds itself in the insights of new materialisms without the all too common attendant rejection of rhetoric.[1] As this chapter will argue,

I believe it both possible and advisable to develop rhetorical new materialisms. Such an inquiry is essential because it may offer a more coherent and less contradictory approach to many of the oft-discussed rhetorically friendly aspects of some new materialisms scholarship, such as Latour's *Dingpolitik* (Latour, "From Realpolitik") or Mol's cross-ontological calibration (*The Body Multiple*; see also, Graham and Herndl; Teston et al.).

Of course, as the citations spread across the last two paragraphs suggest, among many there is no hesitance to adopt the insights of new materialisms. So while my primary aim is to offer new possibility, that new possibility must be slowly built out of grave concerns I have about the general thrust of many versions of new materialisms. In short, I will argue that although most new materialisms are born of the same diagnosis of failure in the history of Western thought, the most popular approaches do not so much escape that diagnosis as reify it, with great cost for rhetorical inquiry. In the sections that follow, I will: 1) outline the diagnostic consensus that recognizes the subject-object dichotomy and other similar Cartesian binaries as the roots of philosophical failure; 2) describe how the most popular new materialisms attempt to solve this problem by instituting new binaries; and 3) explore how these new binaries relegate the status of rhetoric to one of accidental epiphenomenon. Finally, I will close with an all too brief suggestion for rhetorically friendly new materialisms grounded not in object-oriented ontology but rather in thing-oriented ontologies.

Diagnostic Consensus: The Two-World Problem

"New materialisms" is the catch-all inclusive term offered by Coole and Frost in their synoptic collection *New Materialisms: Ontology, Agency, and Politics*. In their introduction, the editors develop a comprehensive articulation of the key themes developed under the rubrics of vibrant materialisms, object-oriented ontologies, epistemology of the concrete, multiple ontologies, etc. Ultimately, Coole and Frost distill their understanding of these combined approaches down to three key features: 1) a posthumanist commitment to taking physical materiality more seriously; 2) a focus on biopolitical and bioethical dimensions of the human; and 3) a renewed engagement with economic materiality (Coole and Frost 7–8). Among these three themes, the first is the primary subject of this essay, *viz.*, the reengagement with materiality and ontology. Although this reengagement takes as many forms as there are new materialisms, a serious and fresh approach to the brute objects of material reality is often a primary feature.

Generally speaking, the broad acceptance of the new materialist turn is predicated on a diagnostic consensus. That is, the majority of new materialisms scholars have come to agree on a central failing in Western intellectual history, the so-called two-world problem (fig. 8.1), which constitutes a series of bifurcations

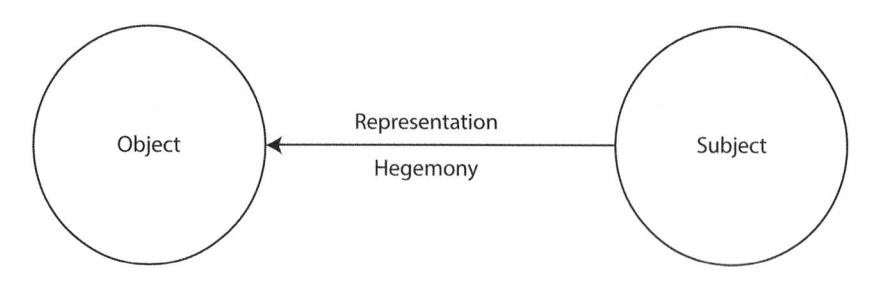

Figure 8.1. The two-world of modernity and postmodernity.

that includes the subject-object, culture-nature, and mind-body dichotomies. These binaries not only establish the core territory of modernism; they create an epistemological crisis. This crisis is what Harman refers to as "the problem of access" (*The Quadruple Object*) and Levi Bryant as "the epistemic fallacy" (*The Democracy of Objects*). The irreversible, unbridgeable dichotomy between the subject and the object forces a constant reengagement with the question of whether or not the subject has access to the object. Elaborating on Latour's critique of modernist epistemology, Bryant argues that "As a consequence of the two world schema, the question of the object, of what substances are, is subtly transformed into the question of how and whether we know objects. The question of objects becomes the question of a particular relationship between humans and objects. This, in turn, becomes a question of whether or not our representations map onto reality" (16). Unfortunately, as scholars familiar with this area will know, postmodernism's rejection of positivism, despite claims to the contrary, does not so much deconstruct this dichotomy as reify it. Latour, of course, identified just this issue as early as 1993. As he notes, "Postmodernism is a symptom, not a fresh solution. It lives under the modern Constitution, but no longer believes in the guarantees the Constitution offers" (*We Have Never* 46). Translated from Latourian, this argument holds that postmoderns do not actually reject the two-world hypothesis. Instead, they privilege the other side, as it were, placing subject over object, words over things.

Bryant follows Latour and identifies a second predominant fallacy of Western thought—"the hegemonic fallacy" (*Democracy* 131). The hegemonic fallacy also arises from the two-world problem and is predicated on the postmodern's binary reversal. When the subject is privileged over the object to the extent that the object becomes an epiphenomenon of the subject—as it does with the death of the referent—then the mirror up to nature has become the bizarre funhouse mirror up to subjectivity. (But note that this mirroring still occurs between a subject and an object, even if that object is epiphenomenal to the subject, as it is in the case of ludic antirealism.) For Bryant, it is this totalizing subject that gives rise to hegemony critiques, and is equally, again, of the two-world problem.

From Two Worlds to Four: The Metaphysical Fallacy

With the broad acceptance of the failure of the two-world schema, thinkers working in new materialisms have set themselves the task of developing new ontological foundations for inquiry. And though the lengthy collection of neologisms in this essay's introduction is suggestive of the variety of proposed solutions, many of these solutions are based in very similar intellectual moves that, taken together, render the two-world problem a four-world problem and replace the epistemic and hegemonic fallacies with what I am calling the "metaphysical fallacy." A careful analysis of proposed solutions in new materialisms, especially object-oriented new materialisms, reveals that efforts to transcend the problem of access ultimately duplicate it on a second (supposedly more authentic) infra-level of engagement. In short, removing epistemology from ontology is not enough. Metaphysics must also be removed or two worlds become four.

I am, of course, not the first to recognize that the influence of metaphysics on Western thought is part and parcel to the influence of epistemology, and that as long as metaphysics is maintained, so is the two-world problem. While most locate the essential turn in new materialisms in the shift from epistemology to ontology, Latour argues for a shift from metaphysics to ontology:

> To go from metaphysics to ontology is to raise again the question of what the real world is really like. As long as we remain in metaphysics, there is always the danger that deployment of the actors' worlds will remain too easy because they could be taken as so many representations of what the world, in the singular, is like. In which case we would not have moved an inch and would be back at square one of social explanation—namely back to Kant's idealism. (*Reassembling* 117)

What we need in a move to new materialisms is the articulation of an ontology outside of both epistemology and metaphysics. Only then will we be able to escape the two-world problem without creating a four-world problem.

So what exactly is this four-world problem? Traditionally, metaphysical inquiry postulates a fundamental separation between noumena (the real essence of an object) and phenomena (the sensual qualities of that object as humans experience them). While epistemic inquiry bifurcates words from things, metaphysics separates things from themselves. That is, metaphysical inquiry postulates that any object is dual and is comprised of those internal features essential to an object's being (noumena), and those features that exist in the object's appearance (phenomena). Of course, this sounds very much like the epistemic fallacy, and it is. However, the attempt to shed epistemology without shedding metaphysics duplicates the problem of access despite removing it from the order of representation. Thus, the metaphysical fallacy is the root of the four-world

112 / S. Scott Graham

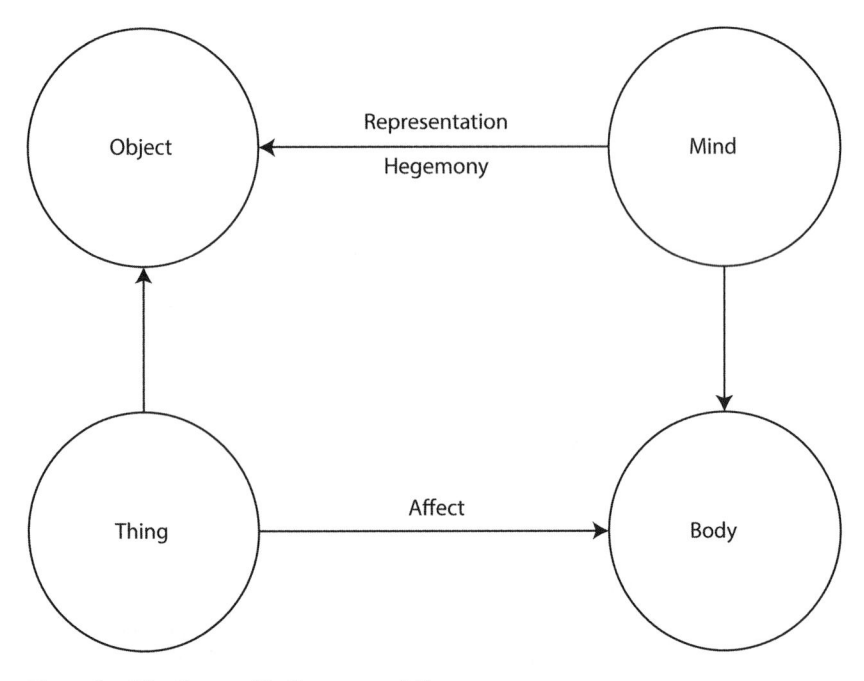

Figure 8.2. The four-world of new materialisms.

problem. When epistemology is thought to be first philosophy, the epistemic fallacy lies directly on top of the metaphysical fallacy and obscures it in debates over representation-qua-correspondence versus representation-qua-hegemony. When epistemology is removed from the equation without also removing metaphysics, a second binary is created between representation (epistemology) and phenomena (metaphysics).

The metaphysical fallacy is enacted and the two-world problem is translated into a four-world problem (fig. 8.2) through the establishment of two simultaneous moves within new materialisms. These efforts include (following my medical metaphor of diagnosis): 1) the thingectomy; and 2) the reverse-Cartesian lobotomy. Each of these moves is further reinforced by demarcations of authenticity that serve to reinforce rhetoric's place as epiphenomenal.

The Thingectomy: Following the desire to overcome the epistemic fallacy, many thinkers working in new materialisms seek out a way to conceive of or demarcate *materia ontologica* from the objects of epistemology. One popular solution comes from Heidegger's thing theory, which posits a dualist unit of being. In short, Heidegger makes a critical distinction between the thing (*Ding*) and the object (*Gegenstand*). The contraposition of *Ding* and *Gegenstand* (literally, that which stands against) highlights the object's necessary participation in the order of representation. The *Ding*, on the other hand, precedes representation, existing in the order of practice and doing. Much clarity is brought to the distinction between *Ding* and *Gegenstand* when we read it against Heidegger's theory of tool-being.

In *Being and Time*, Heidegger distinguishes between *vorhanden* (present-to-hand) and *zuhanden* (ready-to-hand). In the famous example of the hammer, a perfectly functioning hammer articulated into the practice of carpentry is *zuhanden*. Its being recedes from notice, although it is still implicated in an order of activity, a regime of practice—that of carpentry. If the hammer were to break, however, it would become *vorhanden* and subject to the theoretical attention of the carpenter who must now assess and then fix or replace the hammer. For Heidegger, things are *zuhanden* and objects are *vorhanden*. In other words, to be an object, to be *vorhanden*, is to stand against (*Gegenstand*) a subject in the order of representation.

As previously mentioned, this demarcation is found in a wide variety of new materialisms as part of ongoing efforts to circumnavigate the epistemic fallacy. Harman, Bryant, Bogost, and Thomas Rickert all directly employ modifications of Heideggerian thing theory in their scholarship. For example, Harman appropriates Heidegger's conception of things when he notes that "No sensual profile of these things will ever exhaust its full reality, which *withdraws* into the dusk of a shadowy underworld" (*Quadruple* 42, emphasis added). And similarly, Rickert's[2] foreword to *Ambient Rhetoric* prefaces his use of Heidegger in shifting the reader's attention from objects to things:

> The project suggests we take as provisional starting points the dissolution of the subject-object relation, the abandonment of representationalist theories of language, an appreciation of nonlinear dynamics and the process of emergence, and the incorporation of the material world as integral to human action and interaction, including rhetorical arts. . . . World in this sense is not just the material environs, that is, the "'mundane' bedrock of reality, but also the involvements and cares that emerge within and alongside the material environment and that in turn work to bring presence to the environs in the mode that they currently take. World, then, is simultaneously *immanent and transcendent* to each agent—and that includes nonhuman elements" (xii–xiii, emphasis added).

While thing theory and tool-being offer a great deal of potential for both new materialisms and rhetorical theory, their current instantiation in much new materialisms inquiry provides the root of the metaphysical fallacy. Indeed, as Harman notes in *The Quadruple Object*, "The metaphysics presented in this book lays great stress on several key tensions between objects and their qualities"

(26). Furthermore, "although we never touch real objects, we always touch sensual objects. Sensual objects would not even exist if they did not exist for me, or for some other agent that expends its energy in taking them seriously" (74). To bring this point into more relief, I first draw the reader's attention to the added italics in the above passages. The deployment of thing theory is regularly operationalized through the "cult of the z-axis." That is, notions of withdrawal, depth, and/or transcendence are used to make both an ontological and a qualitative distinction between the thing and the object. See, for example, this later passage from Harman: "The *real objects that withdraw* from all contact must somehow be translated into sensual caricatures of themselves" (*Quadruple* 74–75, emphasis added). Similarly, Bryant's *Democracy of Objects* describes objects which "harbor a volcanic reserve in excess of their qualities," and further argues that the "essence of a substance is to *withdraw* from presence" (86). In each of these cases the supposed escape from the epistemic fallacy is predicated on the establishment of a new divide between the object and the thing, a demarcation reified in notions of depth where either withdrawal (Harman; Bryant) or transcendence (Rickert) is the wellspring of reality.

Ultimately, the deployment of thing theory in new materialisms fails on two accounts: 1) as Harman recognizes, Heidegger's *Ding* never fully disengages with the human; and 2) the cult of the z-axis grounds ontological authenticity in reference to the horizon of subject-object entanglement. Regarding the first:

> [T]he opposition is not really between tools on the one side and broken tools on the other, but between the withdrawn tool-being of things on one side and both broken and nonbroken tools on the other. After all, the functioning pragmatic tool is present for human praxis just as the broken tool is present for human consciousness. And neither of these will suffice, because what we are looking for is the thing insofar as it exists, not insofar as it is present to either theory or praxis. (Harman, *Quadruple* 54)

In the second case, the frequent reference to withdrawal or transcendence is its own undoing. Z-axis movement is an essential concept for thing-hood. The essential aspects of a thing are those which recede from or transcend subjectivity and representation. The subject is removed from the equation only to be replaced with the horizon of subjective interaction as a new subject, a new reference object. In distancing itself from epistemology and the subject, the thingectomy still relies on the subject-object relationship as the index of being. The horizon of subjectivity creates the boundaries of the thing.

The Reverse-Cartesian Lobotomy: Part and parcel of the thingectomy is the reverse-Cartesian lobotomy. In short, representation is split from affect once the two-world problem becomes fully four-world. As Harman notes, what I describe as the reverse-Cartesian lobotomy arises specifically from thing theory and the separation of *Ding* and *Gegenstand*. This new dichotomy projects back on the subject and creates two poles of interaction: one representational and another sensual. "Heidegger has no hope that theory can do justice to things. Theory is secondary for him, and thus might seem to arise only from an unnoticed background of pretheoretical practices. Instead of granting priority to a lucid conscious observer, Heidegger sees human existence (*Dasein*) as thrown into a context that is taken for granted long before it ever becomes present to the mind. Consciousness is reduced to a tiny corner of reality, while practical handling and coping become central to his model of the world. Invisible praxis is the soil from which all theory *emerges*" (Harman, *Quadruple* 40, emphasis added). In his further elucidation of Heidegger, Harman presents, perhaps, the most complete reverse-Cartesian lobotomy. Indeed, as he rereads materiality through Heidegger's infamous concept of the "fourfold," he creates a new model of reality that is explicitly four-world. This model makes a firm distinction between the real and sensual profiles of objects in interaction. Theory only emerges (as he says above) from the a priori sensual entanglements as projected from real objects.

This same move is present in Bryant's discussion of information (mind) as an accidental epiphenomenon of sensuality. Bryant replicates the noumena-phenomena or thing-object dichotomy but replaces it with a new vocabulary of endostructure and exostructure. Following many philosophers, Bryant interrogates his theory through a convenient object on his desk, a blue coffee mug. The endostructure of the coffee mug has to do with its internal characteristics and composition as read through the mug's abilities. So a part of the mug's endostructure is coloring power, and presumably also the power to hold and pour liquid. The blueness of the mug is, however, an exostructure. That is, for the mug to be blue the coloring power of the mug must engage in a distributed network that includes certain wavelengths of light and particular neurological structures (photoreceptor cones and visual cortices).

In the distinction between endo- and exostructures, we see once again a thingectomy. Much as was the case with Harman, when this thingectomy is reflected back on the subject a (re)new(ed) mind-body division is instituted. As previously noted, when the thingectomy is reoriented toward the subject, communication becomes accidental and epiphenomenal. The truth of this can be seen in Bryant's theory of information (166). Under Bryant's model, communication is an event wherein one object that happens to have the requisite communicative endostructure perturbs its environment (possibly through using its vocal cords to vibrate the air) and a second object with the appropriate endostructure receives this annoying stimuli and, due to the accidents of the second object's endostructure, the perturbation is interpreted as information. To elucidate this model of communication, Bryant relates a cynical narrative of how he interacts with his cat, pointing out that where he interprets the cat's nuzzles as affection, they are very likely merely a desire for warmth. The cat has perturbed (nuzzled) Bryant, and his human endostructure has interpreted that as information (affection) in a way that has nothing to do with the cat.

Morton's "Sublime Objects" explicitly extends Bryant's OOO to rhetorical theory, arguing for "revising the implicit order of Aristotle's five parts of rhetoric" (211). Arguing for a delivery-first approach, Morton offers a new vision of the fifth canon that simultaneously joins the physicality of mediation and the affective dimensions of rhetorical performances. He argues compellingly that invention, arrangement, style, and memory cannot be thought to precede the medium and that all rhetorical decisions, across canons, must be negotiated simultaneously. I certainly agree, as I have argued elsewhere (Graham and Whalen). However, Morton's fidelity to Bryant's OOO is its undoing. As a footnote to Bryant's theory of information, Morton presents a theory of mediation that bears an uncanny resemblance to Shannon and Weaver's famous transmission theory of communication. As Morton argues, "Delivery deforms what it delivers and the deliveree, stuttering and caricaturing them, remixing and remastering them" (214).

Additionally, Morton's rhetoric tacitly accepts the reverse-Cartesian lobotomy and reinforces the demarcation of authenticity. Morton presents affective response as the anchor of the persuasive, focusing on the sensual at the expense of the representational:

> It would be a good start to look away from the supposed 'content' of rhetoric, and even away from styles such as metaphor or ekphrasis, and toward the most physical form, delivery. Then truly we can say that by generating more sublime objects of tone, pitch, bearing, rhythm, torque, spin, nonlocality, lineation, viscosity, tension, entanglement, syntax, climate, heft, density, nuclear fission, inertia, rhyme (the list goes on and on), rhetoric really does give us a glimpse of real sensual things, things even a cat and an eighteen month old boy can steal, read about and get tangled up in. (227)

Here, again, demarcations of authenticity present a more "real" affective domain from which epiphenomenal theory or representation may arise.

In each of these cases "emergence" has been a key feature. Theory or information (the order of representation) is that which emerges from the more authentic sensual-affective interactions of objects entangled. Indeed, this notion of representational emergence is not just present in the discourse of philosophical new materialists. It is also manifest in Rickert's ambient rhetoric wherein he argues, "Language in this ambient sense *emerges* within a complex ecology of a land, people, and culture, all of which draw from and are co-responsive to one another in such a fashion as to grant a distinctiveness" (180, emphasis added). I would argue that this speaks to the pervasiveness of the metaphysical fallacy in new materialisms. Even when a rhetorician seeks to articulate a flat ontology, s/he ends up replicating the reverse-Cartesian Lobotomy. Indeed this move finds its fullest expression in the following passage from Rickert (which also reflects Heidegger's insights back on the subject):

> Affect is a modality of the entanglement of the world and body. Indeed, this attention to attunement/mood leads to Heidegger's praise of Aristotle's *Rhetoric* as "the first systematic hermeneutic of the everydayness of Being with one another" (*BT* 178). Importantly, current studies in neuroscience can be seen as empirically verifying Heidegger's claims (see Ratcliffe). Mood is not reducible to psychological or conscious cognitive states, to "interior" phenomena, since it is constitutively entangled within and emerges from the environment in which we are situated and therefore also is a prerequisite for intelligibility as such (Ratcliffe 289). . . . Heidegger makes an important contribution to rhetoric in emphasizing that pathos is the ground of logos, not vice versa. (*Ambient* 14)

I would point out, once again, that we see reversal rather than rejection. The distinction between logos and pathos is maintained, but reverses. And again, much as was the case with the thingectomy, the reverse-Cartesian lobotomy is performed with the scalpel of authenticity. Embodiment replaces representation as the authentic mode of engagement with the world. But, of course, as long as "we" are engaging with "the world," the subject-object dichotomy is never truly erased. It is merely rewritten in metaphysical terms.

The Rejection of Rhetoric

Ultimately, the pervasive rejection of rhetoric in new materialisms is a result of the metaphysical fallacy and the duplication of the two-world problem. Whether it comes in the language of Bryant's exostructural-endostructural perturbations, Rickert's ambient rhetoric, or Morton's delivery, rhetoric and representation are time and again presented as epiphenomenal to more authentic affective-embodied entanglements. This authenticity demarcation serves to construe subjects, objects, and their coarticulation in language as epiphenomenal. Not only does this introduce a new binary into new materialisms, it further marginalizes rhetoric. For indeed, in Bryant's account, his rumination on the coffee cup presents a story where the mug has an essential nature (endostructure) of molecular cohesion which has the power to produce an exostructure of coloring, which is recognized by Bryant's exostructure of color vision and interpreted as information by his endostructure. So we have the mug's physics (noumena), qualities (phenomena), and its recapitulation in language (epiphenomena). I therefore must ask how is it that we have moved past positivism at all?

Indeed, the rejection of rhetoric as emergent accidental epiphenomenon is nearly pervasive in new materialisms. The efforts to overcome the epistemic fallacy have resulted in explicit arguments for the removal of not only the problem of access, but also rhetorical inquiry writ large. Pickering, for example, rejects "the linguistic turn" as the avatar of correspondence epistemology: "I take the cybernetic emphasis on epistemology to be a symptom of the dominance of specifically epistemological inquiry in philosophy of science in the second half of the twentieth century, associated with the so-called linguistic turn in the humanities and social sciences, a dualist insistence that while we have access to our own words, language, and representations, we have no access to things in themselves" (26). Similarly, Coole and Frost note a recurrent rejection of textual approaches and the cultural turn as part of the move away from the hegemonic fallacy:

> Everywhere we look, it seems to us, we are witnessing scattered but insistent demands for more materialist modes of analysis and for new ways of thinking about matter and processes of materialization. . . . We interpret such developments as signs that the more textual approaches associated with the so-called cultural turn are increasingly being deemed inadequate for understanding contemporary society, particularly in light of some of its most urgent challenges regarding environmental, demographic, geographical, and economic change. (2–3)

Taken together, the rejection of representation-qua-correspondence and the rejection of hegemony via discourse formations leave little space for rhetoric and rhetorical inquiry. As long as new materialisms are predicated on metaphysics and the metaphysical fallacy, symbolic action will forever be construed as emergent and epiphenomenal and the long-standing binary between language and reality is maintained. So what, then, is the solution?

Toward Thing-Oriented Ontologies

Ironically, I will argue that the bulk of new materialism scholarship is right to look for a future of inquiry in Heidegger's thing theory. What I object to is not so much thing theory, but the use of the authenticity demarcation to separate the thing from the object—the thingectomy. Rather, I would argue, following Latour and Rickert, that thing theory is better mobilized when it collapses the object into the thing. As both Rickert's *Ambient Rhetoric* and Latour's "From Matters of Fact to Matters of Concern" suggest, Heidegger's *Ding* is not defined solely in opposition to *Gegenstand*, but also through the play of gathering and doing. Heidegger's essay "The Thing" takes this question to task through a diligent exploration of that typical philosophical desk-object. Rather than a blue mug, Heidegger tackles a wine jug. Whereas Bryant's mug colors, Heidegger's jug holds, contains. Each focuses on the doing of the object/thing. For Heidegger, however, this doing is more complex and includes multiple doings—actual and potential. In making his case, Heidegger focuses most prominently on a hand-crafted water jug, his exemplar of a thing. In his analysis of the jug, he notes that the jug's being is found in its doing. The jug *takes in* water. It *keeps* water. It *pours* water. For Heidegger, the jug's being is all of these doings and potential doings simultaneously. To this account of doing, Heidegger also adds gathering:

> Neither the general, long outworn meaning of the term "thing," as used in philosophy, or the Old High German meaning of the word thing, however, are of the least help to us in our pressing need to discover and give adequate thought to the essential source of what we are now saying about the nature of the jug. However, one sematic factor in the old usage of the word thing, namely "gathering," does speak to the nature of the jug as we earlier had it in mind. The jug is a thing neither in the sense of the Roman *res*, nor in the sense of the medieval *ens*, let alone in the modern sense of object. The jug is a thing insofar as it things. ("The Thing" 177)

For Heidegger, a thing is a thing insofar as it things thingly. That is, the ontology of things lies at the intersections among doing, gathering, and presence. A thing is not forever locked in the order of representation, but is rather a co-participant in the doing of gatherings. As such, thing, as opposed to object, provides us with a ready-made term for addressing the recalcitrance of being and the ontology of articulated praxis without the doomed attempt of trying to separate *Gegenstand* from that which it stands against.

With this nondemarcated thing as a foundation, I propose "thing-oriented ontologies" as a more productive theatrical and methodological alternative for rhetorical studies that engage with new materialisms. This possible horizon of inquiry is built on three theoretical moves. The first is the active resistance of the thingectomy described above. The second and third are that the ontological orientation must go plural and tiny. In the first case, I embrace Mol's vision of multiple ontologies. As she writes, "*Ontologies*: note that. Now the word needs to go in the plural. For, and this is a crucial move, if reality is really *done*, if it is historically, culturally and materially located, then it is also *multiple*" ("Ontological Politics" 74).

Mol's words here inform my distinction between object-oriented ontology and thing-oriented ontologies. In focusing on the multiplicity of ontology, thing-oriented ontologies do not attempt to fold the particulars of a momentary articulation (metaphysics) into the fundamental account of being (ontology). Object-oriented new materialisms, in contrast, seek to locate both the essential and the accidental on the same ontological plane. The coloring power of the mug is part of the ontology of the mug. The differentiation between endo and exo becomes an unsolvable quandary (the metaphysical fallacy). Thing-oriented ontologies posit a being that precedes metaphysics. It establishes the being of recalcitrant substances (things) and the possibility of articulations (gatherings), but then it stops. Thing-oriented ontologies are stripped down ontologies. They do not seek to account for all reality at all times, but merely aim to articulate the preconditions of being, preconditions from which localized, context (articulation)-specific metaphysics can arise. Thing-oriented ontologies are what Bogost dubs a "tiny ontology":

> Theories of being tend to be grandiose, but they need not be, because being is simple. Simple enough that it could be rendered via screen print on a trucker's cap. I call it tiny ontology, precisely because it ought not demand a treatise or a tome. I don't mean that the domain of being is small—quite the opposite, as I'll soon explain. Rather, the basic ontological apparatus needed to describe existence ought to be as compact and unornamented as possible. An alternative metaphor to the two-dimensional plane of flat ontology is that of spacelessness, of one-dimensionality. If any one being exists no less than any other, then instead of scattering such beings all across the two-dimensional surface of flat ontology, I suggest the *point* of tiny ontology. It's a dense mass of everything entirely—even as it's spread about haphazardly like a mess or organized logically like a network. (*Alien Phenomenology* 21–22)

Tiny thing-oriented ontologies are simple and plastic. Gathering and doing, articulation and action without further specification become the extent of ontological analysis (much like Harman's aforementioned account of actor-network theory).

Given the relative newness of new materialisms and the enthusiasm for their object-oriented variances, there is not a great deal of rhetorical new materialism that move in the direction of thing-oriented ontologies. However, some work that appropriates and updates Latourian and Molian insights hints at the potential of a thing-oriented ontologies approach (Rickert; Graham, "Agency"; Graham and Herndl; Teston et al.). A predominate feature of this work is that it is less oriented toward the uptake of new materialisms into rhetoric and more oriented toward expanding new materialisms' methodologies by adding rhetorical approaches to them.

When rhetorical theorists develop analytic approaches that begin with the symbolic, the affective, and the physical as ontological coequals (as opposed to stripping out rhetoric and adding it back in epiphenomenally), they begin with rhetorically friendly new materialisms. A recent example of work which offers rhetoric as an addition to new materialisms can be found in Rickert's positioning of a rhetorical understanding of kairos as a central analytic for the exploration of space-time. Similarly, Graham and Herndl and Teston et al. explore how stasis deliberation serves as a central feature of ontology formation and cross-ontological adjudication. Furthermore, Kelly and Maddalena offer a truly symmetrical approach to inquiry that combines rhetorical genre studies and Latourian actor-network theory. And, finally, in *The Politics of Pain Medicine*, I offer a rhetorically inflected approach to tropic analysis that serves to more fully capture the nature of black box formation than actor-network theory alone. While none of these, with the exception of *The Politics of Pain Medicine*, explicitly engage thing theory, they each successfully avoid new materialisms' all too common rejection of rhetoric. In so doing, they provide a foundation for future inquiry into thing-oriented ontologies, a future where rhetoric is central but not totalizing.

From this evolving approach, there are many benefits for rhetoric. Chiefly, if the classification of articulations is considered a secondary step of metaphysical methodologies that might (or might not) follow from ontology, then human engagement with the world is not treated as a special case, and language and representation are not the accidental epiphenomena of more authentic precognitive sensual engagements. Things thing thingly. And if in their gathering they gather through electromagnetism and gravity, that gathering is not ontologically distinct from their gathering through representation or ideological hegemony. Put another way, object-oriented new materialisms, as long as they are metaphysical, will always be a footnote to the question of *les mots et choses*, as Foucault put it (and Rickert acknowledges). Thing-oriented ontologies, on the other hand, begin with the argument that *les mots sont choses*. Words are things. And indeed, the thingness of words is all the more evident in ruminations on the etymology of *Ding*. Heidegger, Latour, and Rickert each explores the importance of the historical connection between *Ding* and *Althing* or parliament. I will not rehearse that argument yet again here. What I will say, however, is that it is this very connection that gives thing-oriented ontologies their potential to be a more viable approach for rhetorical inquiry. In Latour's terms, this is the shift from matters of fact (with shades of authenticity) to matters of concern, where humans and nonhumans engage in the politics of nature (things thing thingly).

Notes

1. Certainly the rejection of rhetoric in new materialisms and their forerunners is not entirely pervasive. Nevertheless, even those that embrace something like the rhetorical exhibit a fraught relationship with rhetoric. For example, Latour (with Paulo Fabbri) published an essay entitled "The Rhetoric of Science" in 1981 and then studiously avoided the term rhetoric until declaring it time for resurrection in his *How to Make Things Public* (2005). I would argue that Annemarie Mol tacitly recognizes a role for the rhetorical, while simultaneously and explicitly distancing herself from all things representational.

2. The extent to which Rickert commits the metaphysical fallacy and is complicit in the four-world problem is a fraught question. I read *Ambient Rhetoric* as one part metaphysical/ontological treatise and one part methodological manifesto. As an ontological treatise, *Ambient Rhetoric* is shot through with demarcations of authenticity that shade in the direction of replicating the four-world problem. As a methodological manifesto, I find the work engaging and unproblematic. As a result, I both reject Rickert's metaphysics and celebrate his methodology, thus creating some noticeable dissonance throughout this chapter.

III

Seeing Things

9
Materiality's Rhetorical Work

The Nineteenth-Century Parlor Stereoscope
and the Second-Naturing of Vision

Kristie S. Fleckenstein

London, marvels an anonymous author in 1859, has been infected with stereoscopic mania, a visual virus that spread beyond the British Isles to encompass much of Western Europe ("Since" 79). Bitten by the same bug, Oliver Wendell Holmes Sr.—Harvard doctor of medicine, poet, novelist, and Boston Brahman—celebrated in the pages of the *Atlantic Monthly* the pleasures and rewards of the stereoscope. Writing in 1859 as well, Holmes rhapsodizes that soon people who wish to see Niagara Falls or Buckingham Palace will visit, instead, "the Imperial, National, or City Stereographic Library" ("Stereoscope" 748) where they will find stereo views so vivid that they "cheat the senses" (742), thereby rendering travel no longer necessary. Introduced in 1838 by Charles Wheatstone as an experiment in human bi-ocular vision, the stereoscope transformed a two-dimensional image into a three-dimensional experience, offering the viewer a startling sensation of depth and solidity. Reinvented as a parlor toy in 1851, this unprecedented visual device accrued the attention of the wealthy, becoming a treasured addition to the upper middle class parlor. Further refined in 1861 into a handheld instrument sufficiently inexpensive for widespread consumption, the stereoscope took America by storm, thereafter maintaining its cultural preeminence with some peaks and valleys until its gradual demise in the late 1920s.

Focusing on this philosophical toy, I argue that the materiality of the handheld stereoscope—its physical design and everyday use—functioned as a rhetorical agent, one that, in conjunction with cultural and institutional discourses, persuaded into existence a new way of seeing characterized by disembodiment and hyper attention. Through its tangible construction and quotidian practices, the stereoscope fostered a visual transformation among America's *fin de siècle* citizens, influencing what and how people saw. This intersection between a visual technology and perceptual practices emphasizes the important rhetorical work performed by physical artifacts, reflecting a new materialist ontology that weds the organic to the inorganic. Configuring matter as "active, self-creative, productive, unpredictable" (Coole and Frost 9) rather than either a "brute 'thereness'" (7) or a side effect of textual systems (4), a material orientation invites a consideration of the rhetorical role enacted by artifacts, especially their rhetorical agency, defined as the ability to act and shape attitudes in the world. Jane Bennett emphasizes this very point, noting that "thing-power" calls for "greater recognition of the agential powers of natural and artifactual things" ("Force" 349). Recent work in rhetorical materiality reinforces Bennett's insight. Michael Calvin McGee offers an early version of material and rhetorical reciprocity, mourning what he calls rhetoric's loss "of contact with the brute reality of persuasion as a daily social phenomenon" (25). Rhetoric, he insists, is "'material' by measure of humans experiencing it, not by virtue of our ability to continue touching it after it is gone" (29). Jack Selzer and Sharon Crowley in their collection *Rhetorical Bodies* forward McGee's agenda, embracing an even more capacious understanding of rhetorical materiality with essays attending to the thingness, not just the symbolicity, of such rhetorical phenomena as memorials, DNA, cannibalism, and a *Vanity Fair* cover. In *Rhetorics of Display*, Lawrence Prelli explicitly identifies a species of rhetoric that exists on the cusp between discourse and matter, including in this category rhetorical acts as diverse as discursive descriptions and landscapes. Finally, Barbara Biesecker and John Lucaites in *Rhetoric, Materiality, and Politics* convert McGee's rhetorical materiality into rhetoric's materiality, collecting a series of essays that explore the relationships between words and things.

As this scholarship reveals, the material turn in rhetoric uncovers the role of physical resources, performances, and tools that had been previously hidden by the field's predominant focus on discursive textuality. In this chapter I advance that materialist realignment, and I do so not by highlighting rhetoric's materiality but by highlighting materiality's rhetoric: the persuasive work performed by physical objects. I ask how concrete artifacts act as agents of rhetoric rather than simply as instruments of or for rhetoric. Drawing on scholarship in what Diana Coole and Samantha Frost call the "new materialisms," I contend that the stereoscope possesses agency through its own "immanent vitality" (Coole and Frost 8). Instead of an inert object, the stereoscope as a physical entity is lively, engaging with eager nineteenth-century devotees to argue into existence a new way of seeing characterized by an emphasis on mental rather than physical experiences and on superficial engagement. More specifically, revealing the rhetorical dynamic by which the experience of the stereoscope promoted the emergence of a visual habit, or ingrained protocols of perception, this chapter emphasizes that neither visual technology, vision, nor viewer is neutral. Each affects the other in intricate feedback loops.

Such a claim both complements and resists scholarship investigating the intersection of vision, rhetoric, and materiality. In its concern with the constructed nature of vision, for example, this chapter aligns with Jordynn Jack's investigation of a "pedagogy of sight" deployed in Robert Hooke's seventeenth-century *Micrographia*. As Jack argues, Hooke crafted the book's discursive content to teach his readers how to see and interpret its visual content thereby emphasizing the rhetorical constitution of vision, a premise central to this chapter. But, at the same time, my claim concerning materiality's rhetoric diverges from Jack's innovative work in that I examine not discursive rhetoric's role in shaping vision but material rhetoric's role. Similarly, this chapter's assertion of the stereoscope's rhetoric agency extends and digresses from Brenton J. Malin's investigation of the stereoscope and the marketing materials accompanying its sale and use at the end of the nineteenth century. As he rightly notes, institutional, commercial, and visual arguments "converge" to influence the viewer's experience (404). But left unexplored in Malin's argument are the influences of the stereoscope itself as a lively participant in that viewer's experience, an omission this chapter addresses. Finally, my argument regarding the stereoscope's rhetorical agency both draws on and departs from Jonathan Crary's groundbreaking work on visual technologies, vision, and scientific-philosophical discourses of the nineteenth century. It builds on Crary's concerns with "the problematic phenomenon of the observer" (5) and his acknowledgment of the stereoscope as a particularly important visual apparatus in the emergence of new "techniques" of vision in the nineteenth century. However, my argument departs from Crary's focus on the "technical and theoretical principles" that formed the stereoscope's discursive background. Instead, it explores the stereograph's rhetorical effects "once it was distributed throughout that sociocultural field" (118).

I begin that exploration by establishing the cultural pervasiveness of the handheld stereoscope in nineteenth-century American and Western European culture. Then, I address the stereoscope as rhetorical agent in two steps, contending that the stereoscope's thingness—its construction and everyday use—promoted a way of seeing that paradoxically relied on the user's embodiment—his or her use of the stereoscope—to erase that embodiment; in short, it counseled the user to dismiss all senses except sight. At the same time, the stereoscope's material rhetoric promoted cursory visual commitment to the cardboard spectacles presented to the eye.

Popular and Pervasive: The Stereoscope as Rhetorical Agent

The power of the stereoscope, like the power of all rhetoric and lively matter, worked in conjunction with its *fin de siècle* audience, a point that Coole and Frost emphasize: the stereoscope qua stereoscope constitutes "a complex, pluralistic, relatively open process" within which humans are immersed and complicit with its "productive contingencies" (7). Kenneth Burke refines this matter-human dynamic, contending that all rhetoric is both material and symbolic: it is an action, movement marked by intention. More precisely, it is symbolic action. As symbolic action, rhetoric possesses material substrates and material effects. Rhetoric cannot exist without its animating materiality: voice, body, text, image. But, Burke argues, just as rhetoric is material, so, too, is materiality rhetorical. Human inventions, from the fork to the telegraph, also have rhetorical substrates and rhetorical effects. Burke articulates this directly in his "Definition of Man," noting that humans create technologies that then turn around to reshape them (13). Human tools second-nature their human makers. This naturalization of a "special set of expectations" (13) gestures to the rhetorical agency of objects, an agency that the stereoscope illuminates through its widespread education of the eye. American enthusiast Oliver Wendell Holmes provides a case in point.

Writing without attribution in the 1861 issue of the *Atlantic Monthly*, Holmes declared that the stereoscope was "no toy" but a "divine gift" that carries users into the very presence of all that is most inspiring to the soul ("Sun-Painting" 28). Implicating the stereoscope's rhetorical agency, Holmes claims that this divine gift and its shared stereo views would make all men acquaintances ("Stereoscope" 744) by re-educating the eye to see in this deceptively natural process (742). Mediating between the symbolically rendered world of the stereo views and the human user's physiology, the materiality of the stereoscope's objectness functioned agentively not only to inspire the viewer's soul but also to alter the viewer's visual practices. With the stereoscope's evolution into the parlor stereoscope and the spread of stereoscopic mania, the instrument's physical design conspired with popular use to persuade into being this new way of seeing for an influential number of rural and urban Americans.

The stereoscope's role as rhetorical agent of vision began with its laboratory birth. From its inception, the stereoscope was inextricably intertwined with the effort to understand the mechanics of human vision, as David Brewster highlights. "When we look with both eyes open at a sphere, or any other solid object, we see it by uniting into one two pictures," the Scottish scientist and inventor explains in his 1856 *The Stereoscope* (5). He thus opens the first chapter of his treatise not with the machine but instead with vision to emphasize its priority. The design of Wheatstone's original stereoscope—consisting of a large and cumbersome box-like structure suitable only for laboratory use—reflects the constitution of visual machine in service to the science of vision. However, Brewster's radical redesign of the Wheatstone stereoscope into the attractive and user friendly philosophical toy shifted that dynamic. Brewster's friendly lenticular, or cabinet, stereoscope took the device out of the sole realm of science and into the upper-class parlor, thus increasing the scope of its rhetorical agency. In so doing, the stereoscope no longer served as an apparatus for understanding vision but as an apparatus for shaping vision. The rising consumer economy, and especially the wealthy and middle classes, immediately embraced the new toy, opening up new venues for the instrument's visual-rhetorical suasion. In just five short years after the introduction of the Brewster stereoscope at the Great Exhibition in 1851, the London Stereoscopic Company had formed and sold more than 500,000 cabinet stereoscopes, taking as its goal in an 1854 ad campaign to ensure that there would be "no home without a stereoscope" (qtd. in Trachtenberg 17). That ambitious goal forwarded the invention of the handheld stereoscope in 1861 by Oliver Wendell Holmes.

Called the parlor or American stereoscope, this inexpensive and light weight device, with its adjustable sliding mount that allowed for differences in viewers' optical acuity, exploded across class lines, instigating stereoscopic mania in America. Twenty years after its invention, Dr. Herman Vogel, during his third visit to America, comments that "there is no parlor in America where there is not a stereoscope" (qtd. in "Interpretive Chronology" 60). In addition, there were no parlors in America where there were no stereographs. The production of stereo views underscores the popularity of the stereoscope as well as the range of its rhetorical influence. Between 1860 and 1890 more than twelve thousand stereophotographers took approximately 4.5 million individual images that were then reproduced into more than 400 million stereographs (Darrah). In 1859, looking to the future, Holmes envisioned stereo views on a grander scale than even this, demanding not just individual stereo images, which he named *stereographs* ("Stereoscope" 749), but also libraries: "We do now distinctly propose the creation of a comprehensive and systematic stereographic library, where all men can find the special forms they particularly desire to see as artists, or as scholars, or as mechanics, or in any other capacity" (748).

The combination of the popular stereoscope with the available stereographs contrived to make the visual stereo system a rhetorical agent. As an intrinsic element of Victorian culture, the stereoscope constituted the first mass production and dissemination of representational photographs. Alan Trachtenberg underscores this conversion of the parlor stereoscope into a rhetorical juggernaut. He contends that "with the mass publication of stereoviews of every imaginable subject on earth and in the heavens, the stereoscope became the first universal system of visual communication before cinema and television" (17). Edward Earle goes even further, claiming that the stereoscope constituted the most significant shift in information accessibility since the invention of movable type (11) because it enabled the first widespread distribution of a standardized set of pictures. In sum, the parlor stereoscope united with the stereograph to persuade an eager and complicit audience to form a new way of seeing, one characterized by disembodied vision and superficial engagement.

Hood and Hand: The Stereoscope's Disembodiment of Vision

Characteristic of the rise of industrialization and consumer culture in the West, the stereoscope introduces a type of Victorian cyborg in which the materiality of the artifact and the materiality of the human user acted on each other in reciprocal feedback loops. Two popular ads gesture to this cyborgian union. Both circulated in the early 1900s, and both were deployed to woo new subscribers by offering free stereoscopes and modestly priced stereograph packages. Each ad features two individuals—one woman and one man—with a stereoscope pressed against his or her face. In the first ad, a well-dressed young man smiles merrily from the left side of the quarter-page ad, holding not just a visual device in his hand but, more importantly, access to "the finest scenery and the greatest natural wonders of the world" ("Stereoscope Free"). Similarly, a second ad features a young woman with tidy Gibson-girl hair and pristine ruffled high-necked blouse gazing through her stereoscope. Sitting safely in her parlor, she can experience everything from "A Trip Across the Continent" to, perhaps more daring, "The Destruction of San Francisco," all without mussing her hair or soiling her garments ("Stereoscope and View Offer"). The ads as a whole, but especially the images featured in each, emphasize "the mutual interdependence of material, biocultural, and symbolic forces in the making of social and political practices" (Braidotti 203–4). More specifically, these ads underscore what Judith Babbitts calls the rhetorical and optical agency of the stereoscope: "By peering through a stereoscope, viewers would be introduced to a new field of vision and become a participant in a vast new world, a world no longer bound by actual face-to-face contact. Stereographs would reshape what it was to know and perceive reality" (131). One crucial characteristic of that reshaped perception consists of a paradoxical disembodiment of vision.

Despite its laboratory birth in the physiology of sight and the anatomy of the human body, despite as well its embodied use, the material design of the parlor stereoscope argued for visual disembodiment. Elements intrinsic to the device's physicality combined to discredit sensuous experience and celebrate instead the virtual experience. The first design component spotlighting materiality's rhetorical work consists of the parlor stereoscope's hood (fig. 9.1).

The hood joined with ambient cultural and marketing discourses to encourage a way of seeing that privileged vision by isolating sight from its physiological home in the body. Characterized by its protruding wooden or tin hood, frequently edged with velvet for comfort, the parlor stereoscope fits snugly over the bridge of the user's nose and against the forehead and cheekbones. Designed both to protect the lenses and block light from the eyes, the hood effectively narrows the user's gaze to an equally narrow reality: the stereograph at the end of the mount. Like all rhetoric that conceals some aspects of reality as it reveals others, the hood directed the viewer's attention solely to vision, attempting to reduce the experience of reality to only a single sense. Holmes underscores this rhetorical selectivity, celebrating the stereoscope's ability to produce "an appearance of reality that cheats the sense with its seeming truth" ("Stereoscope" 742),

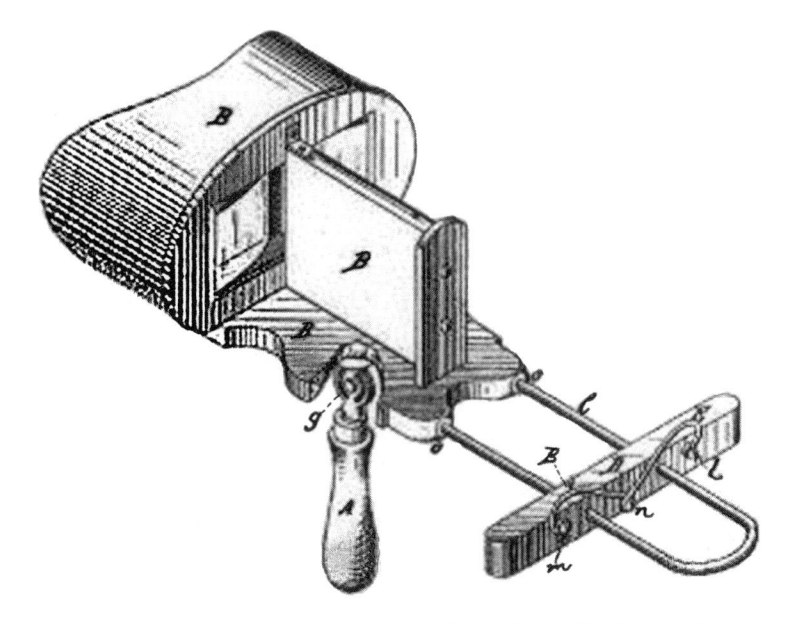

Figure 9.1. The Holmes-Bates Stereoscope, from John Pagliughi and John Ardito, Patent 232649, US Patent Office, 28 Sept. 1880, Web.

finding no downside in the loss of touch, hearing, or smell. Elaborating on this phenomenon in 1861, Holmes praises the "concentration of the whole attention" and the "shutting out of surrounding objects" required by the stereoscope ("Sun-Painting" 14–15).

Within this practice, the only important sense is the visual, which, by its exclusivity, erases, or cheats, the remaining senses. In other words, as a rhetorical agent, the experience of the stereoscope's hood persuades the user to amputate vision from the body by suppressing other bodily sensations. Babbitts notes this exclusivity, claiming that the stereoscope's focus on the visual derived in part from its denigration of the remaining senses. A visual memory secured by the stereoscope avoided the noisome "odors, ear-splitting noises, stifling temperature, and dirty hands and elbows of the 'natives'" that the viewer would be subjected to if physically present in the depicted scene or event (132). The device's hood thus creates a kind of sensory vacuum by which other physiological responses are separated from sight, a point that Meredith A. Bak underscores. Focusing on the widespread use of the parlor stereoscope in American classrooms, Bak argues that the instrument's materiality especially bypassed the tactile (164). The hood on the parlor stereoscope privileged the visual pathway at the same time that it divorced that pathway from its rootedness in the viewer's body.

The second design element revealing materiality's rhetorical agency consists of the handheld quality of the parlor stereoscope. In conjunction with the hood, the handle linked disembodied vision with disembodied reality. If the stereoscope's hood design encouraged the separation of vision from body, then the stereoscope's handheld design invited the user to convert disembodied vision into disembodied reality. Jib Fowles describes this process as devoted viewers "wrenching" a pictured reality from its natural setting and resituating it within "the comfort and security of the viewer's home" (91). One 1909 first-time stereoscope user narrates just such an experience of disembodied reality. While holding the stereoscope to his face in the tidiness of his home, he "seemed let out to the ends of the earth" (qtd. in "Interpretive Chronology" 80). Furthermore, the "ends of the earth" at that moment possessed greater reality than did the tidy parlor. The viewer marvels, "I was taken out to no world of fancy but to the world of fact" (80). Central to this disembodied movement into a disembodied world of fact was the lightweight handheld format of the parlor stereoscope, which impinged only tangentially on the viewer's attention. This physical aspect persuades the viewer to dismiss the device itself, rendering the interface imperceptible. Unlike the earlier version of Brewster's lenticular stereoscope, which required the user to bend over the table on which the weighty instrument was positioned to bring eyes to the stereographed world (fig. 9.2), the handheld parlor stereoscope invited the viewer to bring the world to the eyes.

With an almost imperceptible weight and a wooden handle shaped to fit naturally into the palm, the parlor stereoscope cultivated the illusion of holding the world in the hand. Combined with the exclusivity of vision, the stereoscope's modest weight privileged the pleasures of a disembodied—or virtual—reality over those of an embodied reality. Fowles notes that, by "holding a stereograph first by hand and then in the stereoscope, they [users] could in a most elemental way possess it. It was totally under their control" (91). The physical affordances of the handheld parlor stereoscope advanced the belief that the viewer could, by personal command, enter into the scenes and events displayed, holding dominion over that virtual reality. By so doing, the stereoscope devotee became "invested with an almost inconceivable power" in that virtual world, gaining the fantasy of "omniscience they could only have dreamed about before" (91).

The power of the hand holding the stereoscope to the eyes, the power of the hand selecting new stereographs to insert in the mount, contrived with disembodied vision to valorize a virtual or viewed reality—such is the rhetorical work performed by materiality as lively matter. Holmes celebrates this very characteristic, reinforcing the visual toy's rhetorical agency. When users see the flat stereograph through the stereoscopic device, he claims, "we seem to leave the body behind us and sail away into one strange scene after another, like disembodied spirits" ("Sun-Painting" 14–15). Furthermore, Holmes argues that as "Nature and Art" are stereographed, viewers can abandon the worthless "carcasses" of reality

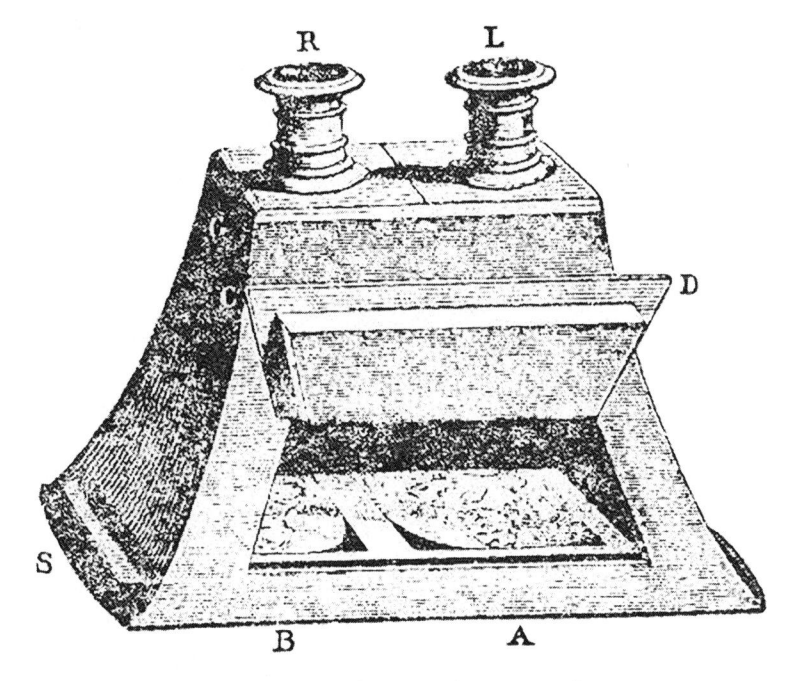

Figure 9.2. The Brewster Stereoscope, from David Brewster, *The Stereoscope: Its History, Theory, and Construction with Its Application to the Fine and Useful Arts and to Education* (John Murray: London, 1856; 67).

because they possess the skin, or the image ("Stereoscope" 748). Only that skin is important. The carcassed reality can be forsaken because the treasure is the disembodied world. Within the safety of their parlors, protected by four walls and societal conventions, viewers could experience without fear of personal injury "nature gone wild" (Green 111). Thus, images of natural disasters, such as the Mill River Flood; the Johnstown Flood; the Grinnell, Iowa, tornado; and the aftermath of the Chicago fire of 1871 were marketed with great success because they could be lived visually—virtually—without physical danger (111). Bak notes a similar phenomenon in the classroom: "While classroom use of the stereoscope afforded pupils new experiences, . . . it did so by reinforcing a new way of seeing that substituted lived experience with mediated vision, thereby obscuring the important distinctions between these two modes of perception" (164). Enclosed in the classroom with reality presented to the eyes through the hand holding the stereoscope and the hand choosing which stereograph to next view, the child experienced a disembodied vision that privileged a disembodied virtual reality. The rhetorical agency of handle and weight thus aligned with the stereoscope's hood to liberate "'minds from the limitations of our bodies'" (qtd. in Bak 164) and "trained students' visual and mental faculties to experience travel without leaving the classroom" (163). Coalescing with other social forces and discourses, the materiality of the parlor stereoscope thus wooed viewers to reconstruct their optical experiences by escaping from their bodies and their realities.

Standardization and Regimentation: The Stereograph's Argument for Hyper Attention

With hood and handle, the lightweight parlor stereoscope paradoxically fostered perceptual habits that privileged disembodiment and a disembodied reality. But equally important to the stereoscope's rhetorical agency are the stereographs themselves. Two attributes of stereographs illustrate materiality's rhetorical work: the sets of standardized views and the typical uses of those views. Both combine to argue for visual hyper attention with its emphasis on immediacy and superficial engagement. Contrasting with deep attention, which consists of sustained attention to a single phenomenon, hyper attention is characterized by rapid shifts in focus in response to multiple information streams. Defined by N. Katherine Hayles, hyper attention seeks "high levels of stimulation" and is marked by a "low tolerance for boredom" (187). Although Hayles acknowledges the evolutionary roots of hyper attention, she aligns its current manifestation with the onset of the digital age that encourages the flitting movement of attention from one visual stimulus to another (188). However, hyper attention characterizes the stereoscopic age as well. Holmes hints at this in 1859, commenting on a model that holds twenty five slides at once, a design feature that enabled the owner to take a guest on a rapid trip through the White Mountains or an equally speedy survey of Old World art. While the owner might "get tired of the unvarying round in which they [the stereographs] present themselves," Holmes claims, the guest will be entranced by the quick movement of the cards. If one experienced a virtual visual world via the stereoscope, one did so at a swift clip via the stereograph, a characteristic that began with standardization.

Standardization encouraged hyper attention by chunking reality into consumable bites. While Holmes draws attention to his collection of more than one thousand stereographs ("Sun-Painting" 15), and one happy consumer celebrates additions to his collection of almost two thousand stereographs ("National?" 45), these numbers hide the standardization of those images in both size and content. Unless consumers were themselves stereo-photographers and thus could create their own unique stereo views, devotees were reliant on marketed stereo images, images that increasingly complied with industry requirements. Standardization worked rhetorically to separate reality into discrete portions, laying out these snippets of reality for easy and quick ingestion. "Stereography," Fowles points out, as a "visual mass medium, captured, segmented and standardized visibility" (92). The most apparent aspect of standardization consists of the typical size and shape of each card: 3½ x 7 inches with a slight curve to enhance the illusion of three-dimensionality. The cards thus stacked neatly or organized themselves into orderly files in a stereograph library. As a common feature of stereos view, the repetitive size persuaded Americans to believe "that the plenum of the visible world not only could be, but should be, segmented, appraised, packaged and sold. The observable became yet another standardized commodity, like bricks" (92). Thus, the regularized shape and size of the stereograph—its materiality—performed rhetorical work by deflecting users' attentions away from the chaos of reality and convincing them to embrace a precise ordering of that reality. Furthermore, as a single bite-size piece of reality coming in a one-size-fits-all package, the stereograph lured users to consume quickly, an ease enhanced by the standardization of contents.

In addition to the size, the stereograph's contents were normalized in two ways, both of which promoted hyper attention. First, to enhance the impression of solidity, stereo-photographers developed a conventionalized style, or a shared manner of presenting subjects (Southall 97). They used a camera angle that situated the subject's head in the center of the scene, focusing the eye on both background and foreground elements to intensify the semblance of depth. They also incorporated long lines, like a street curb, to draw the eye further into the depths of the image (Fowles 91–92). Complementing the conventions of size and style, stereograph companies also regimented the subject matter, duplicating subjects and themes across markets (Southall 97). The millions of commercially produced images thus fell into common categories, including American landscapes, foreign sites and people, art and architecture, and science and education (see Darrah 145–96). Such multifaceted regimentation encouraged users to anticipate in advance what they would experience, enabling them to move quickly through the various available cards. It discouraged the deep attention that Holmes advocates when he urges devotees to contemplate rather than skim their stereo views to enjoy "the beauties lurking, unobserved" in each view ("Stereoscope" 744). Despite Holmes's verbal persuasion, even in 1859, the design of stereographs persuaded users to engage habitually in the flitting movement of hyper attention, a rhetorical impact reinforced by everyday practices.

What the consumer viewed undoubtedly contributed to hyper attention. But how the consumer viewed his or her library of standardized images also cultivated the rushed attention and superficial engagement characteristic of hyper attention. Coole and Frost note that lively matter requires a new focus on the "phenomenology of diverse lives as they are actually lived," with particular attention to physical objects that use humans as humans use them (27). Thus, examining the everyday stereoscopic practices—the material use of the stereographs—exposes additional levels of materiality's rhetorical agency. Hyper attention intertwined itself into the phenomenology of the stereograph's everyday life. Enjoying stereographs was anything but an innocent entertainment; it "involved arrangements of bodies in space, regulations of activity, and the deployment of individual bodies" all of which "codified and normalized the observer within rigidly defined systems of visual consumption" (18). The codified and normalized habit of visual perception characteristic of stereoscopic practices consisted of routinely and mechanically moving from one card to the next, skimming through quickly rather than contemplating deeply. Advice to hostesses of the period explicitly recognized and implicitly reinforced the habit of hyper attention: "While you are arranging the parlor," socially minded homemakers were cautioned, "just have a thought for the visitors who must sometimes wait to see you." A conscientious hostess will ensure the easy availability of objects such as "a stereoscope and views" that will occupy the "stray minutes" a guest might spend alone (qtd. in "Interpretive Chronology" 54). The stereographs, then, became consumable pleasures worthy of a few stray moments of attention. Even Holmes, despite his fervid advocacy of deep attention, reveals the lure of hyper attention in his verbal recreation of a stereographic tour of the world drawn from his own collection of stereo views.

Materiality's rhetorical work circulates throughout Holmes's second essay on the stereoscope, published in 1861. Here Holmes seeks to spark his readers' interest in the stereoscope by taking them on a "stereographic trip" (16). Evoking the movement of his reader-companions who participated in the trip by viewing their own stereographs, Holmes dashes from scene to scene in his faux tour of the world. This quick movement points not only to hyper attention but also to the rhetorical role of stereographic practices in persuading that visual practice into being. For example, in his initial stop at Niagara, for "we must know something of the sights of our own country," Holmes moves the tour in four sentences through two specific stereographs as well as an unnamed variety of "fine views." To keep up, the reader-tourist, at least in imagination, had to mount and remount one stereograph after another without any opportunity for contemplation. Introducing the "numerous views" of Charles Blondin, the nineteenth-century daredevil who crossed the Falls on a rope, Holmes describes two different stereographs of this single figure before moving abruptly from Niagara in New York to the Old Man of the Mountain in New Hampshire. Again, the reader-tourist likewise must rapidly move from stereograph to stereograph to maintain the pace. Later in his trip, Holmes even encourages his entourage to "flit away"—to quickly switch stereographs—in order to savor a steeple in the English countryside (22). The entire stereographic trip is marked by speedy changes in locale matched by equally speedy changes in the stereographs depicting those locales. Thus, the practice of hyper attention that Holmes explicitly denigrates in 1859 he implicitly performs in 1861, taking the reader and viewer around the world in 12 pages.

While parlor practices worked their suasory power over visual habits through everyday practices, so too did classroom practices promulgate a similar hyper attention, revealing the range of the stereograph's rhetorical agency. In the wake of calls between 1890 and 1920 for visual rather than solely verbal education, and in response to concerted marketing campaigns by American stereoscopic companies, stereoscopes became a fixture in most public school and some college classrooms (Bak). By the early 1900s, few towns with populations over 50,000 did not use stereoscopes as common instructional tools in their public schools. Here, as in the parlor, how the students looked at these stereographs was just as rhetorically significant, if not more so, than what they looked at. Bak explains: "In specifying both what children saw in the stereoscope and controlling the viewing conditions, including the length of time to view each image and the order in which they were seen, educators could utilize the device to restrict students' fields of vision" (149) and reshape those fields into new practices. More specifically, Bak contends, the children viewed stereographs in a highly regimented manner. Drawing from instructional articles from the period, Bak describes the movement of stereoscopes and their views as "precisely orchestrated. Like a factory assembly line, views and stereoscopes moved from hand to hand and images shifted from lesson to lesson like interchangeable parts" (143). The visual habit of hyper attention attended these practices, commanding rapid changes in a "mechanized, repetitive pattern of looking" (151). What resulted was a material argument for a visual habit "characterized by disciplined scanning of the image," privileging a survey-assessment movement by which images were consumed but not contemplated. "More than the representations themselves, the stereoscope's impact in shaping students' perceptual patterns—the habituation and mechanization of their binocular vision—is perhaps the device's greatest ideological consequence," Bak concludes (154).

Conclusion

At the epicenter of the nineteenth-century visual experience, the visual stereo system of stereoscope and stereograph provides insight into materiality's rhetorical work. During an era characterized by a frenzy of the visual, the stereoscope performed as a rhetorical agent through its material design and habituated use. It induced new perceptual habits and changed attitudes by blurring the boundaries between what one sees, how one sees, and who one might become as a result of that seeing. As it dominated urban and rural culture, the stereoscope with its attendant stereographs invited people to perceive their realities and communicate about those realities in new ways. Holmes applauds this very change, enthusing that, because of the stereoscope, "the 'morphotype,' or 'form-print,'" achieves a symbolic weight equal if not superior in power to that of "the logotype or word-print" ("Stereoscope" 744). While Laura Schiavo cautions that these stereoscopic lessons "cannot be reduced to the intrinsic logic of the stereoscope and its operative form" (114), a warning that Malin and Crary reinforce, we cannot so easily discount materiality's rhetorical force. As lively matter, the stereoscope functions not as the deterministic "massive, opaque plenitude" Schiavo envisions; rather, it operates rhetorically, "constantly forming and reforming in unexpected ways" (Coole and Frost 10). As this chapter demonstrates, the physical constitution of the stereoscope, the standardization of the stereograph, and the practices common to each highlight materiality's rhetorical work in the stereoscope's advocacy of a disembodied vision organized by hyper attention.

10
Circulatory Intensities

Take a Book, Return a Book

Brian J. McNely

Figure 10.1. The Little Free Library placard and credo. Photograph by author.

Cultural geographer Doreen Massey argues that places are *events*, "a simultaneity of stories-so-far" (130). In this chapter, I explore an ordinary place as a nexus of ongoing events, as a literal simultaneity of stories-so-far: one Little Free Library at the corner of Woodland Avenue and Maxwell Street, near downtown Lexington, Kentucky (fig. 10.1). The Little Free Library movement began in Wisconsin in 2009 to promote literacy and improve communities worldwide. Founders Todd Bol and Rick Brooks established the goal of creating and sustaining 2,510 little libraries—a number that would eclipse Andrew Carnegie's efforts ("Our History"). By 2014, over ten thousand little libraries around the world were stewarded by volunteers and community donations ("Our History"). Here, I explore the events and stories that flow through and near one library, an ideographic[1] account of the multisensory affects and suasive, circulatory *intensities* surrounding ubiquitous everyday objects: books.

To provide this account, I combine scholarship of material cultures and a theory of rhetorical situatedness grounded in an understanding of worldish ambience, entanglement, and disclosure. Rhetorical situatedness emerges from and conditions a cascading set of granular attunements: to material and sensory affects; to object assemblages and potentially embedded moralities (Pink); to movements of rhetors and nonhumans; and to entanglements of past, present, and future events, discourses, objects, and organisms. These facets of rhetorical situatedness intersect, blend, and co-constitute understandings of places as events, of objects as suasive, and of humans as rhetors. Yet rigorously attuning to this ambience may be challenging. According to anthropologist Kathleen Stewart, attunements may emerge from momentary intensities—"regularly, intermittently, urgently, or as a slight shudder" (*Ordinary* 10). In these ordinary affects, Stewart sees a "layering of immanent experience" (6): of intensities dull and sharp, quotidian and monumental. I consider here the ways in which circulatory intensities mark ambient disclosures that constitute our being-in-the-world.

For Martin Packer, the notion of *constitution* evokes regional ontologies—how things and people show up in and through their everyday intensities. Packer traces and complicates inquiries through Kant, Husserl, Schutz, and Berger and Luckman, wherein constitution is "an *epistemological* process in which each individual constructs *knowledge* of the world" (149; emphasis in original). He then traces alternative inquiries through Hegel, Heidegger, Merleau-Ponty, and Garfinkel wherein constitution is "an *ontolog*ical process in which the very constituents of reality—objects and subjects—are constituted" (149; emphasis in original). If the circulatory intensities of everyday life are indeed key moments of ontological constitution, then different approaches to empirically studying the complexities of rhetorical situatedness are warranted.

Kathleen Stewart offers one such approach: Ontological constitution may be found in the ordinary affects of everyday life—in *worlding* ("Atmospheric"). Everyday attunements are for Stewart "an intimate, compositional process of dwelling in spaces that bears, gestures, gestates, worlds" ("Atmospheric" 445). From this perspective nonhumans are relevant not because of how they appear to us, or how they are epistemologically constructed by us, "but because they have qualities, rhythms, forces, relations, and movements" (445) that co-constitute being-in-the-world. In "the everyday work of attunement to worlding," Stewart argues, "spaces of all kinds become inhabited" (446)—by rhythms, forces, relations, and movements—even the smallest spaces, even little libraries that hold, at most, one generous armful of paperbacks. By attuning to rhetorical situatedness, by recognizing intensities, and by tracing ambient circulations, we may better understand how worlds are thrown together (Stewart *Ordinary*, "Weak Theory").

In this chapter, I first explore rhetorical situatedness in worldish ambience, entanglement, and disclosure, where attunement to circulatory intensities may help us discern how everyday worlds are constituted and thrown together. I then consider nonhuman participation and multisensory affects in everyday constitution. I also detail my methodology and methods, a visual autoethnography of circulatory intensities. Through a series of fieldwork vignettes and photographs, I describe how intensities act as visual, sensory, material, and haptic *puncta* in everyday life. Barthes's notion of the *punctum*—the accidental detail or unintentional wound of apprehension and being—signals intensities and layers of "immanent experience" (Stewart *Ordinary* 6) that situate rhetors and mark constitutive processes of being-in-the-world.

Disclosive Ambience (From Situation to Situatedness)

Theories of rhetorical situation have developed significantly since Lloyd Bitzer's influential formulation. I briefly trace those developments, from rhetorical situation to ambient rhetoric, because these theories significantly shape understandings of situatedness. Thomas Rickert's ambient rhetoric frames the coextensive participation of humans and nonhumans; ambience, I argue, moves rhetoric from situation to robust situatedness. Moreover, Heidegger's concepts of thrownness, worldishness,[2] and attunement ground understandings of ambient rhetoric and rhetorical situatedness. Though I embrace Rickert's new materialist, object-oriented perspective on ambience, my focus is the rhetorical situatedness of humans; however, I follow him in resisting subject-object dichotomies. Since we recognize ourselves as rhetors, we discourse with ourselves constantly, framing and adjusting our situatedness *in concert with* everyday worldishness; in turn, we are *worldish*—world-forming. Our situatedness thus travels, adapts, performs, and retreats—comprising, for rhetors, conditions of attunement.

This view is considerably distant from Bitzer's—he argued that situations precede rhetoric (2). Rhetors do not make worlds, but rather respond to a priori reality. Situations, their provenance largely arhetorical, control rhetorics, serving as "the very ground of rhetorical activity" (5). In Contrast, Richard Vatz argued that utterances rise not from a priori facticity but the perceptions of rhetors (154). Ascribing characteristics to a given situation, therefore, is an interpretive move, for "no situation can have a nature independent of the perception of its interpreter" (154). This moves rhetoric from a priori facticity to a phenomenological quiddity of individual perceptions and values. Both perspectives are thus grounded in strong subject-object dichotomies: Bitzer overdetermines a priori reality, and Vatz overdetermines rhetors.

For Jenny Edbauer, rhetoric and its elements—should it have any—are part of lived experience, part of "affective ecologies" that evoke a broader situatedness (5). Edbauer's shift to affect—and from rhetorical situations to rhetorical ecologies—recognizes "temporal, historical, and lived fluxes" (9) of sociality. She argues that "practical consciousness is never outside the prior and ongoing structures of feeling that shape the social field" (10), a perspective that moves rhetoric further toward Rickert's ambience. Yet subtle shifts from situations, elements, and processes to *situatedness* signal ontologies that move, adapt, and become—an ever-present rhetorical imminence, a horizon of internal and external possibility.

"Rhetoric," Rickert argues, "must be grounded in the material relations from which it springs" (x). This materiality is not simply exigence, but a constitutive foundation. This is the fundamental sense in which rhetoric is ambient. Traditional notions of rhetorical situation atomize, individuate, and extract salience, but doing so excludes the constitutive role of ambience in how situations emerge (xi). Rickert appropriates Heidegger's notion of disclosure, a key component in a robust theory of situatedness. Ambient rhetorics thus involve "the always ongoing disclosure of the world shifting our manner of being," where "worlds" are "the mutually achieved composite of meaning and matter," inclusive of everyday "involvements and cares" (xii). Rhetorical situatedness is fundamental to our being-in-the-world because rhetoric is "one of the modalities for *attunement* to the world" (xviii; italics in the original). Ambient rhetorics are part of our "fundamental entanglement" and ongoing disclosure of being-in-the-world (8), and our attunement to ambience conditions how we comport ourselves. Our everyday, therefore, is immersed in layered attunements to disclosive ambience.

The worldishness "of being situated," Rickert adds, "is the means by which we are attuned" (13). But being situated in disclosive ambience brings substantive shifts to conceptions of agency. The things and affects of our environs have palpable suasive potential, but everyday being-in-the-world is grounded in wholeness difficult to consciously individuate (18). This is the point. "An ambient rhetoric integrates the world itself as a necessary part of rhetorical work," Rickert argues, "making rhetorical theory as much about the world around us as it is about human being" (21). Attuning to disclosive ambience thus "situates us differently in the world, evoking other ways of being" (33). Ambient rhetoric fosters a new situatedness, one beyond cherished notions of "coming from somewhere" or "having a worldview" (33). Instead, our somewheres are entanglements-for-now subject to new and shifting disclosures.

Ambient rhetorics foster attunements to such disclosures, which often emerge as circulatory intensities—worldish "relationality, conditionality, [and] withdrawal" (Rickert 204). We are immersed in rhetorical lifeworlds rather than rhetorical situations (213). In *Being and Time*, Heidegger explores concepts of thrownness and worldishness that ground rhetorical lifeworlds. We begin entangled, thrown into worlds over which we have little control—which we often even evade—but through which we are simultaneously consumed by affect and care (132–35). More important, worldishness is mutually disclosing: we disclose ourselves to the world as beings who think about our existence even as worldish ambience discloses its "thereness" to us in myriad ways. The confluence of these disclosures substantially constitutes our being-in-the-world (129), since the "thereness" of the world is part of us (129), and our "thereness" moves with us as potentialities (140). We attune to the ways that worldish ambience discloses itself to us, and we to it, but we often evade everyday disclosures (131). Yet even in evasions (keeping rain off our heads with an umbrella, for example) "the there *is* something disclosed" (131).

Attunements may unfold in fits and starts, through momentary intensities. Regardless, we are *inescapably situated* by attunements to disclosive ambience, and we bring this evolving situatedness with us, as entanglements-for-now, to future entanglements. Attunement, therefore, "is an existential, fundamental way" in which we are our "there" (Heidegger 135). Because the thereness of our being moves with us, we constantly adapt our entanglements-for-now to new worldish possibilities (139). As Heidegger explains, we are a "being-possible," we are walking embodiments of *"thrown possibility"* (139; italics in the original). Rhetoric is a central mode of attunement to thrownness, entanglement, and worldishness, and the subtle shift from situation to situatedness encompasses the conditions of attunement for a given rhetor. Situatedness thus evolves, adapts, moves, and changes as new forms of worldish ambience are disclosed, evaded, and embedded in one's being-potential.

Considering Things | Embedded Moralities, Affective Affordances, Rhythms

The approach to rhetorical situatedness described above has significant implications for perspectives of worldish things. For example, Elizabeth Shove and her colleagues "show how things are implicated in the development, persistence and disappearance of patterns and practices" of everydayness (3). Through their work on material cultures, they contest prevailing views about object agency and the role of things in shaping everyday life (4). Agency, they argue, is thoroughly distributed, emerging from assemblages of humans and nonhumans—a perspective that fosters new forms of inquiry for the role of objects in social life (7). Though such objects may appear stable, like rhetorically situated humans "their social significance and their relational role in practice is always on the move" (8). Objects and artifacts "evolve as they are integrated into always fluid environments of consumption, practice and meaning" (8). People, objects, and everyday practices thus "interact in ways that are mutually constitutive" (23). In this view, things have suasive and agentive potential; objects in everyday life carry deep personal meanings, participate in identity construction, aid cognitive efforts and physical labor, and shape ordinary orientations and gazes.

Sarah Pink brings similar ideas to bear on the anthropology of experience. For example, Pink situates suasive objects within a broader context of "purposeful engagements in an aesthetic, material, sensory, social and power-infused environment" (48). In everyday settings such as kitchens, a theory of materiality and practice helps account for object and sensory assemblages that co-constitute ways of knowing and being (53). Indeed, everyday objects often carry "embedded moralities" (59): traces of previous interactions, and memories of such traces, that may be discerned through patterns of wear, for example. These may represent forms of tactile knowing, learned adjustments from childhood, or applications of normative traditions (59–62). Objects also have affective affordances: doing laundry, for example, is "part of the ecology of things that make the textures, smells and visual appearance of home" palpable for Pink's research participants (76). Overall, Pink is concerned with the routes and flows of such objects and sensory details and how they co-constitute everyday life.

In this regard, a fellow anthropologist, Tim Ingold, heavily influences Pink's work. Ingold argues that a pervasive logic of inversion turns "the pathways along which life is lived into boundaries within which life is contained" (1796–1797). The logic of inversion is fundamentally Kantian, and it is a Kantian view of the world—of enclosure and surfaces—that dominates contemporary science, where the knowing subject is positioned over and against materiality (1798). But the world as lived is processual and mixed (1801): Organisms move through "a world-in-formation rather than *across* its preformed surface" (1802; emphasis in original). As they move, they encounter, engage, and interact with circulatory intensities; in this sense, to be is "not to be *in* place but to be *along* paths. The path, not the place, is the primary condition of being, or rather becoming" (1808; emphasis in original).

Stewart sees these processual developments and co-constitutive engagements with ambience as "the cultural poesis of forms of living" ("Weak Theory" 71). Movements along paths, encounters with weather, and entanglements with humans and nonhumans unfold across everyday processes, through "textures and rhythms, trajectories, and modes of attunement, attachment, and composition" (71). The poesis of everyday life is a bringing-forth, a making, a worldishness. The everyday is often seemingly thrown together, as if Ingold's paths, Pink's affective affordances, and the agentive potential of material objects surprise us by becoming durable forms of coalescence, emergent from ambient environs. Stewart argues that everyday living, perceptions, and notions oscillate in rhythmic potentials—"a *some*thing waiting to happen in disparate and incommensurate objects, registers, circulations, and publics" (72; emphasis in original).

Stewart focuses less on objective representations and more on where things might go: "what potential modes of knowing, relating, and attending to things are already somehow present in them as a potential or resonance" (73).

These post-Kantian approaches to the constitution of everyday life are well and good, but they may be methodologically opaque for many empirical researchers of rhetoric. How do we study something as potentially complex as worldish attunement? How do we follow circulations of objects, uncover embedded moralities, or trace sensory affects? In Packer's notion of constitution, the research focus shifts to practical activity and embodied know-how (167). This emphasis fosters a related shift in objects of study, where everyday assemblages, interpersonal orientations, and sighs and rolling eyes constitute ontological disclosures alongside those comprising traditional forms of fieldwork. Packer argues, then, for "our absorption in everyday social interaction, and our inescapable entanglement in the material world" (201). In the following section, I describe my methodology and methods for studying circulatory intensities in and through the Little Free Library, and the relationship of such intensities to rhetorical situatedness.

Worldish Attunements | Methodology and Methods

As Clay Spinuzzi argues, methodologies frame and guide the values and theories of empirical studies, while methods are modes of investigating phenomena (7). My methodology in this project was analytic autoethnography, a qualitative approach that acknowledges and incorporates the researcher's subjective experience and that stems from ethnographic traditions grounded in symbolic interactionism (see Anderson). Analytic autoethnography does not necessarily reject the epistemological assumptions of ethnographic research, as do some forms of evocative autoethnography. The methodology looks inward (at the subjective experience of the researcher) to see outward, "to an intellectual constituency informed by social theory" and imbricated in social life (Atkinson 403). Rigorous autoethnography, like traditional qualitative approaches, "provides reports that are scholarly and justifiable interpretations based on multiple sources of evidence" (Duncan 31).

Scott Hunt and Natalia Ruiz Junco suggest that "individuals' actions of the present moment emerge from understandings of pasts and anticipations of future selves pursuing future lines of action" (371). The present may therefore "be very spacious" (371). Here, autoethnography is a methodology for tracing the spaciousness of an evolving present by considering my experience with the circulating entanglements (Rickert), routes (Pink *Situating*), intensities and trajectories (Stewart *Ordinary*), and lines and meshworks (Ingold) through the disclosive ambience of the world in and around one Little Free Library. Autoethnographers, Leon Anderson contends, should be candid, "vividly revealing themselves as people grappling with issues relevant to membership and participation in fluid rather than static social worlds" (384). This approach does not simply document one's experience—analytic autoethnography should use empirical data to provide broader insights about social phenomena (Anderson 387).

I follow Elizabeth Chaplin in conducting visual autoethnography; both Chaplin and Jon Wagner see photography as a way of visually documenting and presenting situated experience. Wagner argues that photographs may help researchers establish a visual baseline in fieldwork (80), providing "an optically etic account" of particular objects of study that may "also serve as a record of material circumstances," potentially providing emic points of view as well (81). In my fieldwork, photographs act simultaneously as ideographic and nomothetic forms of evidence: they reveal my research perspective on everyday circulations of material objects and affects while also offering presentations of a site, materiality, and visible-sensory field that may be productively compared to some 10,000 analogous sites around the world.

This project was motivated by a disengagement from material things, the circulations of those things beyond my own life, and their participation in broader movements of sharing and literacy. After two household moves in three years, the physical and psychological weight of my family's material goods was palpable. Before settling into our home in Lexington, I seized an opportunity to simplify—to let go of books I had read or would never read before they made their way onto new shelves, and into new forms of permanence in my life. Fascinated by the mission of the Little Free Library and inspired by a minimalist challenge to let go of one "thing" each day for one month, I resolved to donate at least one book each day to the little library nearest my home in December 2012. I visited rain or shine, through snow and wind, on Christmas Day and New Year's Eve. In total, I moved forty-eight books and nine DVDs out of my home, through the little library, and on to points unknown. By February 9, 2013, all my donations had turned over, circulating out of my life and into others'.

I generated three forms of data: book circulation patterns, fieldnotes, and photographs. My research question was simple: what would following the circulation of books tell me about the world and about rhetorical situatedness? Consequently, I kept meticulous records of library holdings: my daily contributions, items in circulation since the previous visit, and new contributions from others. More important than circulation patterns, however, were fieldnotes documenting experiences in a spacious present of disclosive ambience—the objects, people, organisms, weather patterns, and movements that flowed through and near the Little Free Library during fieldwork. Overall, I wrote thirty-four fieldnote entries (7,650 words over 277 paragraph-separated units), covering each day of fieldwork during December and three additional visits in January and February. Each entry details circulation patterns, interactions with others, and sensory engagements and apprehensions. Finally, I composed 118 photographs: a minimum of two each day during the fieldwork period (with a mobile phone), and a series of more detailed explorations of the spatial and sensory field composed with a digital single-lens reflex (DSLR) camera on three different occasions. Photographs augmented circulation patterns, establishing a visual baseline of daily holdings that helped me trace movements through the library. And photographs also augmented fieldnote entries, providing qualitatively different details about my environs.

As fieldwork progressed, I focused on forms of movement beyond the books with which I had earnestly begun. I explored additional circulations—of people nearby and through the library, of implicit discourses and forms of capital, of cars and bikes on the street, of weather through my clothes and skin, of sentiments and entanglements in the periphery and outside my conscious attention. I asked: what are the circulations, practical activities, and intensities that co-constitute this little, thrown together world? And though my approach was focused on the rhetorical situatedness of humans, my fieldwork practices rejected subject–object bifurcations. Studying places as events, the embodied and haptic interactions with suasive things, and circulatory intensities of nonhumans beyond subject–object distinctions is fully congruent with my methodology and methods. A similar study, for example, might have focused on the vibrant materialities (Bennett) circulating through and near the library—the influence of books on other books, rather than on the rhetorical situatedness of humans.

My analytic approach was systematic, but cognizant of—and resistant to—attempts to force theory from data. Following Bonnie Nardi (Zachry), I was interested in understanding sensibilities and themes. Ultimately, I applied Barthes's theory of the *punctum* as an analytic method for exploring everyday intensities and their role in rhetorical situatedness, worldishness, and ontological constitution. Of the data, I asked: How might circulatory intensities act as visual, sensory, material, and haptic *puncta* in rich tapestries of disclosive ambience? Such uncoded, accidental, and even unintentional details, I argue, coalesce in a spacious present that pulls together and weaves past, current, and future circulations of rhetorical situatedness, and in the process, constitutes ontologies.

Suasive Circulations | Constitutive Worldishness

My analysis yielded two themes across several *puncta*: first, the suasive potential of ordinary objects, and second, worldishness apprehended through circulatory intensities that constituted the Little Free Library and that situated my rhetori-

Figure 10.2. Current holdings, December 21, 2012. Photograph by author.

cal being-potential. Through vignettes from my fieldwork, I explore my evolving understanding in light of the theoretical perspectives developed thus far.

Suasive Circulations

> December 2, 2012
> When I left yesterday, I had ordered the holdings from left to right, roughly tallest to shortest. When I opened the library today, things were almost flipped! None of the books that I added yesterday were taken, but I think that perhaps at least one other book was taken. I reordered the books again, from left to right, tallest to shortest.

↬

During fieldwork, I was obsessed with the appearance of books in the library. On just the second day, I was flummoxed to see disorder, to think that someone had ransacked the holdings and left them in disarray. How could a patron reasonably peruse titles when the holdings were disordered, when spines were difficult to see, when the "natural" orders of things (left to right, tallest to shortest) were disrupted? I recognize that my personal fastidiousness is largely to blame for this needless worry. But as McLuhan argued, all media work us over. My past, present, and future vision for how books should be arranged and presented *worked on me*, and each day influenced my tactile interactions with the library. I would not photograph the holdings until they were properly aligned, and I fussed over the arrangement of books throughout the project.

> December 5, 2012
> The library is at its highest capacity since the project began, for sure. More contributions than lendings, on the whole. I wonder how much I'm gaming the project, since so many of the contributions are my own?

༄

> December 6, 2012
> The library is at its highest capacity by far today. Someone dropped several trade paperbacks in the box since my last observation. Ironically, someone left a copy of *All the King's Men*—ironic because I chose my copy yesterday evening to drop off today. I'd say that there are 10–12 new books since yesterday—my guess is that they were all contributed by one person. [. . .]
>
> My main question at this point is how long it will take for some of this inventory to lend. I don't know how many books here I would consider really desirable, but at the same time, there are some solid works—some classics—that some folks may want to read. I think for tomorrow I should just bring one book, or even a DVD.

༄

By day five, I wonder whether I am "gaming the project," as if my daily contributions of books will subversively influence patrons or disrupt some internal vision I have of circulatory normalcy. And I worry about future circulations. How long will it take for these books to move out? What kinds of objects are desirable to others? Why did I have to choose Penn Warren's opus today? Am I burdening the library with works no one will want? Again, circulations, current capacity, and the decisions I have made about titles and arrangement *work on me*. I worry, and care. I think about how I can provide complementary titles. I consider contributing a DVD, primarily because I feel it will be more attractive to patrons. I react to movements in or from another patron, and I consider ways of effecting movements out.

Constitution and Attunements to Worldishness

As fieldwork progressed, my attunements to the disclosures of worldish ambience intensified. I became interested in circulations of weather events, patrons, sounds, and sensory affects. I detail, therefore, the *puncta* of such circulatory intensities and I reflect on the ways in which they situated me and constituted a world.

> December 7, 2013
> As I arrived at the library, I noticed three people standing directly in front of it, gathered around what appears to be a small pushcart or walker. As I ride up, I guess that these folks are unhoused, or lightly/transiently housed. Each wears a hat and large coat, and most of their clothing looks worn to threadbare.
>
> I lean my bike underneath the library as I normally do, but I don't have clear access to the library yet. At this point, they notice me—two men and a woman—all I judge to be at least in their 40s, more likely in their 50s. The woman looks at me and beams, expressing to me how happy she is that the library exists. I concur, then I ask if they are picking up or dropping off. They note that they're picking up.
>
> The man nearest me says that he's checked out *The Three Musketeers*. I tell him that I think that's great, and then he asks me if I've read it. I confess that I haven't but that I'd seen the movie. He asks me if it's about bank robberies, and I tell him that no, it's about a group of French swordsmen. At this point, the woman rejoins the conversation, expressing once again her gratitude for the library. It's clear to me how much this little service means, and they all nod agreement that it's important to them. More important, they express happiness that it's something there for all.
>
> Shortly after our conversation, they head off down the sidewalk, moving toward Woodland Park. I was truly thrilled to see folks today, and to have a chance to talk with someone about how they use the library. So far, this project has been a rather lonely pursuit—I know that there are people contributing and lending, but counter to nearly all of my research, I haven't actually had a chance to *talk* to another person about how and why this little library is meaningful. I sincerely hope I meet others before the month is over!

I met others, but I did not have a similar encounter. Disclosures of worldishness shape perceptions, situate rhetors, and magnify intensities. I was keenly aware of the contrasts between these patrons and me. I thought later that day, for the first time, about the library as an emblem of social capital; here is an assemblage that promotes literacy and free exchange. And yet here is an assemblage that represents privilege, forms of social capital, perhaps even guilt. In my fieldnotes three days later I wondered if the library might even support local economies for the unhoused—a mechanism for obtaining free goods to sell. I have no answers, but this moment changed me, and changed my perspective of the library.

December 8, 2012
One thing I've not noticed yet are DVDs. Jen [my wife] had brought up a box from the basement yesterday with several DVDs that she thought we might want to part with. For example, after my dad died, Leslie [my stepmother] gave me a bunch of DVDs that my dad liked, but that she didn't care for. I'm not sure what she expected me to do with them, but I took them nonetheless, just to make things easier for her.

These are moments in which worlds are thrown together. A box of DVDs, brought up from the basement; a reminder of a conversation in my dad's home in Atlanta, a day after he died, and me taking a box of DVDs from my step-mother, not because I wanted them, not because my dad wanted me to have them, but because I knew it was one small give-and-take in which saying yes was far easier than saying no. Such objects do not matter at such times. Who cares? Yes, I'll gladly take these DVDs—John Wayne and WWII films and westerns. My stepmother had life insurance claims to file, bills to pay, distant friends to notify, closer friends to thank and lean on and cry among. I'll take this box of DVDs and drive it back home, and I'll figure it out later. It sits in the basement, the taking and the storing part of the ambience conditioning my rhetorical situatedness. And then a circulatory intensity: the box resurfaces four years after my dad's death, the routes and circulations of things widen—from Atlanta, to Texas, to Indiana, to Lexington, to a Little Free Library where the provenance of these DVDs will never be known, but where they may be appreciated nonetheless.

December 11, 2012
As I was finishing tidying up the presentation and arrangement of the library before taking my daily photo, a crossing guard from the nearby school—dressed in her bright yellow, reflective coat and carrying her Stop Sign and large orange cone—stopped to speak with me. I thought perhaps she had something to say about the library, but instead she wanted

Figure 10.3. The Little Free Library, looking down Maxwell toward an eagle's perch. Photograph by author.

to alert me to the eagle perched on top of the telephone pole at the nearest corner of Woodland and Maxwell.

I looked up, and sure enough, there it was, facing away from me, looking down, over its left shoulder, at the traffic on Woodland or at kids scurrying to school or at a squirrel. I asked her if she'd seen the eagle before, if this was a regular roost; she said that she had indeed seen it previously, on the pole opposite, and that she'd taken some good pictures. She then moved off up Maxwell toward the park, presumably to get into her car after her crossing guard shift.

I did not look up and around until several days into my fieldwork. I did not notice, for example, that two used bookstores operate within 200 feet of the Little Free Library. And while I could not help but notice weather events—I biked each day, in sometimes freezing wind, rain, ice, and snow—I rarely noticed other organisms, and I was not open to their disclosures. But I am not ashamed to say that this was my favorite moment of worldish disclosure, a glimpse of unnoticed potential, a shift in my research gaze, a turn in my rhetorical situatedness. I had been focusing on and asking questions about the circulations of humans and things; meanwhile, circulations of a different kind surrounded me, and helped constitute my world, even as I unintentionally evaded them.

Figure 10.4. Circulations, disclosures, and attunements in rhetorical situatedness. Photograph by author.

Openings | Studying Rhetorical Situatedness

In this chapter, I explored the circulatory intensities that move through one little library. Circulations include weather patterns, nonhuman organisms, sounds, objects, other humans, and the practical activity of one researcher and other patrons. In visiting the library each day, in tracing the circulatory intensities that surround and move through it, my practical activity was both ordinary and an exploration of worldish ambience, constitution, and rhetorical situatedness. I am a different rhetor for having been immersed in these circulations, for attuning to elements of the everyday and formulating research questions that I would not have generated otherwise. In studying rhetorical situatedness, then, we must attend to circulations beyond discourses, and we can do so empirically, with careful methods such as those described here.

Notes

1. Ideographs, in rhetoric, are value words often used in political oratory. *Ideographic* methodologies, in qualitative research, focus on individual cases. Ideographic approaches contrast with nomothetic approaches, which focus on generalizable populations.

2. While Rickert uses the terms "worldliness" or "worldly," common translations of Heidegger's *Weltlichkeit* and related adjective *weltlich*, I prefer Magda King's translation: worldishness and worldish. As King notes, the terms "worldliness" and "worldly" have definite meanings in English. For Heidegger, though, humans are "worldish, spaceish, timeish, i.e., world-forming, space-disclosing, time-originating" (370).

11
On Rhetorical Becoming

Laurie Gries

In this chapter, I explore the ontological notion of becoming as it relates to visual-material rhetoric. Rhetoricians have long been interested in the ontology of becoming. Nathan Crick, in fact, insists that "the connection between rhetoric and the ontology of becoming . . . is present at the very origins of rhetoric" (22). Most typically, in a Western context, this concern has to do with the identity formation, subjectivity, and civic development of human beings as well as the health of democracy. We might interpret, for instance, the purpose of progymnasmata in ancient Greece as teaching pupils how to become rhetorical and develop public virtue—a notion emphasized by David Fleming, who argues that rhetoric's ongoing educational function is to help students become rhetorically self-conscious and flexible civic actors ("Becoming"). We might also read the sophist rhetorician Protagoras as being committed to the ontology of becoming, as he believed that "all things are in motion" and that "the verb 'to be' must be totally abolished."[1] This recognition of flux, Crick argues, is evident in John Dewey's own belief that the power of discourse lies in its ability to move the individual self (and thus a democratic public) toward unknown possibilities. From a new materialist perspective that believes in a democracy of things (i.e., all things have equal ontological footing), human subjects are not the only ones who experience rhetorical becoming. Rhetoric is a distributed event that unfolds *with* time in and across networks of complex, dynamic relations. At the heart of this process is rhetorical transformation—a virtual-actual process of becoming in which rhetoric unfolds and alters reality in unpredictable, divergent, and inconsistent ways. Nonhuman things, such as new media images, also experience rhetorical becoming in that their potential to spark identification, persuasion, and collective action is constantly materializing via their multiple and diverse encounters. This chapter asks what we might discover about visual rhetoric by acknowledging a new media image's rhetorical transformation.

156 / LAURIE GRIES

Figure 11.1. Obama Hope poster, designed by Shepard Fairey, 2008. Photograph by Steve Rhodes, 2008.

In relation to visual rhetoric, several iconic images could be discussed to study rhetorical transformation: Mona Lisa, Rosie the Riveter, Uncle Sam. As evident in a simple Google Images search, all these images have led complex rhetorical lives as they have been remixed and appropriated for various reasons. Yet, Obama Hope, Shepard Fairey's now iconic, stylized rendition of Barack Obama,[2] is, perhaps, the most contemporary quintessential example of such rhetorical transformation. Obama Hope, in its most widely recognized form, first entered into circulation in late January 2008 in an effort to help then-Senator Obama become the next US president (fig. 11.1). Today, digital reproductions and remixes of this image can be found on more than two million websites while numerous physical renditions can be found tattooed on human bodies, plastered to urban walls, and waving at protests across the globe. As it has circulated and transformed with time and space, it has become, among many other things, an international environmental and political activist, a popular cybergenre for launching social and political critique, and a spark of political enchantment for people both within and beyond US borders. Obama Hope has also become an educational force, as it has surfaced in scholarship about not only new media literacy, art, and presidential history, but also, as evident in Jeff Rice's recent work with noetic space, rhetorical theory. Considering such ontological instability and unpredictable rhetorical becoming, how ought scholars think about visual rhetoric in a digital age?

In the following sections, I demonstrate how nonmodern and chronotopic perspectives of time and space can help elucidate a visual thing's virtual-actual dimensions and distributed ontology. I also, and more particularly, advocate for thinking about visual things, such as Obama Hope, as *single, multiple images* that acquire thing-power as they circulate with time and space. For visual rhetoric scholars, such theoretical moves are useful for a number of different reasons, only two of which I discuss here. First, as Finnegan and Kang note, iconoclasm often acts in subtle ways in theories about public rhetorics—this iconoclasm limits our understanding of how images materialize and affect consequences in the public sphere (379). Acknowledging an image's distributed ontology and accounting for its rhetorical transformation helps scholars move from iconoclasm to iconophilia, a respect for not only an image itself but also its movement, its transformations, and its ability to construct publics (Finnegan and Kang 395).

Second, such theoretical attention is useful for elucidating how new media images become rhetorically divergent in a globally networked culture. Mary Queen has argued that electronic texts are visibly unstable; they "change not only because they are ephemeral—forming and dissolving simultaneously—but also because they are mobile: they circulate and, in the process of circulation, they encounter and are transformed by other forces" ("Transnational" 475). Especially with digital remixing burgeoning as both an important twenty-first century literacy practice (Lessig) and a global activity of creative and efficient information exchange (Navas), the same can be said for images that are both "born digital" and become digital as they are uploaded to the Internet for various reasons. Yet, while remixed, circulating images have received increased rhetorical attention in recent years thanks to scholars such Robert Hariman and John Lucaites, rhetorical theories have yet to catch up with new media images circulating and functioning in a digitally saturated climate. Here, I thus unpack the notion of rhetorical transformation in efforts to deepen our understanding of how new media images become rhetorical in a digital age.

Circulation and Transformation

To be clear at the outset, becoming, as I am referring to it here, can be understood as a virtual-actual process in which any given thing (better thought of as a multiplicity) "changes in nature as it expands its connections" through its *constant*[3] production with time and of space (*Deleuze and Guattari* 8). Typical perceptions of matter view material things as inert, whole objects with analyzable compositional elements that distinguish them from other solid entities. When we study objects such as books or photographs from such perspective, we tend to stand over or in front of the object, gaze at it from a distanced perspective, and attempt to identify its fixed internal properties in order to determine its possible rhetorical meanings. The object is studied as a static entity before us both in terms of its essence and location in the world. Such perspectives reinforce a static model of discourse structure in which we "view meaning as an object contained in the text, accessible to an 'objective' description, capable of spatialization and thus open to simultaneous comprehension of all its parts" (Phelps 139). As a consequence of this static model, we often refrain from acknowledging how discourse experiences rhetorical transformation and from accounting for its constant yet often-unpredictable change and movement.

Within rhetorical study, this methodological dilemma is as troublesome for images such as Obama Hope as it is for other kinds of discourse, largely due to transmission models of delivery. In our everyday understanding of delivery, as Collin Brooke has noted, we speak about objects being delivered in a specific context (*Lingua* 170). More particularly, we think of someone transmitting some thing to someone else in a precise moment and a specific place. Our mailperson delivers mail to us at our houses; we deliver conference papers to a room (hopefully) full of colleagues. Such perspectives entrap us in thinking about delivery in terms of a fixed rhetorical object, a knowable author, a knowable audience, and an identifiable immediate situation. Such transitive thinking about delivery also perpetuates the notion that intended audiences are passive, albeit interpretive, receptors of delivered things. In a viral economy and participatory culture, in which both intended and unintended audiences play an interactive role in remixing, appropriating, and spreading images, we know that "delivery" is not something that is so direct or controlled. We also know that digital things are rarely stable in and of themselves. Wikipedia, as Brooke notes, is one clear example. With no stable, discrete object existing in the form of a deliverable physical product, Wikipedia is an instance of active performance in which information is constantly being revised and updated (Brooke). Yet, if we take a long view, we can also see that images such as Obama Hope are often in flux in terms of location, form, medium, genre, and activity. As such, it would behoove us to think about not only electronic texts but also visual things as *"circulating, not some thing to be circulated"* (Brooke 192). In this intransitive model, performance, or enactment, constitutes reality as visual things are not only constantly taking place (Brooke 192) but also on the move and undergoing constant change.

Suffice it to say, even as we may intellectually know this to be true, it is still difficult to envision the dynamic flow of visual things typically categorized as still (photograph, poster, painting, etc.). In visual rhetoric, such difficulty stems, in part, from a habit of *"freeze-framing,* that is extracting an image out of the flow, and becoming fascinated by it, as if it were sufficient, as if all movement had stopped" (qtd. in Finnegan and Kang 395). This habit is reinforced by a lack of theoretical perspectives and research methods that enable us to study images as a dynamic network of distributed, unfolding, and unforeseeable becomings.[4] Jenny Edbauer Rice's work with *rhetorical ecologies* is useful in this regard in that it draws our attention to the fluidity and circulation of rhetoric as it is embedded in the "ongoing social flux" that constitutes society (9). As Edbauer Rice explains, "networked life" is constituted by flows of historical and cultural forces, energies, rhetorics, moods, and experiences that emerge between spaces of contact in between humans and their organic and inorganic surroundings. Rhetoric is a distributed act that emerges from between these affective encounters and interactions, not among individual discrete elements (author, text, audience) in any given rhetorical situation. In this theoretical sense, rhetoric is a "process of distributed emergence and as an ongoing circulation process" whose circulatory range is affected by the social flux of forces, energies, encounters, etc. (13). A rhetorical ecological model is productive for visual rhetoric, then, because it challenges us to imagine how images emerge and flow within networks, fields, forces, affects, and associations.

The notion of *rhetorical transformation* discussed here is intended to be productive in similar regard. By rhetorical transformation, I am referring to the process in which things become rhetorical in divergent, unpredictable ways as they circulate with time and space and acquire thing-power. Thing-power, according to Jane Bennett, refers to a thing's "curious ability . . . to animate, to act, to produce effects dramatic and subtle" (*Vibrant* 6). This ability—which we might also think of as a thing's "rhetorical can-do-ness," to borrow Sharon Crowley's phrase (*Toward* 55)—does not derive solely from an actualized image's rhetorical design nor is it a static affair, especially when it comes to images that experience viral circulation. Rather, as images materialize in different versions and enter into divergent associations, they become rhetorically diverse as they enter into a dance of agency with other entities (human and nonhuman, abstract and concrete) to catalyze change. From this new materialist perspective, agency is a doing, an enactment generated by a variety of components intra-acting within a particular phenomenon (Barad 235). Intra-action signifies that when two things come into a relation, they each are mutually transformed. Therefore, while an image may acquire thing-power during an event, a relation, this power is ephemeral; it changes when image materializes in different supports or encounters different entities. In addition to acknowledging an actualized image's interior relations (design, content, arrangement, etc.), then, simultaneously zooming in on an image's emergent exterior relations helps discover how something becomes rhetorical with time and space as it participates in a distributed dance of agency with other entities and alters collective life. Such alteration includes, as many scholars have noted, establishing a particular gaze (Deluca and Demo; Mulvey), producing a multiplicity of visual realities (Vivian), and negotiating civic identity (Hariman and Lucaites). Yet, visual things also become rhetorical when they reassemble collective life as they draw people and other things into relations to achieve various purposes. As an immanent concept, rhetorical transformation acknowledges that such rhetorical becoming is a spatio-temporal, distributed process that intensifies with each new actualization and with each new encounter.

Rhetorical transformation, as a process, is unique to singular images and can only be disclosed by tracing their distinct, albeit divergent, rhetorical lives. This process can seem quite simple, short lived, and inconsequential if an image does not spread and/or transform widely nor leave many traces of rhetorical activity. However, in regard to an image such as the Mona Lisa, which first materialized between 1503 and 1506, this process can be quite complicated, as it has been transforming in terms of genre, media, form, and rhetorical function and circulating across the globe for centuries. With a new media image such as Obama Hope, which took on a plethora of rhetorical roles in countries as disparate as the United States, Turkey, and England within just a few months of entering into circulation, rhetorical transformation can also be quite convoluted. Research methods such as iconographic tracking[5] can help recover the rhetorical transformation of images with such complex, convoluted lives, but how are we to understand this process on a theoretical level? In a general sense, as I have argued elsewhere,[6] thinking intuitively about visual rhetoric helps us theoretically understand this dynamic process. To think intuitively, after all, is to perceive reality as change and mobility—a world in flux constituted by an entangled web of creations, or becomings, each moving toward something new. Yet nonmodern and chronotopic perspectives of time and space also help make theoretical sense of an image's rhetorical becomings.

From a modern perspective, visual things are conceived as bounded, stable entities—marked by solidity—that move through time and space only upon influence of a force or another agent. This movement is thought to obey fundamental and invariable laws of motion and is thus deemed somewhat predictable and controllable. When we adopt nonmodern perspectives, as Latour explains, "we do not fall upon someone or something, we do not land on an essence, but on a process, on a movement, a passage" (*We* 129). From a new materialist perspective, we also land on becoming, the opening up of events into an unknown future. From this perspective, materiality itself is perceived as a fluctuating flow of matter and energy, events and forces in which all things are "relatively composed" (Bennett 349). This flow, or movement, especially on the Internet,[7] does not take place in homogenous space; it does not entail the linear passage of a fixed entity from point A to point B. Rather, movement is nonlinear and entails the production of space and time. In this spatio-temporal sense,[8] circulating images experience a virtuality of duration—"the qualitative change that every movement brings not only to that which moves, but also to the space that it moves in and to the whole into which that space necessarily opens up" (Terranova 51). From this nonmodern perspective, the open-process of becoming cannot help but take place. Visual things do not just move inconsequentiality and unchanged through space and time; they are both impacted by and impact that which they encounter. Despite their stable appearance at a given moment, then, visual things—especially those that experience viral circulation—constantly exist in a dynamic state of flux and are always generative of change, time, and space.

Virtual and Actual

While nonmodern perspectives of time and matter help us understand how visual things exist in flux in a general sense, this perspective does not help explain how images actually undergo rhetorical transformation and experience a distributed ontology. Thus, it is also useful to think about an image's virtual-actual constitution and its variability—its ability to exist in "different, potentially infinite versions" (*Language* 36). An image's virtual-action constitution can perhaps be elucidated most easily by thinking about the relation between an image and a picture. "An image," W. J. T. Mitchell explains, is "an immaterial entity, a ghostly, fantasmatic appearance" that "comes to life" in a material support, i.e., a picture (18). As an immaterial entity, an image can transcend media and thus survive a picture's destruction (16). It also can transform across different material supports while still maintaining its recognizability. For example, take a look at figures 11.2, 11.3, and 11.4, consisting of pictures downloaded from Flickr, in all of which the Obama Hope image materializes. In some pictures, Obama Hope materializes in similar, even seemingly exact, ways as it did in Fairey's "Hope Poster" and is thus easily recognizable if you are familiar with Fairey's work. Yet in other pictures, such as the mural in Figure 11.4, Obama Hope is barely recognizable. One has to be intensely familiar with the stylized portrait of Obama to recognize its presence. Nonetheless, as evident here, the Obama Hope image haunts and transcends all of these pictures.

While an image may be an immaterial entity, an image is a real thing that stimulates material consequences, including its own actualizations in diverse material supports. In this generative sense, we might think of an image as a virtual entity (Vivian 2007; Mitchell 1994) that undergoes a multiplicity of actualizations to become something new. As Steven Shaviro explains so clearly, the virtual is like a field of unexpended energies, or a reservoir of untapped potentialities, that makes the actual capable of coming into existence ("Kant"). The virtual does not predetermine the actual. Instead, the virtual can be understood as a creative force that affords each materialized version to appear or manifest as something new,[9] "something that has never existed in the universe in quite that way before" (Shaviro). In Deleuzean terms, I understand this process of actualization to be one of differenciation[10] in which a creative process of divergent

Figure 11.2. Beacon by OVO, 2008.

Figure 11.3. Obama for Presidente poster, designed by Fred Hidalgo, 2008. Photograph by Jason Anfinsen, 2008.

Figure 11.4. Obama Graffiti: Hope. Photograph by Franco Folini, 2009. CC BY-SA 2.0.

variation takes place. In regard to photographs, murals, or any other material support, this open process of materialization, to reiterate, is not preordained or determined by a virtual image. Although virtual potentials are an ever-present dimension of any given entity that contributes to how an image is dramatized in space, actualization is a divergent process that is dependent on a diverse array of influential external factors, or exterior relations. Such relations involve a wide ecology of human interventions but also nonhuman things such as external light that influences an actualized entity's color, or technologies that shape its production and distribution, just to name a few. Because a virtual image has potential (especially in a viral economy) to enter into a wide range of exterior relations at seemingly simultaneous moments, its actualizations are divergent and multiple. The actual, we must keep in mind, then, is not a singular entity; it is a multiplicity, constituted by heterogeneous materializations with virtual-actual dimensions. During the process of actualization, divergent paths of development constantly unfold in different series, directions, and spatial configurations as well as different time frames, tempos, and patterns. Actualization is, in other words, a mode of constant (but not continuous) individuation in which multiple varieties materialize with time and space.

Some of the versions in which images actualize are obviously quantitative. For instance, when the Obama Hope image manifests in a specific mural (fig. 11.5), it is actual, objective, and extensive in that its actualized self can be easily

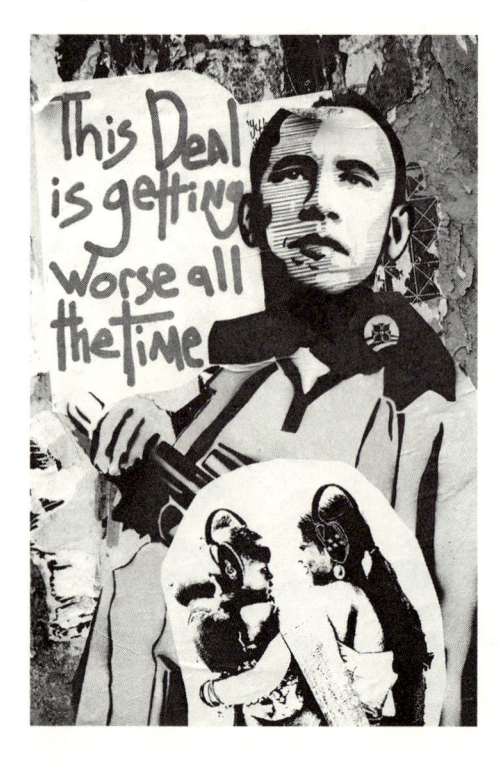

Figure 11.5. Obama mural in Los Angeles, created by Free Humanity. Photograph by Lord Jim, 2011.

identified as differing in degree, represented, and counted by the human eye or a machine (Tampio). Other manifestations, which Deleuze calls qualitative, are not so easily identifiable, as they are subjective and intensive and cannot be easily defined, counted, and quantified (Tampio). For instance, when I speak about the Obama Hope image, a mental picture may come to mind as an actualized form in my imagination, but that picture is not necessarily objective in that it can be measured, nor is it the same one that likely materializes in your brain. While any given image observable in material support is at once qualitative and quantitative, virtual and actual, the ontology of a single image that experiences[11] not only viral circulation but also viral transformation is especially distributed across qualitative and quantitative dimensions. As such, we need to understand that, as Annemarie Mol puts it, "reality is distributed" (96) and that images such as Obama Hope are "single multiple," meaning both one and many (142).

Single and Multiple

In *The Body Multiple: Ontology in Medical Practice*, Mol uses the example of atherosclerosis to explain how a single disease can be a multiplicity in both senses described above. As her ethnography of this disease in a Dutch university hospital makes evident, atherosclerosis does have some sense of coherence in that via a range of coordinations or tasks—such as making images, performing case studies, etc.—it forms and maintains some sense of identifiable whole. Yet, without being so totally fragmented that it cannot go under a single name, it concurrently has multiple versions, depending on factors such as who is discussing it, when and where they are discussing and treating it, and what apparatus they are using to treat it. While some of these versions are easy to locate in print materials or x-rays, others are subjective and cannot always be ascertained even as they have a consequential presence. Some folks, for instance, who have in mind and are affected by their own conception of atherosclerosis, are not always able to totally access and define their understanding of it. While singular, then, in that it has an actual body, this disease is also multiple, many. As such, from the perspective of what Mol calls empirical philosophy, we can think of atherosclerosis as a body multiple—a multiplicity constituted by heterogeneous versions that emerge with their own spatio-temporal configurations yet hang together to give the disease a sense of whole.

Images such as Obama Hope are also body multiples. As a virtual entity that first actualized in Mannie Garcia's "Obama Photo" and then Shepard Fairey's Obama posters, the image has since manifested in many different versions in a variety of media, locations, and genres. It has also transformed many times over in terms of form and/or function, depending on what associations it enters into. In the United States, within months after it entered into circulation, for instance, Obama Hope was materializing in fields of grass, on building facades, and on a wide range of apparel meant to catalyze support for Obama. Yet within these same months, parodies of Obama Hope began to surface in what have now become known as "Obamicons," which actually worked to critique Obama and his political policies. In addition, in places like Africa, Turkey, and China, Obama Hope surfaced on a wide variety of things such product packages, restaurant billboards, and posters, where it worked to sell everything from "Obama Biscuits" to local fare to banking services (fig. 11.6). In France and Germany, on the other hand, remixes of Obama Hope showed up plastered on urban streets and hanging from hot air balloons in image events put on by Greenpeace to fight for environmental justice. In this distributed sense, Obama Hope has been able to maintain a sense of whole, as evident by its recognizability across these actualizations. However, with time and space its reality has become increasingly distributed, as each of its actualizations has taken on a life of its own and shaped collective life in divergent ways.

Because Obama Hope's complex and ongoing rhetorical life exploded like a firework of activities across the globe at lightning speeds, it is difficult to make chronological sense of this single, multiple image's rhetorical transformation. Chronotopic perspectives of spatio-termporal matters, however, can help account

Figure 11.6. Obama Biscuits, 2013. Photograph by author.

for a single, multiple image's distributed ontology and rhetorical transformation. Chronotope, as a concept, recognizes the relativity of time and space. As defined by Bahktin (1981), a chronotope refers to the intrinsic connectedness of temporal and spatial relationships that are artistically expressed in literature (84–85). However, chronotopes can also be thought of as distinct, yet interlaminating spatio-temporal configurations that unfold during any given phenomenon. This spatio-temporal process—what Paul Prior and Jody Shipka, drawing on Bahktin, describe as chronotopic lamination—does not unfold in regular, predictable patterns and thus cannot be totally foreseen. Yet, if we trace the multiple lives of a single image, we can begin to map out how a single, multiple image experiences rhetorical transformation as it acquires thing-power and flexes its rhetorical muscles in divergent ways.

This point is especially important to understand for a theory of visual rhetoric founded on the ontological notion of becoming. Typically, we might think of becoming as one continuous process that exists into eternity; yet the rhetorical transformation of a new media image unfolds at differing speeds and in different spatial configurations, depending on what material forms it takes on, whether these manifest in physical or cyberspace, and any number of institutional, economic, political, or personal forces that shape their design, production, distribution, and maintenance. At any given time, for instance, the Obama Hope image may be concurrently actualizing on the streets of Santa Fe in a pro-Obama mural that takes five hours for artists to create; in a mosaic created out of credit cards that takes three days to complete; or in a digital remix composed in Photoshop over the span of forty-five minutes. While the mural may stay in tact for only two months before it is painted over by folks with dissenting political views, the mosaic may be preserved in a craft museum or personal home and live for one hundred years. The digital remix, on the other hand, may be uploaded to a website where it remains visible for five years but then disappears when the site becomes inaccessible, only to remain in some person's digital file until her or his computer crashes and all files are lost. Such differenciation does not happen in a neat, easily mappable, linear fashion. Yet, with a chronotopic eye toward futurity, a single, multiple image's divergent rhetorical life can come to light both in our rhetorical theories and our research methods. We simply need to make rhetorical transformation the center of our focus.

Conclusion

Rhetorical transformation, as I have been discussing it here, is not specific to new media images per se. Many material things become rhetorically consequential in divergent and unpredictable ways with time and space. As more and more people gain access to the Internet and as remix becomes more and more popular as a transnational practice, however, the rhetorical transformation of single, multiple images such as Obama Hope is bound to intensify. Some of this transformation will surely be humorous and seem rhetorically insignificant. In 2012, for instance, a PhotoFunia-generated montage fooled many people in urban London into thinking an enormous mural depicting *Game of Thrones* character Tyrion Lannister with the word "(P)imp" written below had been painted on a wall (fig. 11.7).

Yet, Obama Hope has also taken on serious roles that continue to unfold nearly eight years after the image first entered into circulation. Obama Hope, for instance, has frequently surfaced in political posters to critique Obama's failed campaign promises. As Justin Vaughn and Jennifer Mercieca have noted, such critiques ought not be surprising for a president with such heroic expectations, especially since "Obama's campaign promises were ambiguous and arguably unachievable by any measure" (11). Yet, Obama Hope has also unpredictably manifested on protest banners to criticize Obama's military use of drones, in political cartoons to satirize Obama's decision to seek Congressional approval for military action in Syria, and in Obamicons to praise Vladimir Putin's negotiations to remove Bashar al-Assad's chemical weapons arsenal. In addition, in countries such as Australia, Mexico, and Germany, Obama Hope has, respectively, become part of the pro-hemp movement, taken a role in rallies against US deportation poli-

Figure 11.7. PhotoFunia montage of Pimp Obamico, creator of montage unknown. Original Pimp Obamicon by Jan Jesko Mantey.

cies, and acted in protests against the US National Security Agency (fig. 11.8). Such continued proliferation of Obama Hope's rhetorical transformation demonstrates how many new media images are constantly on the rhetorical run, participating in collective life in important yet unexpected ways.

As a way to bring this chapter to a close, such continued proliferation also demonstrates why certain new media images deserve a more prominent place in rhetorical history. Rhetorical history, as David Zarefsky has pointed out, often focuses on four concerns: the history of rhetoric, the rhetoric of history, the historical study of rhetorical events, and the rhetorical study of historical events. In historical studies of rhetorical events, which is most relevant here, discourse is typically studied "as a force in history" (Zarefsky 30). Yet much of the time, the force of discourse is isolated to specific moments in history or specific contexts, a scholarly move that often ends up narrowing and limiting its projection (Marback 64) and overlooking its "madness, excess, and ecstasy" (DeLuca and Wilferth). Images such as Obama Hope remind us of the many rhetorical events and the wide expanses of history there are to recover, at least when we look to the future to trace the multiple and divergent rhetorical becomings of a single, multiple image. As a final thought, then, how might rhetorical history be enriched if we put single, multiple images and their rhetorical transformations at the center of our studies? What rhetorical discoveries might we stumble

Figure 11.8. *Yes We Scan*, Rene Walter, 2013.

upon by following new media images at rhetorical play across time and space? From a new materialist perspective, as we begin to think more seriously about the rhetorical ontologies of things, these are just two of many questions certainly worth exploring.

Notes

1. These quotes are taken from Socrates's account of Protagoras's philosophy in Plato's *Theatetus*.
2. As Shepard Fairey now admits, Obama Hope is a remix of a Mannie Garcia photograph, which was taken in 2006 at the National Press Club.
3. *Multiplicity* here refers to the state of things in which no totality or unity exists, only multidimensional relationality. *Constant* refers to the fact that "now" is not a static moment in time but rather is a "now" always undergoing a process of transformation.
4. I use the phrase "networks of becomings" to emphasize that an image does not unfold in a single-threaded, sequential, continuous manner but rather along divergent and seemingly simultaneous spatio-temporal channels.
5. See my article "Iconographic Tracking: A Digital Research Method for Visual Rhetorics and Circulation Studies," *Computers and Composition*, December 2013.
6. Ibid.
7. In *Network Culture*, Terranova defines the outernet as "the network of social,

cultural and economic relationships which criss-crosses and exceeds the Internet—surrounds and connects the latter to larger flows of labour, culture and power" (75).

8. Here, I draw on Jeff Rice's (2011) work with Henri Lefebvre to emphasize that "'spaces are produced' as a variety of forces come into contact with one another on an everyday basis" (11). These forces include institutional, economic, and political factors that construct a network or set of networks, yet also "non-instrumental or non-structural modes of communicative organization: feeling, sensation, and intuition" (12). Yet, I also draw on Steven Shaviro's work in *Without Criteria* (2009), who in commenting on Whitehead's "reformed subjectivist principle" reminds us that "Time is not given in advance; it needs to be effectively produced, or constructed, in the course of subjective experience. . . . Time is produced in and through experience; and experience, in turn, is implicitly temporal" (77). Such subjective experience is not limited to human entities, but is extended to all entities, which, according to Whitehead, are subjects (77).

9. Here, I diverge from Deleuze's monist perspective of the virtual, which suggests that discrete entities emerge from a single virtual substance. My thinking of the virtual is thus more in line with what Levi Bryant calls a virtual proper being, which is a dimension of every individual thing that acts as a generative mechanism. See Bryan's *The Democracy of Objects*.

10. Deleuze makes distinctions between differentiation and differenciation. While differentiation entails the "determination of the virtual content of an Idea," differenciation refers to the "actualisation of that virtuality in species and distinguished parts" (*Difference and Repetition* 207).

11. While experience in this discursive use may seem anthropocentric, from a new materialist perspective, an image does undergo experience in that it actively participates in events. In addition, if we take a long view of an image's rhetorical life, we can observe that it undergoes constant change, depending on how it materializes, whom it encounters, and how it works (engages in a physical or mental activity). Just like we say that a company experiences change, then, we can say that images experience transformation as they circulate with time and space.

12
So Close, Yet So Far Away
Temporal Pastiche and *Dear Photograph*

Kim Lacey

Six or seven years ago, my mom and I met for lunch at a restaurant not far from our first family home. Since neither of us had seen the old house since we moved out of it, we thought it would be fun to go see what the old neighborhood looked like. We had a hard time locating the house, and we especially felt out of place driving very slowly down what had become an unfamiliar road. When we found it, it was a mild letdown. Located in the east side of Detroit, the house and surrounding neighborhood looked like the rest of the city—worn down and empty. I had not seen the house in person since we moved from the city to the suburbs in 1988, and my family relied on shared memories and photographs to document our old home. My personal childhood memories of the locale were alarmingly different than what I was seeing in front of me that cold January afternoon. Sure, the flowers were not blooming on the side of the house (it was winter, after all) and my neighborhood friends were not outside (they had all grown up or moved away), but the vividness of the "home" I recalled was absent. Even though the surroundings looked somewhat familiar and the basic structure of the neighborhood was intact, that house no longer looked anything like the photographs or the memories. We looked, we recalled, and we drove away. Even though we only parked out front and did not venture to the door or even peek into the backyard, I felt a deflated sense of that part of my childhood escaping. There was something about the mismatch between the mental pictures and the existing place that I could not pin down, an affective response that I was having trouble expressing.

More recently, my husband and I moved into a new apartment, bringing with us loads of mementos (i.e., garbage) that we will never use again. On a mission, we cleaned out our storage unit in one cathartic (i.e., exhausting) weekend. Many of the tokens had lost their symbolic value—why had I kept that flair from my waitressing days at Red Lobster? What use would our old business cards serve? And that fourth-grade leaf collection—why? These small pieces of our past represented fleeting time, but the affectivity connected to it was missing. These were no longer valuable mementos; instead, they became trash I was gleefully tossing in the bin.

These two examples led me to wonder about the shaping of memory through things, time, places, and affective response. Because they were tucked away in boxes, the smaller, more personal mementos garnered a somewhat limited response. There is action required to surface that memory—it is not every day that I think about those Red Lobster pins. Conversely, memories of a childhood home are not limited to that East Detroit bungalow. I do not need to drive down there just to think about my family's first home. "Home," in this situation, becomes more abstract but at the same time more universal—it is a place that has changed, shifted meaning, expanded. Home is a concept to which most anyone can relate, but the strong affective ties we attach to certain concepts like "home" are curious. Can the meaning of "place" be conveyed through different media?

In this chapter, I explore the ways *Dear Photograph* allows us to question how we manage the "things" of our past and the ways we attempt to resurrect their importance for our personal memories of a place. As described in one of the blurbs on the book's cover: "*Dear Photograph* is a nostalgia-bomb-bursting, brain-cell-twisting, heartstring-pulling roller coaster ride into the emotional unknown" (Pasricha qtd. in Jones). The photographs in this collection are not just a single image. Instead, they are what I am calling a "temporal pastiche," an intertextual combination of time, place, and affect. Each Dear Photograph is a layering of two individual images, one older photographic print aligned with the current condition of the same place. As a result of this layering, we see the past and present simultaneously. More importantly, the *Dear Photograph* project shifts the ways we interact with material memory.

Ontologically, *Dear Photograph* performs within the space of "what was" and "what is"—or, as I will refer to it here, "the meanwhile." The space of the meanwhile in *Dear Photograph* acknowledges that a place, person, or object has undergone obvious change. As I will explain shortly, a Dear Photograph is merely concerned about the present, the past, and what happened in between. In both *Alien Phenomenology* and in his "Seeing Things" talk—discussing *Dear Photograph*, no less—Ian Bogost refers to the in-between as the "meanwhile," a way to understand the concept of ontography. Yes, this collection of essays is focused on rhetorical *ontologies*, but Bogost's extension of Graham Harman's term *ontography* is beneficial for understanding the complex relations of time and place in *Dear Photograph*. Bogost suggests we see "ontography" as something that reveals "object relationships without necessarily offering clarification or description of any kind . . . a record of things juxtaposed to demonstrate their overlap and imply interaction through collocation" (Loc 845). *Dear Photograph* can be seen as a form of place-based, as opposed to verbal, collocation—these are places that hold particular memorial value to particular people. Bradford Vivian, for one, has suggested the importance of community meaning-making throughout the process of understanding memory (13). For *Dear Photograph*, such meaning-making occurs within a smaller community (perhaps as small as two people), sharing a reference to a particular place with an attached memory. These communities cannot, however, see these places without attaching the memory. What is important to recognize about *Dear Photograph* is its reliance on the recognition of passing time, or the meanwhile. This representational meanwhile relies exclusively on the juxtaposition of the two objects—it could not exist without either.

It is this connectedness to time *and* place that interests me in this chapter. Leaning on Kevin Lynch's coupling of architecture and memory, Gilles Deleuze's and Henri Bergson's theories of time, and Svetlana Boym's concept of nostalgia, I will question the implications of these layered photographs that are connected temporally *and* topographically. How does the temporal and topographic gap between the layered photographs explore the connection between the material "thing" (the photograph itself) and a site-specific memory? As others have clearly articulated (e.g., Blair; Haskins; Landsberg), places and objects have special, reflective value in the creation of personal and rhetorical memory. The Dear Photograph images specifically perform this reflective value through the combination of the old and the new. The individual images, while still meaningful, would not capture the passage of time or the emotion that they do when they are combined and layered on top of one another. Together, the layered photographs persuade viewers that something has happened in the meanwhile—something between the past photo and the present place.

Finally, each Dear Photograph also offers another dimension—affect. In addition to the photographs, submitters are asked to include a short note addressing the past. These notes-to-past-selves help viewers begin to understand how the photograph functions as material memory within the meanwhile and through suggestion of collocation. While these small quips do not let the viewer in on all the secrets, we begin to understand the rhetorical importance of the space between "what was" and "what is". In what follows, I will continue to examine the "meanwhile" and will argue that the "things" that comprise *Dear Photograph* can be understood as rhetorically charged examples of time, place, and affect.

The Place Is the Thing wherein I'll Catch the Location of Me

The symbolic nature of standing in the same place as someone else runs deep. Across the street from Ford's Theater, where President Lincoln was shot, is displayed the bed in which he died. Rookie athletes revel in the fact that they get the opportunity to run plays in the same spots as their heroes. When recalling momentous occasions, the phrase "in this exact spot" represents the combination of place and memory. Family stories are prefaced with it ("I met your grandmother right here") and it is used to identify precious personal experiences ("it is in this exact spot I was standing when we said goodbye"). Returning to these places of import allows us to feel a connection to a past, to hold onto some physical representation of something as immaterial as memory.

As important as the physical places can be, however, *Dear Photograph* illustrates how a representation of a place can create a similar response. Documenting places in photographs has become an increasingly important priority for the general public. Visually based social networks like Snapchat, Tumblr, and Instagram encourage users to capture and share even the most mundane aspects of their lives through photographs. Digital photographs are automatically embedded with geolocation information, permanently tying a photo to a specific place. Although the process of geolocation happens at the code level, and not on the surface of the photo itself, the application FourSquare more explicitly ties place and photograph by asking users to "check in" to places and to share photos of their experience at the establishment. A FourSquare user, for example, might check in at a local restaurant and then share images of her meal or the dining area. Once a very deliberate way of capturing momentous events, the snapshot is now a way of documenting the very things of our everyday lives. Rather than being limited to a specific number of exposures on a roll of film, digital snapshots have few storage limitations. Even though photography is not disappearing, the medium of the printed photograph is becoming rarer.

As a result of the dwindling availability of film, there is now something precious in holding an actual print, an experience on which *Dear Photograph*[1] draws (fig. 12.1). In 2011, twenty-one year old Taylor Jones started *Dear Photograph* through a happy accident (Jones 1). After dinner one night, his family decided to flip through some old photo albums. While perusing the photos, one of them caught his eye—Jones realized his brother was sitting in the same chair and in the same spot as he was in that photograph. He held up the photograph, aligning the chairs and countertops as they were in the photo, snapped the "before and after" shot, and added a small caption: "Dear Photograph, I wish I had as much swag now as I did then" (Jones 3). He posted the image on his Tumblr blog only intending to share it with his friends; instead, it went viral and a phenomenon was started.

Taking a Dear Photograph is easy . . . well, sort of. Jones provides the rookie with a set of nine steps, including such directives as: "Make sure to get your hand in the picture. It shows that you stood at the original spot where the old photo was taken," and "Check carefully to make sure the real-life background matches the edges of the photo from the past" (Jones 5). In these instructions, the emphasis on place is critical, but equally important is the implication of

Figure 12.1. The image that launched *Dear Photograph*. Photo courtesy of *dearphotograph.com*.

the medium of photography. To more completely understand *Dear Photograph*, I want to focus first on the different objects and media involved in capturing a successful shot: a physical place, a photographic print, a digital snapshot capturing both which is then posted on a blog or, as with the examples used in this chapter, printed in a hardbound book. In the McLuhunian sense, the medium is critical to understanding this project's relation to time, place, and affect; fortunately, we do not have to look far for a clarifying example.

Dear McLuhan: The Photo Really Is the Message

To commemorate the twelfth anniversary of the 9/11 attacks, AT&T released an advertisement in the likeness of a *Dear Photograph* (fig. 12.2). The New York City skyline forms the background of this photograph. In the foreground, there is a hand holding a phone (likely supported on the AT&T network) that has been aligned with the space left by the absence of the Twin Towers. Whereas a true Dear Photograph would have pictured the standing towers, the Twin Towers, represented by two large beams of light, can be seen on the screen of the phone. The words "Never Forget" were included with the image that was distributed via AT&T's Twitter account. This image caused a great deal of backlash, primarily for trivializing a tragedy with an advertisement (Stern). Nonetheless, this image captures the importance of the medium for a successful Dear Photograph.

AT&T ✓
@ATT

Never Forget pic.twitter.com/74Br2rBL3A

Figure 12.2. AT&T Twitter advertisement. Photo courtesy of *twitter.com/att*.

At the risk of sounding too cutesy, part of the charm of a Dear Photograph is the condition of the photograph itself. Whether it is vintage black and white, or a 1970s print tinged with too much red, the photograph itself, regardless of its content, kick-starts nostalgia. Presumably, we can and will continue to be able to look at our digital photos from any device. However, using a digital device to display an old photo derails the context of the *Dear Photograph* project itself; rather than noticing the quality of the photograph, we are instead focused on the device. And even though Instagram might be capitalizing on old-timey filters in an attempt to reclaim the look of a photographic print, it still operates within digital spaces.

Each Dear Photograph relies almost exclusively on the medium of photography, stopping short of the means through which they are shared. Both the *Dear Photograph* blog and book are used as interfaces for the photos themselves; and although McLuhan might argue that these interfaces change the way we view or understand each Dear Photograph, I suggest that it is more important to focus specifically on the medium of the photograph against and within a place of topographical import. Furthermore, this juxtaposition of photo and place deepens the significance of each Dear Photograph's temporality.

The Temporal Pastiche

The success of *Dear Photograph*, at least from a framing standpoint, relies on two physical objects: the old photographic print and the current condition of the locale in which that print was taken. It is this reliance on "things" that creates the rhetorical appeal of each Dear Photograph. What we see in the Dear Photograph is the past (the photo) and the present (current condition), both contributing to the implication of a meanwhile, an idea I will explain shortly. It is this immaterial third object—the meanwhile—that is critical to understanding the effect of the Dear Photograph. Indeed, one could create a Dear Photograph with Photoshop or with historically iconic images, as is the case with Sergey Larenkov's *Link to the Past*. What lies between the photograph and the current time of the Dear Photograph reifies a sense of passing time of something personally relevant. I am not discounting the importance of iconographic images on national memory, but for the purposes of this chapter, I will remain primarily focused on the personal memory.

To help understand how *Dear Photograph* captures personal memories through time and place, I turn to Pierre Huyghe, an artist whose work often relies on reenactment. *Third Memory* began as the title of one of Huyghe's performance pieces, recreating scenes from well-known films; but eventually Huyghe began to refer to this liminal space of recreation as "third memory." Third memory is "the displacement of an event onto its representation so as to create a new object of translation. . . . It is through the montage, the way we combine and relate images, that we can create representation of an event that is perhaps more precise than the event itself" (qtd. in Barikin 5). A Dear Photograph is not a reenactment; such an event would ask for things to be as close to the original as possible. On the contrary, a Dear Photograph succeeds because it illustrates change through material representations of passing time—it is a temporal pastiche. To suggest that *Dear Photograph* is a temporal pastiche emphasizes the strong interaction between past and present through which memory, experience, place, and affect all collide. For *Dear Photograph*, third memory (not to be confused with Barthes's "third meaning") is a way of understanding the implications of such a pastiche. Thus, the third memory becomes a way of translating the past of the older photo into the vernacular of the present established via the Dear Photograph. In this case, the temporal pastiche is not defined through a typical three-way division of past, present, and future; instead, *Dear Photograph* uses the concept of the "third memory" as a way to interrogate the time between the past and the present.

Another way of considering the interconnectedness of time and place is by looking at Frederic Jameson's idea of "cognitive mapping," a concept inspired by his reading of Kevin Lynch's text *What Time Is This Place?* At the start of

Lynch's text, he examines the inability of individuals to draw, from memory, accurate maps of places with which they have been intimately familiar (Lynch 21–23). For Jameson, the inability to recreate the place from memory signals one's disassociation and alienation from that space (51). To quote Jameson at length: "Disalienation in this traditional city, then, involves the practical reconquest of a sense of place and the construction or reconstruction of an articulated ensemble which can be retained in memory and which the individual subject can map and remap along the moments of mobile, alternative trajectories" (51). *Dear Photograph*, then, is an attempt at the reconquest. Each "Dear Photograph" image yearns for a place that is at the same time both familiar and alien. By layering the two, the temporal pastiche reconquers a past through the present all while creating a space of great importance in between.

At this juncture, the *Dear Photograph* project warrants a critical look at certain theories of time and how they inform the temporal pastiche and the meanwhile. One of the complications of this task is that *Dear Photograph* plays within the past and the present, leaving the future unknown or even unimagined. The three waves of time—past, present, and future—must all be rethought for this project. Not only do these three waves need rethinking, the reliance on only the past and the present necessitates a critique of the "meanwhile" and a questioning of the importance of the future.

Over and Over Again: Recapturing Time

In *Cinema 2*, Deleuze states that "time simultaneously makes the present past and preserves the past in itself" (98). Certainly this statement is applicable to linear time, but *Dear Photograph* does not operate solely in the present. Instead, the temporal pastiche relies on the consistency of the present *with* the past—they are relying on a dual preservation within each other. We can think of Deleuze's time as a series of marked limits. Deleuze invites us, his readers, to think of three specific aspects of our own lives, say, childhood, adolescence, and adulthood. These three periods probably blend into each other, likely because they each have bolstered the subsequent phase in our life. The mistakes we make in adolescence shape the decisions we make and the maturity we reach in adulthood. Even though these three phases build on each other in chronological time, when we think back on them, we can only see them simultaneously. To clarify, as we experienced these phases, we likely imagined them occurring horizontally, like a timeline. Our childhood occurred over a number of years and was marked by a certain point on the x-axis of passing time. Following that conception, our adolescence and adulthood subsequently lie further to the right of our youth. We "look-back" across that axis to see what has passed, quite like looking in the rearview mirror as we drive a long distance down a freeway.

But this looking back is not as simple as looking through that mirror. What we see when we try to recapture time is an equal representation of these moments; rather than lying horizontally as when they first occurred, the remembered events are mentally stacked vertically. *Dear Photograph* interprets this vertical time almost literally—the past and the present are purposely stacked to illustrate change. *Dear Photograph* allows us to view several points in time simultaneously—we can recognize a familiar past through the lens of a familiar present. For Deleuze, this is a critical discourse of time—we only view the past as one of several simultaneous presents. What *Dear Photograph* does with these simultaneous presents is allow us to dive into the meanwhile, connecting the current-present to past-present in the photograph. Deleuze argues that when we look into the past, we must choose between regions (or accents) via points of view (or peaks). These peaks allow us to see all the events related to a specific occasion from one vantage point—our current present. As our gaze falls on the Dear Photograph, we are able to visualize, quite literally, the formation of the past through this current-present.

Unlike Deleuze, Bergson suggests that time is not made of distinguishable past, present, and future moments, but that the three are always part of each other—the present is becoming past as it simultaneously becomes the future. Whereas Deleuze notes that we can only look at the past from a privileged standpoint, Bergson takes the stance that time is formed by process of unzipping. According to Bergson, time is a constantly formed and reformed trinity: past, present, and future. Essentially, these are not individual entities, as they are simultaneously becoming one another via one another. Because of this interdependence, one might recognize time as a linear entity, a repeating formation of future becoming present, present becoming past. However, distinguishing between these becomes nearly impossible, as these three are all represented within each passing moment. In attempting to define the notion of past by stating "whether the past has ceased to exist or whether it has simply ceased to be useful," Bergson is ultimately questioning the present: if it is immediately becoming past as it is formed, wherein does the present lie (149). Bergson's statement is not a question of the value of the past, but rather insists on the value, or, essentially, the probability, of a present. We simply "define the present in an arbitrary manner as *that which is*, whereas the present is simply *what is being made*" (Bergson 149–50, emphasis in original). This is the critical illusion of time according to Bergson—the present is "being made" as it is at the same time disappearing. Therefore, for Bergson, the disappearing present seemingly never exists—it is only "being made" into the past. Time, then, never actually has a present; and, if the past has also "ceased to exist," how do we access *any* time? If a present is never available, to label linear time becomes nearly impossible, for if there is no present "being made" into a past, there cannot be progression.

Returning to Bergson's question of the importance of the past: what complicates the idea of a past ultimately is not the formation of the present, but rather the way one accesses a personal history, or memory. To examine this idea, Bergson designates three important processes through which one can examine time and, ultimately, one's personal history: pure memory, memory-image, and perception. Just as the past-present-future trio functions only as a result of its component parts, "perception is bound to expel the memory-image, and the memory-image to expel pure memory" (134). When one attempts to recall an event in one's past, one must "detach [oneself] from the present in order to replace [oneself] first, in the past in general, then, in a certain region of the past" (134). Bergson continues by noting that just as the present is illusory, this return to certain regions of the past "still remains virtual; [one] simply prepares [oneself] to receive it by adopting the appropriate attitude" (134). Time, then, is a personalized history. One has the ability to maneuver between actual time—which is occurring immediately and accessing a past to which the individual only has access—or virtual time. This notion of maneuvering through time becomes increasingly apparent when looking at a Dear Photograph—virtual time is always available *within* actual time. *Dear Photograph* demonstrates that we can choose whether, when, and how we want to utilize the present, and in the case of *Dear Photograph*, how to connect with the past.

That the individual has the ability to connect a present moment to an event in one's past suggests that time and progression are specifically initiated by the individual. One does not lose the present to the past, but instead only recognizes the present *through* the past. The move to connect memory to the past indicates that there is a desire to link it to *something*, to materialize its importance. Jacques Derrida notes the importance of an event's impact once its presence has passed, calling this recurrence "hauntology," defining it as "repetition *and* first time, but also repetition *and* last time, since the singularity of any *first time*, makes of it also a *last time*. Each time it is the event itself, a first time is a last time" (*Marx* 10). Because *Dear Photograph* relies on both the old photograph and the current condition of a certain place, that layering becomes a physical representation of a haunting, not a mere apparition.

New Owners, New Memories

Selecting just one Dear Photograph to discuss is difficult—in fact, it is difficult looking at many of them in one sitting without tearing up a bit. The example I chose speaks across all the theories discussed above (fig. 12.3). In the overlaid photograph, there are two children, presumably brother and sister; she looks to be about five and he looks a year or two younger. They are sitting on the steps of a deck or maybe a front porch—it is difficult to tell from the picture—holding

Figure 12.3. Siblings on steps. Photo courtesy of *Dear Photograph*, Taylor Jones, 2012.

hands and smiling at the camera. In the background, we can see what those steps look like now. No longer the white and blue of the overlay, the steps have been painted brown. While there is greenery in both images, it is hard to imagine that they are the same plants in both. The note-to-self captures a longing: "Dear Photograph: No new owner will ever truly know the steps of that house: who walked down them, fell up them, and was loved while sitting on them" (Jones 103). What I like so much about this example is the importance of that meaning to the photographer and the new homeowner's ignorance of it. Yes, the new homeowners likely have memories of their own from those steps, but this specific Dear Photograph relies on the combination of space and place so artfully that it is practically a universal example of what it feels like to leave something behind and move on.

This leaving something behind and moving on is not entirely the case—if we truly left it behind, the *Dear Photograph* project would not hold value. Instead, my interest lies in the return, the revisit, or what Svetlana Boym calls nostalgia: "a mourning for the impossibility of the mythical return" (8). In the example, the impossibility of the mythical return rests with the new owners. Having moved out of the house, those stairs will never hold the same ontological value as they did for the woman who created the Dear Photograph. That 'impossibility' is one of the mysteries of re-creating a scene for a Dear Photograph. It is a physical manifestation of what was, what is, and what happened in between. It is, as Boym also infers, "Janus-faced, like a double-edged sword. To unearth the fragments of nostalgia one needs a dual archeology of memory and of place, and a dual history of illusions and of actual practices" (xviii). Each layer of the Dear Photograph can function as a stand-alone token of memory; it is not until they are combined that the rhetorical impact of these elements expands across time and place.

Conclusion

All things considered, *Dear Photograph* is not a project that can sustain itself. As we accumulate more and more digital items, the physical printed photograph is falling by the wayside. The materiality of the photograph adds a layer of affective response perhaps unlike those of digital prints and reproductions. I do not intend to end this chapter by suggesting digital prints are not proper objects of memory—hardly so. I am, however, focused purely on the idea of a photographic print as something we can hold while saying "in this very spot." The past has fleeted, but holding the physical representation of what once was there bridges the nostalgic gap, if only to be captured in another photograph. There are, however, several layers of irony to this story. First of all, the *Dear Photograph* project was born digital—the layered photographs are submitted electronically and originally posted on the blog of the same name. People who submit Dear Photographs are contributing to the demise of such a project. Digital photographs, while prevalent and personal, might not be able to set the stage for the nostalgic milieu. The printed photograph reminds us of a time long gone. With film companies like Kodak and Polaroid shuttering some of their operations, the print itself (not withstanding what is captured in it) suggests dead media and old memories. And while it is true that one could achieve a similar layered photograph using digital images, here is yet another example of the medium delivering the death notice to itself.

Note

1. I use the term "Dear Photograph" to represent both the project as a whole as well as the individual photos within the larger project. To differentiate, I use italics (*Dear Photograph*) when referring to the whole, but not when referring to individual examples (Dear Photograph).

IV

Assembling Things

13
Assemblage Rhetorics
Creating New Frameworks for Rhetorical Action
Jodie Nicotra

> Any actant has a chance to win or lose, though some have more weaponry at their disposal. Winners and losers are inherently equal and must be treated symmetrically. The loser is the one who failed to assemble enough human, natural, artificial, logical, and inanimate allies to stake a claim to victory. The more connected an actant is, the more real; the less connected, the less real.
>
> Graham Harman, *Prince of Networks*

As anyone who has stubbed a toe on a piece of furniture can attest, it doesn't take an academic to point out that things have their own suasive force. A table might not literally say, "Hey, watch where you're walking, pal," but its material properties of solidity and resistance to movement interact with the momentum of fleshy, bony human limbs in ways that persuade the owners of those limbs to step more carefully next time.

A strain in rhetorical studies has been theorizing the rhetoricality of the material world for some time now. In her body of work on public memorials, for instance, Carole Blair has analyzed how the designed, material properties of various memorials work rhetorically on viewers. From the concrete curves of Maya Lin's Civil Rights Memorial, which jut out into the pedestrian walkway just far enough to disturb pedestrian rhythms, to the Salem Witch Trials Memorial that forces viewers to walk on the engraved defenses of the women condemned as witches, Blair extends the familiar methodology of rhetorical close reading to the material world.[1]

Blair's work—along with that of rhetorical scholars like J. Blake Scott, Jenny Edbauer Rice, Debra Hawhee, Michael Bernard-Donals, Clay Spinuzzi, and a number of others—is part of a growing attention to the material that has been gathering momentum for decades, but has suddenly seemed to snap into place in a variety of distinct but connected disciplines: philosophy, rhetoric, political theory, sociology. Cynics might grumble about what is already being called "the material turn" as just a product of capitalist logics operating within scholarship, the academic equivalent to the latest killer app or New York Fashion Week. But the "turn" to the material (or more accurately, the *return* to the material, with a less positivist difference) is more than the Next Big Sexy Thing—rather, the material changes in our communication technologies have altered our habits of perception such that the suasive force of the material has simply become more obvious. As Anne Wysocki writes of the sudden visibility of writing technologies, "part of what has changed the warp and woof that used to seem so steady underneath us is precisely that we are now aware of the warp and woof . . . of the complex weaves of writing [and other modes of communication] as a material practice" (2). From mobile computing to social media, it is clear to even the casual observer that these technologies have had profound, material effects on the way we think, communicate, and organize our lives.

The work of Bruno Latour, Graham Harman, Jane Bennett, and other "new materialists" has pushed the thinking on materiality in ways that offer intriguing possibilities for rhetorical studies. If in Blair's work the material properties of various nonhuman substances and objects remain rather comfortably under the control of the designer, materiality for the new materialists is considerably wilder. Their work suggests that things are never just things, present in themselves, but are instead bound up in countless discursive and material networks, the complexity of which can be concealed and explained away thanks to our current "partition of the sensible" that posits humans as active agents against a background of nonhumans and things. Whether referred to as "networks," "web," "mesh," or "assemblages," the point is that they can never be fully understood or grasped in their entirety at any given moment: as Harman argues, pushing on Heidegger's concept of *Zuhandenheit* ("readiness-to-hand"), things are caught up in countless relations of use, not all of which (or even most of which) have to do with human purposes. Similarly, Bennett, drawing heavily on Latour, Spinoza, and Deleuze and Guattari, argues for and performatively demonstrates "assemblage thinking," a mode that aims to disrupt the persistent binary of human agents operating on and against a passive world of nonhuman animals, plants, bacteria, and inorganic substances.

In assemblage thinking, nonhumans and material objects are equally bound up with human actions in events. All actions come about not as products of deliberate human decisions, but from a heterogeneous, distributed agency of many actants, both human and nonhuman. As an example, Bennett presents the 2003 North American blackout, an event that emerged from the assemblage known as the electric grid: "a volatile mix of coal, sweat, electromagnetic fields, computer programs, electron streams, profit motives, heat, lifestyles, nuclear fuel, plastic, fantasies of mastery, static legislation, water, economic theory, wire, and wood" (25). Despite the customary after-the-fact attempts to assign agency in the form of blame for the blackout, Bennett argues that it would be impossible to separate out one or a few elements of this assemblage, as it was the interaction of all these components and the "slight surprise of action" from which the event emerged. Assemblages like that involved in the blackout, Bennett argues, have their own dynamic force and directionality apart from the will of the individual (human) components that might be involved.

Given what Bennett and other new materialists argue—that it is impossible to know or grasp all the forces at work in a given event—what good might assemblage thinking be for rhetoric, a field distinguished by its pragmatic orientation, and invested in both the analysis and conduct of strategic action? Could it have the potential to help us answer the most basic but biggest and difficult of rhetorical questions: what causes large-scale attitudinal and relational adjustments? For instance, why do most Europeans believe in anthropogenic climate change, but most Americans do not? Given the growing attention to the clamor of things, a continued faith in the power of discursive persuasion and straightforward rhetorical agency (a notion attacked for years from all sides) no longer seems possible, as assemblage thinking presents further challenges to the presumption that humans are more or less in control of their messages. But it also seems unproductive to simply blackbox the complex workings of events and obviate the possibility for deliberate rhetorical action. Attending more rigorously to the role of the nonhuman, nonorganic world in matters of persuasion necessitates a series of reattunements; these in turn require the interruption of customary modes of perception, followed by the development of new habits of attention. Rhetorical studies needs to develop methods and strategies for understanding, as the epigraph by Harman suggests, how what we deem as rhetorical "winners" have managed to assemble human and nonhuman allies so as to achieve "victory." Understanding a thing that takes place as a being caught up in assemblages—rather than as a product of linear cause and effect—points the way toward providing a richer framework for rhetorical action. So too does broadening the scope of analysis to include nonhuman actants.

In this essay, I use two different examples to think about the potential use and value of "assemblage rhetorics." The first is personal, a phenomenological account of uncovering (by accident) the complex entanglement of habits in material and discursive networks, through the humble force of trash. Through this example, I aim to show how assemblage rhetorics practically reveal themselves. But since this accidental revelation of assemblages does not provide a sense for how assemblages might affect more deliberate rhetorical action, I discuss a second compound example: a set of concepts and principles (permaculture) that deliberately employs and negotiates assemblages to design systems, and one formal organization (the Transition Network) that productively uses permaculture principles to further its rhetorical goals. Using these examples, I demonstrate that attuning to assemblages helps us reconceive rhetorical action as something that requires a deliberate and intentional attention to all of the elements of the system (both human and nonhuman, organic and inorganic) in which one hopes to intervene, an attention gained through repeated interaction and empirical observation and experimentation.

The Force of Trash

Few things illustrate the complex rhetorical pressures of the material world better than trash. Perhaps this is because, as Gay Hawkins argues in *The Ethics of Waste*, the multitude of practices involved with deciding what waste is and finding ways to manage it are deeply connected to what constitutes us as selves (4). Hawkins claims, "It is impossible to change waste practices without implicating the self in a process of reflexivity, without asking people to implicitly or explicitly think about the way they live" (5). One's waste practices can thus serve as a site for personal reflection on ethics, as the title of her book implies. However, waste straddles an interesting line between the intimate and the cultural: while the production and management of waste clearly involve some of the most fundamental personal habits, they are also culturally specific practices, yoking together (through deeply rooted habits) laws, cultural and personal norms, and a multitude of small decisions and practices involved in deciding what is useful and what is not, sorting what is part of us from what is not. Trash, in other words, is a particularly lively assemblage, and as such provides a rich site for examining assemblage rhetorics.

The assemblage that we call trash, which typically remains outside ordinary consciousness, most vividly reveals itself when something changes—for instance, when one is suddenly thrust up against a foreign system, as I found out when I moved to Finland for a sabbatical year. The material pressures of waste revealed themselves in fairly short order upon my arrival: before I'd furnished the apartment, found bus schedules, even located a place to buy food, the trash exerted a primal anxiety, a low-lying but insistent pressure. Random bits of detritus began piling up on the kitchen counter: a used Kleenex, the foil lid from my yogurt container, the plastic container itself. Containing organic waste like banana peels to avoid a population explosion of the fruit flies that came with the apartment presented a constant problem.

The stress of uncertainty about how to manage waste in an unfamiliar culture immediately summoned to attention a multitude of ingrained habits, actions that had become so embedded in the sense of my world's order that they had fallen from conscious view (confirming Hawkins's aphorism that habits "bind us to the world at the same time as they blind us to it" [14]). At home, I had over time developed a series of habits around managing waste. These habits were the product of scores of various material and discursive factors specific to my particular circumstance, including the architecture of my house and yard (spacious enough to accommodate multiple bins for sorting and storing different categories of waste); the kinds of products available for purchase in local stores (whether they came in packages that had to be trashed, recycled, or possibly stored, for instance if they were glass jars with good screw-top lids); my exposure over the years as a middle class consumer to many rhetorical acts persuading me of the virtue of recycling; the dozens of arguments and small negotiations with family members about who dealt with what kinds of trash and how it was dealt with; my municipality's rules and schedules for trash pickup and recycling, themselves products of hundreds of negotiations and discursive acts involving a wider public; etc. In turn, each of these factors include their own subsets of specificities: for instance, our categorization of what counts as trash is bound up with the organization of technological and economic structures that render some things valuable, others not; the space in my house and yard is afforded to me thanks to my job as a tenured university professor; and so on *ad infinitum*. The system as a whole had a sensuous presence, a literal material heft: the weight of the bag from the diaper pail, the compost container's stink of coffee grounds mixed with onion peels, my perpetual newspaper-and-Windex campaign to keep the outside of the trash can free of streaks, the space that the four metal bins for plastic took up on the porch, the distant rumbles and clanks of the recycling truck on Tuesday mornings prompting a stressed-out scramble to get the bottles and paper out to the curb.

In the context of habituated use, such assemblages necessarily withdraw, and so the weight of the trash assemblage did not become apparent until I was no longer embedded within its various material and immaterial components. Its sudden absence brought with it anxiety, a disorienting lightness magnified by the material evidence of a new series of systems in the Finnish apartment: three diminutive plastic bins tucked away on a rollaway cart under the sink. Innocuous as they were, these three bins served simultaneously as a material point of contact with a new trash assemblage, a cathection for all my trash-related anxieties (why were they so *small* and what were they supposed to hold?), and as a seed catalyst for a whole new set of attitudes, habits, and practices related to trash. The dinkiness of the trash bins and the ever-hovering fruit flies exerted the need to take the trash out more frequently than I was accustomed to, which in turn bumped me up more often against the trash removal system installed by the apartment building and municipality, fostering my awareness of these systems through repetition. I developed new relationships to biodegradable trash bags, coffee grounds, and vinegar-and-soap fruit fly traps. The trash bins affected not just my practices of disposal, but also of consumption: I began buying smaller amounts of food more frequently, mindful of the practical need to avoid storing or throwing away large quantities of leftovers and packaging, which in turn meant that I was forced into more frequent personal and public transactions. Hence a proliferating series of individual practices, habits, and ways of organizing time arises from the most mundane of objects.

Through the repetition of waste-related actions, the Finnish trash assemblage gradually revealed itself in more detail, beyond the trash bins that had been my initial point of contact. Initial befuddlement at the absence of an obvious place to recycle aluminum cans and glass bottles led to a discovery of Finland's container deposit legislation, which provides cash incentives to return plastic and glass bottles for refilling and aluminum cans for melting down and reusing. The metaphoric collapse of containers and cash in turn revealed and fostered a host of symbiotic relationships: the people who comb through city trash cans for cans and bottles, the picnickers in the city park who nonchalantly chuck their beer cans on the sidewalks for the men who cruise around collecting cans in their bicycle baskets.

As it happens, the Finnish trash assemblage also has tentacles in law: namely, the Waste Act of 1993, revised in 2011 to reflect the Ministry of the Environment's National Waste Plan for 2016. The Waste Act among other things mandated a 50 percent reduction of all municipal trash, with the onus on the municipalities to figure out ways to do this (hence the inclusion of separate containers in each apartment for recycling, and prominently placed biowaste, cardboard, and paper bins in common areas). But while clearly the law adds an imperative element, the assemblage that we might name "trash in Finland" is not a one-way causal arrow. Rather, it has a momentum and force of its own that galvanizes different material interactions and ultimately encourages different habits.

Thus, the enactment of a new relationship to trash was more than a rational decision resulting from my attention to and abstract belief in some discursive influence like "it's good to recycle." I did not consciously decide that I should rethink how I "do" trash. I could not have held onto my old systems for dealing with the trash even if I had wanted to, since the material affordances of the new trash assemblage simply did not allow for it.

A conclusion by *reductio ad absurdum* might posit that since the Finnish trash bins served as the locus and catalyst for my initial persuasion, *they* were the rhetorical agents. But while this gives more shrift to the force of the material, arguing this would simply displace one mistaken single locus of agency (a human agent) with another (the plastic bins). In both cases, agency is seen as both unidirectional and single-pointed. Rather, thinking through this example shows that while what we might call persuasion is practically enacted as a change in personal habits, this change emerges as one result of an interaction of a multitude of material and discursive things. Finnish waste, metonymized by the three kitchen trash cans, articulated me as a subject by reshaping my relations not only to trash, but to a whole other host of practices: a kairos of the assemblage.

Trusting the Chicken: Permaculture's Attunement as Design

As I hope my description of negotiating new trash assemblages reveals, the formation of ethical sensibilities and political changes relies partly on micropolitical changes to human relational capacities: the blocking of habituated forms of interaction, and what Bennett, in *Vibrant Matter*, describes as "a cultivated, patient, sensory attentiveness to nonhuman forces operating outside and inside the human body" (xiv). Seeing assemblages, and thereby developing possibilities for intervention, requires a process of attunement, both to habits and to the material and immaterial forces at work in an assemblage. While, as the Finnish trash assemblage example demonstrates, this is perhaps easiest to do when something interrupts or rubs up against one's habits in a way that reveals them as habits, too often (as with my own experience) such interruptions are a happy accident—had I not moved to Finland, I may never have attuned to trash in the way I did. More useful for those thinking about rhetorical agency and more deliberate rhetorical action would be the cultivation of practices that would help us attune to assemblages.

Bennett suggests in another essay that to understand and perhaps devise a way to counter the naturally subtractive nature of habituated perception (which conceals the workings of assemblages and the call of the nonhuman) we might do well to study hoarders: people who obsessively collect and accumulate things. Bennett invites us to see hoarders less as victims of psychopathology than as people who are preternaturally sensitive to the material agency of things. In the balance of subject-object relations (in which the subject is typically considered the more active party), Bennett argues, the psychic balance of hoarders has tipped to the side of the object, the "call" of which they find irresistible. Hoarders, argues Bennett, are predisposed to "an exceptional awareness of the extent to which *all* bodies can intertwine, infuse, ally, undermine, and compete with those in its vicinity" ("Hoard" 256). While she is not recommending hoarding as the answer to our insensitivity to material agency, Bennett suggests that studying hoarders and others who are uncannily sensitive to the call of things "might shed light on the role that a not-quite-human form of effectivity might be playing in maintaining the over-consumptive, ecologically disastrous society that I inhabit" ("Hoard" 268–69).

Like Bennett, I am invested in developing practices to cultivate an attunement to assemblages, though I am interested in practices that aren't a) accidental (as in the attunement to the trash assemblage described above), or b) typically considered as pathological. How might we become more attuned to assemblages in a way that is useful for rhetorical production? One example of deliberate practices meant to cultivate an attunement to assemblages comes in the form of the design practices of the concept known as "permaculture."

Permaculture is based on the idea of systems design through a process of attunement. It is especially oriented toward systems that involve the production of food, though any intentional space can be designed using permaculture principles. A portmanteau of "permanent agriculture" (or simply "permanent culture"), permaculture was articulated in the late 1970s by Bill Mollison and David Holmgren, who saw a need to move away from the instrumentalist approaches typical of industrial agriculture: as Mollison writes in *Permaculture: A Designer's Manual*, "Permaculture design is a system of assembling conceptual, material, and strategic components in a pattern which functions to benefit life in all its forms" (ix).

As this definition suggests, permaculture is invested in intentional design. But the agency of permaculture designers does not arise like that of *The Fountainhead's* Howard Roark, from individual genius and will-to-execute—or like traditional conceptions of rhetorical agency, which posit an active subject acting on and through a passive world of things and other humans. Rather, permaculture design requires the designer to be keenly attentive to all of the systems operating in a given place: natural systems like climate, soil, geology, waterways, and sun position; the presence and activities of local animals and plants; the attributes, knowledge, and interactions of its various human inhabitants; and the nuances of the already-existent forms of infrastructure—economic, agricultural, industrial, civic, engineered, etc.

Permaculture trains designers to see in terms of assemblages rather than hierarchies. Mollison critiques the visual metaphor of the trophic pyramid, in which plants are at the bottom and keystone predators, including humans, are at the top. The trophic pyramid, he argues, not only presents an impoverished view of life systems, but is also based on bad science; it ignores basic aspects of life systems that can be empirically observed by even a casual observer, like the complex interactions between species, the "recycling" work performed by growing and mature organisms, and the complexity of food chains. Permaculture designers are enjoined to see less in terms of hierarchies than interactive food webs and feedback loops. As an example, Mollison points out that many species not immediately edible by humans can be made edible once they are processed through other species: "Herons, themselves edible, eat poisonous toadfish, and goats will browse thorny and bitter shrubs. Thus we can specify these useful conversions before blindly eliminating a life element *of any type* from our diets" (30). Training oneself to see in terms of assemblages, in other words, reveals sources of value that that would be hidden by a way of thinking informed by hierarchy and unidirectional causality.

Through attunement to the systems of a place arises one of the foundational attitudes of permaculture, cooperation—specifically, that "Cooperation, not competition, is the very basis of existing life systems and of future survival" (2). Practically, this attitude translates into an affirmation of whatever elements happen to be in a given system. If boulders or jagged outcrops exist in a landscape that is being designed, the permaculture designer does not see them as nuisances to be removed or mitigated. Rather, as the *Permaculture* manual decrees, "the problem is the solution": "Features only become 'problems' when we have already decided on imposing a specific site pattern that [a given feature] interferes with" (15). Instead of seeing such features as problems to be overcome, the designer attunes to the potential affordances provided by these features (shelter from wind, shade, niches for particular helpful organisms, etc.). The same goes for what typically is known as "waste"—in permaculture, there is no such thing as waste, only outputs that can feed some other part of the system.

As the heron and goat example above suggests, permaculture designers are encouraged to attend more closely to the nonhuman elements of the system apart from their direct use value to humans. The more complex an organism, the more possible connections and interactions it can make that we cannot ever possibly know. Mollison uses the example of chickens (a staple of permaculture design for their many behaviors—like scratching and foraging for bugs—that are incidentally helpful to farmers):

> If we consider the number of possible connections to and from an element such as a chicken, we can see that these potential connections depend on the information we have about the chicken, so that the complexity of a system depends on the information we have about its components, always providing that such information is used in design. . . . [T]hus in permaculture we always suppose that the chicken is busy *making connections itself*, about which we could not know and, of course, for which we could not design. We must simply trust the chicken. (31)

To paraphrase Deleuze and Guattari (paraphrasing Spinoza), the gist of this permaculture principle might be restated as "we don't even know what a chicken can do." Trusting the chicken requires letting go of preconceived notions of how chickens might be useful. The effects of *not* trusting chickens are apparent in industrialized farming, which has attuned to only one or two aspects of chickenness, hence reducing the rich complexity of the chicken assemblage to meat and egg-producing machines. The problems with cutting off the rest of the assemblage are apparent in the (bad) design of the industrial system, which among other things produces visibly miserable and diseased animals, huge amounts of pollutants in the form of chicken waste, and palliative measures like beak snipping to discourage typical chicken behaviors. Thus, rather than simply relying on what we think we know, permaculture design requires cultivating attunement to situations through repeated practices of empirical observation and experimentation.

Transition: Attunement to Assemblages as Rhetorical Action

While permaculture as a formalized concept or set of principles has been around since the 1970s, most of its application has been scattered and small scale, far outside of the mainstream. But recently permaculture has gotten more traction through its application in an organization called the Transition Network ("Transition"), which advocates attunement to assemblages and employs assemblage rhetorics to accomplish its goal of preparing communities all over the world to be responsive to potential challenges to embedded habits of daily life. Hence Transition demonstrates what deliberate rhetorical action through attunement to assemblages might look like.

Founded by Rob Hopkins in 2005, the Transition Network aims to support "community-led responses to climate change and shrinking supplies of cheap energy, building resilience and happiness" ("Who We Are"). As the name suggests, Transition is based on the idea that some kind of significant change to everyday life—most likely in the form of prohibitively expensive energy or global warming—is coming, and that it is critical to prepare for it ahead of time. But unlike typical Western responses to potential catastrophic change (which in my current state of Idaho tend to involve bunkering away large quantities of ammunition, weapons, and foods for individual or family-unit survival), Transition's emphasis is on proactive, practical *community* preparation for change.[2] Such preparation comes with a clear rhetorical challenge: how is it possible to persuade communities consisting of people who likely have differing beliefs, values, and goals to become invested in the process of proactively preparing for as-yet abstract change?

The Transition Network is philosophically and practically informed by the principles of permaculture, as the process of designing "initiatives" makes evident. The design of each initiative relies upon an attunement to the human and nonhuman assemblages unique to each potential community. For instance, island initiatives (like the Lopez Island Initiative in Washington's San Juan Islands) must identify and respond to a very different set of systems than do city initiatives like the PDX Initiative in Portland, Oregon. An initiative can only work if the organizers have successfully attuned to the resources available to them in their particular circumstance.

Thus, by necessity, the Transition Network as a parent organization cannot take on a traditional prescriptive or top-down role. Though informed by a clearly stated philosophy and set of goals (i.e., to pave the way for thoughtful and proactive change across a wide range of communities), the Transition Network as an organization functions less as a traditional rhetorical agent with a controlling message delivered on a one-way channel than as a nurturer and facilitator of community-led networks. As Hopkins writes, "We have already been seeing a structure emerging organically over the last two-years and what we propose . . . is based on a deepening and supporting of this emergent model, on the principle that self-organization, innovation and action are to be encouraged and supported where they arise, supported by a distinct set of principles and clear guidelines" ("Who We Are"). Transition likens itself to the process of baking a cake: while every cook's creation "will be unique, reflecting his or her abilities and culture, and the local resources available," there are "certain time-proven stages" to successful baking. In its written materials, Transition lays out these stages and ingredients and lets various "bakers" create as they will.

Unlike many other environmental organizations (Greenpeace, PETA, Earth-First!), which rely on more traditional agonistic rhetorical tactics and are deeply invested in agency (especially as it inhabits the name of the organization), Transition aims to be indiscernible. Hopkins includes as a kind of guiding principle a quotation from the artist Jean Dubuffet: "Art does not lie down on the bed that is made for it; it runs away as soon as one says its name; it loves to be incognito. Its best moments are when it forgets what it is called." Likewise, he suggests, "Perhaps our work preparing communities for transition should similarly be constantly reinventing itself and forgetting what it is called: a creative, engaging, playful process" (50). This emphasis on dissolution is reflected even in the way the Transition Network lays out its stages. The organization recommends that the founding groups for each transition initiative include a plan for their own dissolution, so as to allow the community to eventually take over.

In this sense, Transition is deeply pragmatic—one might say that it is less invested in getting it *right* than getting it *done*. For instance, Transition's initiative in Sandpoint, Idaho, gets its politically divided community (tea party Republican loggers, California liberals who relocated to buy lakeside vacation homes) involved in Transition through projects like the community garden in the center of town, tapping a common interest in growing food (whether that be under the guise of "local is better" or "food security"). The several members of Transition on the Sandpoint City Council were encouraged by the mayor (a Transition sympathizer) to remove references to their Transition membership and local initiative from their applications. Talk related to the initiative in City Council meetings focuses not on the coming catastrophes of peak oil and climate change (which would be called out as liberal buzzwords by more conservative Council members), but on the need for "food security" for Sandpoint and "community self-reliance." While another organization with similar investments might be quickly called out for particular political motivations, the Sandpoint Transition Initiative has managed to achieve a surprising amount: perhaps what Harman, channeling Latour, might name a "winner."

Conclusion

Studying Transition's explicit and implicit rules and guiding principles might suggest a potential framework for reconceptualizing rhetorical action. Such rhetorical action would operate less as a result of traditional rhetorical agency (i.e., an active human subject acting on a passive world of nonhuman objects) than as an attunement to and negotiation of assemblages. Using such a framework, rhetors would plan for attunement as an explicit part of the process by deliberately attending to all of the components in a given situation—human, nonhuman, nonorganic, immaterial, and affective factors alike—in order to "feel out" the possibilities for action. Identifying these components, as well as recognizing established habits and patterns, might suggest natural courses of effective rhetorical action (like the perhaps apocryphal landscape planners who watched how people walked to and from a newly constructed building and used the naturally worn paths as guides for more formal sidewalks). Such attunement requires what might be thought of as "flex-ability," the capacity to act *in medias res* or on the fly, without a completely formed plan. Rather than a specified set of outcomes, rhetors might instead aim for a particular *directionality*, viewing a rhetorical strategy not as a once-and-for-all action, but rather as continual attunement to a process that is beautifully complex, multivariate, and ever evolving.

Notes

1. See Blair and Michel, "Rhetorical Performances;"see also Blair, "Contemporary."
2. Currently there are 1,130 registered Transition Initiatives in various stages of development.

14
Objects, Material Commonplaces, and the Invention of the "New Woman"

Sarah Hallenbeck

In her 1896 bicycling memoir, Women's Christian Temperance Union President Frances Willard describes a conversation she had with a fellow bicyclist in which the two "rejoiced together greatly in perceiving the impetus that this . . . machine would give to that blessed 'woman question' to which [they] were both devoted" (38). Citing the new machine's likely impact on American women's health, physical confidence, and personal relationships, Willard suggests that long sought social changes would come about not because of women's direct advocacy, but because of their performances aboard the bicycle. "A reform often advances most rapidly by indirection," she notes, adding, "an ounce of practice is worth a ton of theory" (39). Though Willard's commentary initially strikes one as a commonsense celebration of a new technology's capacity to change the lives of its users, her insistence on the persuasiveness of "practice" over "theory" suggests a tacit commitment to the power of material rhetorics to change the very terms of the argument surrounding the "blessed woman question" to which she refers.[1] More specifically, Willard gestures toward the object of the bicycle itself as materializing—and enabling embodied performances of—particular arguments that reformers had long struggled to make in response to "the woman question."

In the final years of the nineteenth century, when new objects like the bicycle were emerging with startling regularity within a new consumer economy, it is little wonder that Willard attended so carefully to the social impact of an object like the bicycle. Americans were surrounded by objects—elevators and light bulbs and dishwashers—that their grandparents would scarcely have dreamt of encountering. They were exposed to unprecedented advertising that encouraged them, for the first time, to construct their identities around their possessions rather than around their work ethic, family name, or personal achievements (Schneirov 5). Objects, both as consumer items and as identity markers, occupied a new and growing niche in late nineteenth-century culture, and Willard's observations suggest that she viewed them not merely as *reflections of* social change, but as *active creators and shapers* of the new arguments that would enable social change to occur in the first place. And certainly, social change was afoot, inextricable from the changing material landscape Willard described. It is not surprising that the so-called bicycle craze that hit both North America and Europe in the early 1890s coincided so closely with the coining of the term "New Woman" in 1894 by novelist Sarah Grand. The term, which referred to the increasingly energetic, educated, independent young women of the day, quickly entered circulation on both sides of the Atlantic, signifying a creature distinct in body and mind from her weaker, less assertive nineteenth-century foremothers.

Though Willard was not an avowed "new woman," she rejoiced in the social transformations that American women—including New Women—were enacting in the changed material landscape of the 1890s. For instance, in her memoir she notes the impact of the bicycle on the dress reform movement, which had long floundered due to reformers' primary focus on advocating, but not always donning, reform dress. When bicycling made garments such as the bloomer and the "health" corset a practical near-necessity for three million American women who had taken up the new activity by the mid-1890s (Dodge 42), however, dress reform gained momentum. As Willard puts it: "the graceful and becoming costume of the woman on the bicycle will convince the world that has brushed aside the theories, no matter how well constructed, and the arguments, no matter how logical, of dress-reformers. . . . [E]re long the comfortable, sensible, and artistic wardrobe of the rider will make the conventional style of woman's dress absurd to the eye and unendurable to the understanding" (39). This observation of the power of a highly visible object—in this case, a clothing item—to "convince," to make the conventional "absurd" and even "unendurable," suggests that Willard had harnessed a form of rhetorical agency that, as rhetorician Casey Kelly has noted, consists of "the capacity to recognize moments in which socioeconomic and cultural structures are vulnerable to reinterpretation and so groups of individuals may act to resignify the social order" (205). Indeed, simply in learning to ride the bicycle herself and then describing her experience in a memoir, Willard was demonstrating her awareness of the vulnerability of such structures, publishing her actions so that other women might, collectively, be inspired to enact change with their bodies and "resignify the social order" by riding the bicycle.

In rhetorical terms, Willard and other women bicyclists at the end of the nineteenth century acknowledged, on some level, the discursive power of *order* writ large. Their embodied enactments of social change are suggestive of what posthumanist theorists such as Bruno Latour, Donna Haraway, and Karen Barad describe as a *performative* understanding of agency. Such an understanding unseats language as the primary means of agency or rhetorical action, acknowledging objects, bodily practices, and material configurations (such as women riding bicycles) as important mechanisms through which meanings (such as understandings of women's "natural" capacities) emerge. Within such an understanding, language no longer precedes order, imposing meaning on it from without; discourse emerges from order and is articulated through performances like those Willard describes in her book. As Barad puts it, in a performative vein, "the primary semantic units are not 'words' but material-discursive practices through which boundaries are constituted" ("Posthuman" 818). According to this configuration, then, American women's efforts aboard the bicycle functioned discursively during the late nineteenth century, reordering gendered boundaries through repeated, highly visible performances.

As Nathan Stormer argues, rhetoricians might draw from this posthuman theory of agency in order to better account for the conditions of possibility that enable the emergence of different forms of rhetoric—that enable the "boundaries" of which Barad speaks to shift. If, as Stormer advocates, we "[understand] rhetoric as a historical product of practices, rather than as a natural faculty inherent in a cultured human mind, body, or language" (258), we might take as our project the ways that particular material-rhetorical configurations enable the emergence of rhetorics such as those Willard celebrated in her account of the bicycle. Such configurations are not *necessarily* discursive, but are constantly evolving and only become so in particular performative regimes. For instance, whereas a contemporary American woman standing with a bicycle and smoking a cigarette might convey, to those who see her on a city street, a wide and fairly unpredictable array of meanings about her gendered, classed, and political identities, a late nineteenth-century American woman doing the same thing conveyed very particular meanings about herself, functioning as a sort of material argument akin to the "image vernaculars" that Cara Finnegan has argued are common within particular historical and cultural contexts. Like the images of Abraham Lincoln that Finnegan describes, the bicyclist's body, her bicycle, and her cigarette constituted a concept uniquely legible to her contemporaries, functioning together discursively to convey her status as a particular "type" of woman: the generally urban, middle-class, educated "new woman."

In this essay, I consider how such a culturally discernable figure emerged and speculate about the impact she had on the nineteenth-century gender order. In doing so, I take up Stormer's call for historians of rhetoric to refocus their attention toward the history of practices rather than on the words of human subjects. Following Stormer in defining articulation as a material manifestation of the Greek concept of *taxis*, or textual arrangement (260), I investigate how the bicycle and other objects, together with the fairly stable range of practices they facilitated during the late nineteenth century, *articulated* (and did not reflect, follow, or even simply enable) changes in the late nineteenth-century gender order.[2] I ask: how did particular material arrangements involving women, bicycles, and associated material objects function as texts legible within a particular historical moment because of the consistency of their arrangement? How did they, during this historical moment, constitute a rhetoric that articulated the cultural shifts Willard observed?

Importantly, this project extends feminist rhetoricians' efforts to consider what Jessica Enoch describes as "the rhetorical process of gendering," to include "the everyday rhetorical processes that create difference and grant privilege" (115). Such processes are inextricable from materiality, and feminist rhetoricians have begun to consider how physical spaces (Mountford, Johnson, Enoch), chronological times (Jack), and imbrications of all of these material elements together (Jack) are implicated in their production and maintenance. Such projects engage in a performative account of rhetoric that understands practices rather than words (or practices in conjunction with words) as central to the production of gendering. Whereas previous scholarship highlights the role of discourse in shaping or defining objects, bodies, and the spaces and times to which they are permitted or denied access, however, my study of nineteenth-century bicycling examines the ways that objects and bodies articulate *with each other* to produce meaning, independently of language.

I examine the discursive performances enabled by configurations of mundane objects that come to function, within particular historical contexts, as what I describe as *material commonplaces*: repeated assemblages of particular elements that, because they achieve a relatively consistent and highly visible physical relation to one another, articulate particular relations among those elements. Like the verbal rhetorical commonplace, which David Bartholomae describes as "a culturally or institutionally authorized concept or statement that carries with it its own necessary elaboration" (626), material commonplaces function within a cultural context as stable concepts that, because they appear common and mundane, require no explanation or elaboration. Like verbal commonplaces, they are produced and sustained through repetition and visibility, through particular bodies and objects assembled in ways that enable a consistent range of performances; they wane in rhetorical power as the linkages between them become multiple and diffuse.[3] And like the visual rhetorical figures that design scholar Hanno H. J. Ehses has considered, these material configurations "manifest themselves in vividly concrete ways" (61)—functioning as representations of somewhat general or universal relations, but also enabling particular meanings to emerge about the concepts they inhabit. Ehses uses rhetorical figures to motivate design students to explore different facets of Shakespeare's *Macbeth*; similarly, I demonstrate how different material assemblages articulate particular relations among the elements they bring together. In general, I extend the work of scholars who have considered how classical rhetorical concepts manifest themselves in visual contexts constructed by rhetors, demonstrating how these same concepts operate in a larger material order that generates discourses beyond the purview of individual human rhetors.

What are some material commonplaces that may explain Willard's convictions about the power of the bicycle to generate social change? How were these commonplaces articulated in performance, and what sorts of gender relations did they alternately enhance, complicate, or challenge? As I argue, three different material articulations functioned as rhetorical commonplaces during the late nineteenth century: Ordinary bicycle+man/tricycle+woman, Safety bicycle+man+ Safety bicycle+woman, and small man/robust woman+bloomers+Safety bicycle. I associate each of these commonplaces with particular rhetorical tropes—*antithesis, gradatio,* and *antimetabole*—in order to delineate how each materialized different arguments about men's and women's bodies. As I suggest, each material trope facilitates a distinctive construction of gender relations—highlighting distinctions, enhancing overlaps, or producing reversals between the sexes. In general, considering how the relations among objects/bodies are in part articulated through their relative qualities helps to track the evolution of arguments and social meanings available in a material-rhetorical world.

Ordinary bicycle+man/tricycle+woman=antithesis

Throughout the 1880s, bicycling remained a highly masculine undertaking, dominated by young, mostly urban middle and upper class professionals who sought to demonstrate their strength, skill, and bravado aboard a machine notoriously difficult to master: the high-wheeled "Ordinary" bicycle first introduced to Americans during the mid-1870s. Riders of these machines associated high wheels both with faster racing and with greater skill; traveling downhill, the machines could be toppled easily, causing "headers" that could seriously injure a rider. New cyclists worked hard to learn how to maneuver their bicycles; once proficient, they joined exclusive clubs in which members demonstrated their prowess through races and stunt riding. One member of the Washington, DC–based Capital Bicycle Club, for instance, bragged in a newsletter of having put together "a most ingenious combination of obstructions" including "a gully about six feet deep, having steep sloping sides and a narrow bottom, which would just receive a wheel."[4] Similarly, members often bragged of their average ages, heights, and wheel heights in order to emphasize their manliness and skill. Among a group averaging 23 years of age and five feet, ten inches in height, the author reports that the average height of the front wheel was 52.7 inches—about four and a half feet tall (2).[5] Such examples demonstrate the extent to which the high-wheeled Ordinary of the 1880s articulated a particular form of youthful, athletic masculinity among its riders, who considered riding a modern antidote to the boredom and lack of physicality they encountered in their sedentary day jobs.

By mid-decade, however, bicycle manufacturers were beginning to sell tricycles as alternative machines to riders who sought out greater safety and ease of learning. Though initially they advertised these machines to older men and boys, women quickly took to the tricycle. Aboard the three-wheeled machine, women could enjoy much-needed exercise and recreation alongside their male counterparts, who expanded their riding to include leisurely runs on paved streets wide enough to accommodate the tricycle. The Capital Bicycle Club's newsletter of 1888, for instance, reports that on a run in which wheelmen were accompanied by "a number of lady friends," "[t]here was no very rapid riding, ten miles an hour being the maximum speed," making for "an enjoyable and beneficial tour . . . confined wholly to carriage roads."[6] Though male Ordinary riders continued their intrepid stunt and endurance riding among themselves, and while a few ladies' tricycle clubs did materialize, riders often socialized together on their respective wheels, and the advertising image of riders alongside each other aboard two significantly different machines became a popular way for manufacturer advertisements to emphasize the romance of the new activity (fig. 14.1).

In general, the 1880s relation of *man+Ordinary bicycle, woman+tricycle* offers an example of how material-discursive articulations functioned during the late nineteenth century as rhetorical figures highlighting the differences between the sexes. More specifically, in rhetorical terms the common sight of the Ordinary and the tricycle together represented a material *antithesis*, whereby the two machines, with their strong gender affiliations and highly differentiated mechanical structures, amplified the perceived differences between male and female riders and downplayed the similarities. Antithesis functions as a stylistic device with a particular syntax that highlights oppositions by presenting contrary ideas in a balanced relation to one another (Lanham 184). However, as Jeanne Fahnestock has argued, antithesis often "reconfigure[s] the nature of an existing opposition, either pushing the terms apart into mutual exclusion or placing them as extremes on a connecting continuum" (58). For instance, when Goethe notes in his famous verbal antithesis that "Love is an ideal thing; marriage a real thing," the distance wedged between "love" and "marriage" is the consequence of the parallelism of the other elements in the sentence, as love and marriage are not inherently opposed to one another. Similarly, the implied opposition between the female tricyclist and the male bicyclist is in part the result of their parallel positioning in relation to one another, as the two machines attempted to ride alongside one another or as they inhabited the same historical and physical context.

As apparatuses viewed in conjunction with one another and with their (differently positioned) riders, these two machines possessed in their pairing a sort of visual parallelism that, like verbal antithesis, invited contemporaries to complete a predictable pattern reinforcing distinctions between men and women.

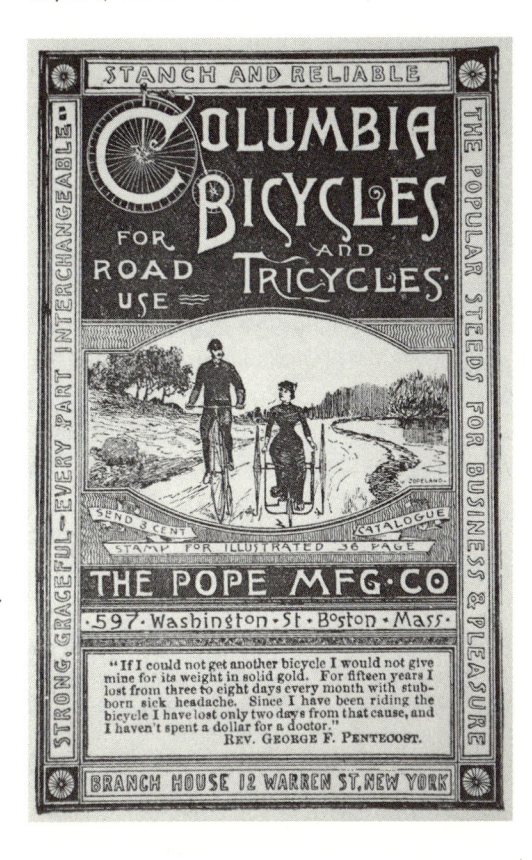

Figure 14.1. Pope advertisement, 1885.

The male Ordinary rider physically towers above the tricycle rider, who sits erect and refined between her wheels rather than above them, almost protected or encaged by the two wheels of her machine. Because she does not straddle the machine, she does not need to change her long skirts for riding, thus allowing her to don clothing that further confirms her physical distinctness from her male companion. Because her machine is easy to ride (and is confined mostly to established paths and roadways), the tricyclist is able to take in the scenery with ease. The Ordinary rider, in contrast, must constantly attend to his machine and demonstrate his skill, sitting aboard a device so tall and dangerous that a "header" could mean serious injury. The machines each materialize what Madeline Akrich refers to as a "technological script," whereby an object inhibits certain behaviors by its users and encourages others. In general, the scripting of these machines limits the experience that riders of each sex can have, re-enforcing gendered commonplaces about women's and men's separate "natures," including their apparent differences in size, stamina, and skill.

Safety bicycle+man+Safety bicycle+woman=Gradatio

Given the significant disparities in design and use between the Ordinary and the tricycle, men and women aboard their respective machines experienced some difficulty when attempting to ride together. Though records like those belonging to the Capital Bicycle Club indicate the increasing presence of women at club rides and social events, the Ordinary and the tricycle themselves materialized nearly separate spheres for their riders. As Caroline Minna Smith wrote in an *Outing* article, "tricyclists do not enjoy long runs of any kind. The bicycle-rider finds it a little tedious to accommodate his speed to the three-wheel, and to a lady rider the exertion of keeping up for a long distance is somewhat fatiguing" ("Women as Cyclers" 318). This incompatibility between the material objects themselves and the practices of the riders aboard them ultimately yielded a third machine that better reflected the practices of its riders, both male and female: the Safety bicycle, which resembles the bicycles of today with its equal-sized wheels and comparative ease of riding. Aboard the Safety, male riders could accompany their female friends without having to balance or concentrate as much as previously, and women riders could accompany their male friends without straining so hard to keep up. In sharing a common experience, they would articulate new overlap among themselves, troubling the material *antithesis* enacted in the relations between the Ordinary and tricycle riders.

Significantly, however, men's and women's Safeties were not just alike. Although they suggested greater commonality than their predecessors, the subtle differences between men's and women's Safeties materialized and maintained small but perceptible arguments about the different capacities of men and women. In contrast to the larger antitheses of the Ordinary and tricycle, these subtle differences suggested a *gradatio*, whereby differences *in kind* between men and women were replaced by gendered differences *in degree*. Within this framework, entities that might be perceived as wholly separate or distinctive from one another (in this case, men and women) could be understood as overlapping and connected. Because men's and women's Safeties shared the same basic structure and height and required similar levels of skill for riding, they materialized far greater overlaps between men and women than did the Ordinary and tricycle.

Nonetheless, particular features of Safeties for men and women maintained some distinctions in posture and speed, offering a gendered *gradatio* among riders. For example, the masculine machine's crossbar, which provided needed stability (fig. 14.2), was lowered to a "drop frame" on the women's models to accommodate skirts (fig. 14.3). This yielded a less stable wheel for skirted women, who were thus less able to engage in particularly strenuous or fast riding. In addition, many women's machines had wire "skirt guards" over their rear wheels to prevent garments from becoming caught in the chain or the spokes (Figure

Terre Haute Manufacturing Co.
Terre Haute, Ind.

MODEL A...GENTLEMEN'S

The
Celebrated
Standard
High-Grade

Price, $75.00

Figure 14.2. Damascus Bicycle Company Gentlemen's Safety Bicycle, 1897 catalogue, Indiana State Library.

Terre Haute Manufacturing Co.
Terre Haute, Ind.

MODEL D...LADIES'

The
Celebrated
Standard
High-Grade

Price, $75.00

Figure 14.3. Damascus Bicycle Company Ladies' Safety Bicycle, 1897 catalogue, Indiana State Library.

14.3). These skirt guards often weighed up to five pounds. As a result of this and the weight of the drop frame, women's bicycles were heavier than their masculine counterparts—often up to ten pounds heavier.

Other features of the Safety bicycles differentiated appropriate riding posture for men and women. Although both groups were warned of the dangers of "scorching," or leaning low over their wheels, men's racing seats were streamlined with a long, narrow pommel and only a small seat area on which to rest (fig. 14.2). Hence, riders were tacitly invited to assume a scorching posture, leaning forward over the pommel. In contrast, women's seats were wide and soft, with only a very small pommel to support riders leaning forward in a scorching position. A racing posture was difficult, as women were compelled to sit tall on their bikes—a position that reinforced their status as recreational, rather than athletic, riders. Similarly, handlebars materialized appropriate masculine and feminine postures. Women's handlebars spread high over the front of the wheel, discouraging any stooping. Men, however, could choose from a variety of handlebars, from those that forced them over the top of the wheel to those that kept them upright (fig. 14.4).

These features of the Safety bicycle, articulated in the activities of male and female riders on outings together, materialized a blending—but not a dissolution—of masculine and feminine bodily positions and physical capabilities. Because of the overlapping features of the Safety machine, the male and female rider were able to ride together more easily than the Ordinary and tricycle rider; novice riders were subject to the same learning process and were called upon to exert the same amount of attention to balance and propulsion. However, because of the distinct gendered features of their bicycles—seats, handlebars, and crossbars—men's and women's bodies were not situated identically in relation to the machine. Omnipresent on city streets and in popular magazines across America, the Safety bicycle as object suggested a material *gradatio*, or overlapping, of masculine and feminine qualities, whereas its predecessors had upheld through a material *antithesis* the commonplace of physical distinctiveness between men and women.

Small man/robust woman+bloomers+Safety bicycle=antimetabole

Though Safety bicycles were initially too expensive for all but the middle and upper classes, by the mid-1890s, the price had declined and the activity was spreading throughout the country. In addition to the romantic contexts implied by the advertisements for the tricycle and Ordinary, women were bicycling to jobs, running errands, and forming all-women social groups for riding. The *gradatio* between male and female bicyclists was joined by another material commonplace, the *antimetabole* produced through fears over the reversals of male and female

Figure 14.4. Damascus Bicycle handlebar options for male and female riders, 1897 catalogue, Indiana State Library.

bodies in domestic and professional space. Cartoonish images of large, robust women on bicycles alongside cowering men without bicycles suggested the impact of the bicycle on the social order. As Fahnestock notes, *antimetabole* consists of two parallel phrases with the key terms reversed in the second sitting. A famous example of verbal antimetabole is John F. Kennedy's famous line from his inaugural speech: "Ask not what your country can do for you, but what you can do for your country," in which the reversal of "you" and "your country" produces a striking effect. Fahnestock further notes that though classic antimetabole involves carefully constructed phrasings like Kennedy's, the trope can be "relaxed from its ideal syntactic configuration and still perform the same conceptual and argumentative work" (125). That is, it can function to confuse previously clear boundaries, to create a sense of balance and completeness even when the idea conveyed is new and unsettling.

Though intended to be humorous rather than to reflect a lived reality, numerous cartoons emerged lampooning women's bicycling featuring emasculated men and their robust, athletic wives. For example, one ad from an 1897 issue of *Life* magazine depicts a young woman on her way outdoors for a ride, standing apart from her family. Her husband, meanwhile, sits centered in the living room space in an armchair, surrounded by screaming children. The juxtaposition between the two—one standing and mobile, the other stationary and physically hindered from leaving—reverses the equation suggested by *Ordinary bicycle+man/tricycle+woman*, suggesting the new interchangeability of spaces and bodies. The effect is one of redistribution, clouding, and the eroding of oppositions or assumptions previously in place; the frailty of women, the naturalness of their location within domestic space, is upset in the process. A similar image—facetiously titled "The New Woman Wash Day"—features a man laboring over a laundry pail as a young woman dressed jauntily in bloomers towers above him, cigarette in mouth and foot planted gracelessly on a chair. In the background sits a bicycle awaiting the young woman's use. This juxtaposition of bodies reflects the anxieties of many Americans who feared the dissolution of existing domestic arrangements; the presence of bicycle dress signals the agency of the bicycle in enacting this dissolution. Such images—enacted in various locations, but always involving a robust woman bicyclist and a small, put-upon man—were plentiful during the 1890s, functioning in their repetition as a commonplace that materialized the clouding of gender relations.

Significantly, the prevalence of these caricatures created negative associations among women, bicycles, and bloomers. Women bicyclists could be "read" as texts connoting carelessness, selfishness, and a ridiculous masculinity; their allegiance to their families could be more readily questioned on the basis of their clothing and their decision to bicycle alone. As a result, riders disassociated themselves from objects, such as the bloomer, that contributed to this implicit material commonplace. Whereas in 1895 a *New York Times* author proclaimed that "there is no question in my mind that in a year or so a woman riding in skirts will attract as much attention as one in bloomers did a year or two ago" ("A Plea for Bloomers" 15), two years later the bloomer had receded in popularity, replaced by a variety of shortened and convertible skirts. Women bicyclists—aware that by wearing the bloomer garment they articulated a material commonplace that situated them as emasculating Amazons—sought to distance themselves from this negative association.

Though initially quite popular, the bloomer's credibility waned because of the increasing cultural imperative for women bicyclists to demonstrate their conventional femininity through bicycle dress. Functioning as antimetabole, the gender role reversals that appeared frequently in popular representations of women bicyclists and their husbands and beaus impacted the ways that women riders could be "read" even if their husbands and beaus were not actually present.

Figure 14.5. "The New Woman Wash Day."

Whereas contemporary material commonplaces—accomplished through antithesis and gradation—operated to establish distinct differences between women and men, this figure blurred gender boundaries but ultimately functioned to regulate gendered women's behaviors.

Each of these material commonplaces—Ordinary+man/tricycle+woman, Safety bicycle+man+Safety bicycle+woman, and small man/robust woman+bloomers+Safety bicycle—materialized a particular narrative about the "proper" or "natural" relationship between men and women in the late nineteenth century. Each emerged at the junction of the physical properties of the objects themselves, the relations among objects, and the associations that developed through their representations. The tricycle's bulk, lack of maneuverability, and dress-accommodating seat design did not, by themselves, constitute an argument about women's capabilities and limitations; in conjunction with the high-wheeled Ordinary and two gendered riders acting in concert with one another, however, an argument emerged that gained particular clarity for those whose associations were colored by meanings circulating within the advertisements and commentaries of a particular historical context. Together, the objects and performances attained a discursive status that was maintained as long as its contexts of use remained consistent—as long as men continued to ride the Ordinary rather than the Safety, and as long as women, more than older men or children, were associated with the tricycle. When the articulation faded because it was no longer sustained through repeated performance, its absence influenced a new articulation: the mutual performance of women and men riding the Safety bicycle. Through this new articulation, women became "new"—changed in ways that were visibly present for their contemporaries and for themselves, and thus subject to a new range of arguments, constraints, and potentialities both positive and negative in nature.

Though feminist rhetoricians have often explored the ways gender norms are constructed, maintained, and transformed through discursive activities related to material, spatial, and temporal conditions, this example considers the ways that *objects themselves* are discursive in their interanimation. It suggests the extent to which gender is constructed through object relations, demonstrating how the material world produces rhetorical effects that exceed and distort the intentions of individual rhetors. An object-oriented approach to the rhetorical processes of gendering introduces a vast and dynamic field of object-agents—such as tricycles and bloomers and bicycle seats—that contribute to the stubborn maintenance of gender difference and to gendered power imbalances.

Similarly, other, more recent material rearrangements might be understood as producing effects regarding not only gender, but also racial, sexual, and political dynamics. For instance, delineating the discursivity of material relations might help us to account for the impact of Title IX on both collegiate classrooms and athletic fields. A woman dunking a basketball or kicking a soccer goal denaturalizes cultural linkages between men and these actions; through repetition and visibility, these actions create new linkages that shift the ground on which gender relations are constituted. Alternatively, the election of the first African-American president of the United States situates a previously marginalized body in a symbolic position of power, whose highly circulated image in conjunction with objects culturally agreed upon as "presidential"—at White House press conference podiums or boarding Air Force One, for instance—enables new arguments to emerge about race as readily as President Obama's own words on the subject. These are questions that might be considered through the lens of discursive objects, which wield persuasive power in conjunction with embodied performances, and which can be harnessed by groups seeking to produce particular sorts of changes in the social order.

By examining the particular material articulations to which the world—with its ever-changing array of objects and bodies, situated in relation to one another—is subject, we can better account for the means by which social change is accomplished, distorted, or muddled despite the best intentions of individual rhetors using rhetoric deliberately and forcefully. Furthermore, in examining object arrangements as rhetorical tropes like *antithesis*, *gradatio*, and *antimetabole*, we can speak more precisely of the particular arguments that grant temporary, but always shifting, rhetorical stability to a volatile, object-filled material world.

Or to put it another way, we can build upon Frances Willard's excited observations of the necessity to engage in "practice" as well as "theory."

Notes

1. The "Woman Question" was a term used to refer to widespread anxieties about the sort of education and training women's bodies and minds were equipped to handle.

2. Like Stormer, I draw from posthumanist scholars such as Haraway and Barad in my use of the term "articulation" more than I do from cultural studies theorists such as Stuart Hall and Chantal Mouffe, understanding articulation as engaged specifically in the production of culturally discernible bodies, such as the bloomer-wearing new woman sitting aboard her bicycle, smoking her cigarette.

3. For instance, the bicycle+bloomer+woman+cigarette linkage remained consistent during the late nineteenth century, constituting a single, culturally legible concept, but over time, a broader array of women came to ride bicycles in a wider range of contexts. As a result, the articulation of new woman performances lost its coherence and the commonplace's discursive power waned.

4. See Capital Bicycle Club, Washingtonia Collection, Series 2, Box 4. Public Library. Washington, DC

5. See Capital Bicycle Club, Washingtonia Collection, Series 2, Box 4. Public Library. Washington, DC

6. See Capital Bicycle Club, Washingtonia Collection, Series 2, Box 4. Public Library. Washington, DC

15
Encomium of QWERTY

James J. Brown Jr. and Nathaniel A. Rivers

> I'll try hard not to give in
> Batten down to fare the wind
> Rid my head of this pretense
> Allow myself no mock defense
> As I step into the night
>
> The Shins, "Saint Simon"

Prologue

The vicious attacks are numerous:

> You might then naively expect that the QWERTY keyboard was designed so that most typing is done on the home row. You would be wrong. Only 32 percent of strokes are on the home row; most strokes (52 percent) are on the upper row; and a full 16 percent are on the bottom row, which you should be avoiding like the plague. Not more than 100 English words can be typed without leaving the home row. The reason for this disaster is simple: QWERTY perversely puts the most common English letters on other rows. The home row of nine letters includes two of the least used (J and K) but none of the three most frequently used (E, T, and O, which are relegated to the upper row) and only one of the five vowels (A), even though 40 percent of all letters in a typical English text are vowels. (Diamond)

In the face of such violence, here stands the QWERTY keyboard layout, nearly 150 years after Christopher Sholes and Amos Densmore's 1878 patent for the Remington No. 2 typewriter. If you are reading this on your computer, look down and you will notice that six letters sit in the upper left-hand corner of your keyboard: Q-W-E-R-T-Y. These six letters serve as a synecdoche for anything from the poor design of your keyboard to a vast mythology about a conspiracy to slow down typists.

The QWERTY keyboard layout as we know it was likely born in the summer of 1878 with the publication of US Patent No. 207,559. By the age of 20, in the autumn of 1898, our young hero had become king by virtue of the formation of the Typewriter Trust, which used its financial clout to standardize not only a typewriter but also the keyboard layout you use today (Yasuoka). King QWERTY advanced quickly to a secure position of prominence. More than a century after its coronation, QWERTY still stands between writers and their various screens, but we have too often taken it as an impediment, as something to be overcome. Howard Gardner urges us to avoid this posture. He grants that some study their keyboards (whether for music or text), seeking out those that feel just right or that allow their fingers to "glide over it with no wasted motion" (Gardner 49). Gardner does not count himself among this group, but he also sees the keyboard as an active participant in his writing and piano playing:

> I pay essentially no attention to the quality of my keyboards. All of my attention is focused on the message, musical or literary. . . . *And yet*, even with my focus so intently on the message, the experience of my fingers on keyboards feels like more than simply a means to a desired end. In the creation of both music and text, if I could bypass the keyboard and directly transmit mental signals to an instrument or to the computer, I would not want to do so. (Gardner 49, emphasis added)

Gardner does not evoke QWERTY directly, but we take his insistence on the importance of any input device as our starting point. We will demonstrate that the peculiar and persistent keyboard layout with which many of us interact daily is not something to be bested or blamed but rather something to be lauded. QWERTY is heroic.

Our defense of QWERTY is, thankfully, not the first. Recent treatments of this great rhetorical device have worked diligently to undo the false histories that attempt to sully QWERTY's reputation. Perhaps you have heard the story, for it emerges everywhere from scholarly journals to cocktail parties: "You know, QWERTY was designed to slow down typists. The hammers in the typewriter kept getting jammed." This pleasing story appeals to our cinematic impulses. Perhaps a QWERTY biopic would even include a battle with substance abuse. But this story assumes an "intelligent designer" behind the most famous keyboard layout in technological history. A closer look at the evidence suggests that this famous story takes some liberties with the facts. Koichi Yasuoka and Motoko Yasuoka go a step further in their detailed account of why the received history of QWERTY should be corrected: "It's nonsense" (161). Yasuoka and Yasuoka lay out a laundry list of scholarly accounts that repeat the QWERTY myth, but most importantly they demonstrate that early users of QWERTY were not even typists—they were telegraph operators. Slowing down telegraph operators would have hindered QWERTY's adoption, since the person typing would have been unable to keep up with the dots and dashes coming across the wire (170).

Edward Tenner is slightly more circumspect in his treatment of QWERTY's history. Stopping short of accusations of "nonsense," he reminds us that no one really knows the complete logic behind the QWERTY layout. As he explains, a purely alphabetical arrangement of keys was revised in the move from the Remington No. 1, which hit the market in 1874, to the release of the Remington No. 2 machine four years later:

> Nobody has been able to reconstruct Scholes's and Densmore's reasoning completely. It would probably be necessary to find an operating Model 1 or 2 typewriter and experiment with combinations of letters. The QWERTY keyboard, as it came to be known, was clearly a compromise. On the middle row of text there was a nearly alphabetical sequence: DFGHJKLM. The last letter was later moved to the bottom row, where the original C and X were also later reversed. On the top row was a vowel cluster (UIO) out of alphabetical order. Scholes and Densmore were both familiar with newspaper type cases, arranged not in alphabetical order but roughly according to letter frequency. The QWERTY keyboard did not follow these patterns but was conceived in a similar spirit. (Tenner 200–201)

At the very least, Tenner is one of many who points out that QWERTY was not designed purely to slow down the typist and that the design was the result of a collection of forces and actors. Thierry Bardini calls these forces "stochastic," and it seems clear that QWERTY emerged from a complex scene of humans and technologies.

Technologies such as QWERTY find no stronger ally than Andy Clark, who argues that the human experience of the world (and, by extension, its action in the world) "is an ongoing construct open to rapid influence by tricks and . . . new technologies" (Clark xx). The musician's keyboard is not simply a tool for creating music, but is part of the iterative process of being a musician as such. QWERTY is likewise and precisely such a (new) technology that, as the record shows, burst onto the scene and stayed there. It sticks around because the mergers it cultivates are so intimate as to disappear into the background of human action. "Such tools," Clark argues, "are best conceived as proper parts of the computational apparatus that constitutes our minds" (6). As we shall see, a significant part of QWERTY's lineage are the human users through which it reproduces itself. What we also see here is that the human itself is a continual construct ontologically similar to QWERTY or any other object.

Humans merge with tools, Clark writes, and so we must extend the same ethical courtesy to them as we do our fellow humans. Merger is the key term here. While at times he describes the mind as incorporating or offloading or distributing, Clark consistently treats the extended mind in terms of relations, intimate mergers, with real bearing on the identities (and ontologies) of all those involved and entangled. Clark's world is a messy but lively one. And so surely QWERTY must celebrate, or maybe smugly smile to itself, when Clark writes, "There is no informationally constituted *user* relative to whom all the rest is just *tools*" (192). *See, I told you so,* QWERTY might reply: *you and I are mates.* This intimacy is praise twice over. Not only that QWERTY is a good tool, but that QWERTY is a necessary partner. What is particularly impressive about QWERTY is the extent to which it is merged with humans, tying its fate to ours.

QWERTY is thus linked to objects like pencil and paper, cortical implants, and video game controllers. But these comparisons are not enough to fully praise QWERTY. A full encomium—one that tracks a hero's lineage and accomplishments—must account for QWERTY's uniqueness in such mergers. QWERTY, not the human mind, is our story's hero, but the story continues to get mangled. QWERTY has not a cause but allies with whom it moves and acts and extends its network: machines, letters, keyboards, designers, ergonomics, typists, secretaries, students, researchers, buttons, wrists, hands, fingers, habits, ruts, neural pathways, symbol systems, and even inertia. We need to take a closer look at the particularities of QWERTY, starting with its stock, its lineage.

Lock, Stock, and Barrel

Of a heterogeneous lineage, QWERTY's relations spread across a network of ancestors. QWERTY has many parents and many aunts and uncles, brothers and sisters, and cousins. It is related to rifles, sewing machines, pianos, and telegraphs. It has of course been said that QWERTY was simply designed by human hands, but this is not entirely accurate. Such an assertion is also praise too little for QWERTY, and it is certainly praise too much for humans. QWERTY was surely a means by which human hands manipulated human hands, but QWERTY does not just work for us. It works for itself and for other machines, and those machines moved the humans that made QWERTY necessary. QWERTY got here the same way we got here: the forces of selection, of the available genetic material, of the environment, and of nurture—of the hands of parents and siblings and cousins and neighbors. We pay tribute to it and honor QWERTY simply in acknowledging in the first place that it has a family history as complex, convoluted, and branching as any other.

In the autumn of 1872 QWERTY was not yet QWERTY. It was QWERTU. It wasn't until the Sholes and Glidden Serial No. 1, released in 1874, that QWERTY emerged after a complex series of business maneuvers and keyboard compromises. Stamp reports, "right before their machine, dubbed the Sholes & Glidden, went into production, Sholes filed another patent, which included a new keyboard arrangement" (Stamp). Sholes was unsatisfied with the placement of the letter Y. He wanted it nearer the center of the keyboard, next to the T. It was previously located where the P now stands. After even more corporate repositioning, the Remington Standard Type-Writer No. 2 was released in 1882. This machine marks the arrival of the QWERTY keyboard arrangement that sits beneath our fingertips today.

But the story of QWERTY's stock is more complex than this last minute shifting of the Y key, and a number of friends and foes have continually shaped this famed keyboard. QWERTY can count Mark Twain as an early friend, who typed in 1874 of "this new fangled writing machine" having "several virtues." As with any intimate coupling, his relationship with the typewriter was a contentious one. In a letter to Densmore, Yost and Company, he pleads with the inventors not to use his name in promotional materials and refuses to endorse the machine:

> GENTLEMEN: PLEASE DO NOT USE MY NAME IN ANY WAY. PLEASE DO NOT EVEN DIVULGE THE FACT THAT I OWN A MACHINE. I HAVE ENTIRELY STOPPED USING THE TYPE-WRITER, FOR THE REASON THAT I NEVER COULD WRITE A LETTER WITH IT TO ANYBODY WITHOUT RECEIVING A REQUEST BY RETURN MAIL THAT I WOULD NOT ONLY DESCRIBE THE MACHINE, BUT STATE WHAT PROGRESS I HAD MADE IN THE USE OF IT, ETC., ETC. I DON'T LIKE TO WRITE LETTERS, SO I DON'T WANT PEOPLE TO KNOW I OWN THIS CURIOSITY-BREEDING LITTLE JOKER. (CLEMENS)

There is, we note, more than faint praise for QWERTY even in this complaint. QWERTY and its partner the Remington are already coming into their own, generating, or "breeding," curiosity. Clemens's friends and family want to know what it does. And we can see this "little joker" already at work in just such a letter.

QWERTY even charmed Clemens's family members, finding its way into a letter to Twain's brother, the first thing he tried to type. Across the top of the letter his daughter Suzie, who beat him to the typewriter, banged away at the keys for a brief moment. And there, across the top of the page in a string of letters, QWERTY appears. It is, of course, not a huge surprise: a child's fingers would have been drawn there, called to engage the keys. Twain's letter speaks to the seductive power of the keyboard and the allure of QWERTY, which is always there in the margins and beneath our fingers. In the beginning was QWERTY. And it is this beginning, banging, and striking that gets at what it has always got: to the heart of QWERTY, a keyboard arrangement kept tightly yoked to history, to humans, and to machines. This letter typed by many hands embodies the lineage of QWERTY.

QWERTY has its own history inasmuch as that history is not reducible to one cause: it has many sources from which its distinctiveness emerges. Yasuoka and Yasuoka write, "The keyboard arrangement very often changed during the development, and accidentally grew into QWERTY among the different requirements" (161). While we would quibble with their use of "accidentally," which suggests a privileging of purposeful human action, they do get at the complexity of how QWERTY came to be. One such requirement, or as we say, ancestor, was the American Morse Code system. QWERTY is closely related to the unique relationship between the letters S, E, and Z in that system. The letter S was represented by a series of three dots (. . .) and the E is one (.). This is a common letter pair. However, the SE pair is three dots followed by a pause and then a single dot (... .) and could be easily confused with the letter Z, which follows the same pattern (... .). The surest way, then, to differentiate SE from Z is the other letters following it. Being able to quickly type SE and Z allowed for the following letter to come sooner, lessening the chances of confusion. Thus, telegraph operators, described by Jimmy Stamp as "early adopters and beta-testers," are part of the stock of QWERTY: their hands shaped it (Stamp).

But more hands than these count QWERTY as progeny. In 1873 associates of Sholes met with representatives from Remington & Sons, manufacturers of, among other things, sewing machines and firearms. Looking to diversify and utilize excess factory space following the Civil War, Remington eventually signed a contract that resulted in the Sholes and Glidden Type-Writer (Yasuoka and Yasuoka 165). This corporate liaison had mechanical consequences. The trial version of the Sholes and Glidden Type-Writer looked very much like a sewing machine, complete with a carriage-return operated by a foot pedal (fig. 15.1). The family resemblance comes as no surprise. Remington made sewing machines, which served as stock for the production of Remington's first typewriters. Friedrich Kittler, in *Gramophone, Film, Typewriter*, makes much of QWERTY's ancestry. Born of a gun manufacturer, Kittler argues, "The typewriter became a discursive machine-gun" (Kittler 191). Not taking coincidence as explanation enough, he adds, "A technology whose basic action not coincidentally consists of strikes and triggers proceeds in automated and discrete steps, as does ammunitions transport in a revolver and a machine-gun, or celluloid transport in a film projector" (191). Kittler also writes, "A spatialized, numbered, and . . . also standardized supply of signs on a keyboard makes possible what and only what QWERTY prescribes" (229). Kittler here implicitly grants QWERTY a lineage that shapes it above and beyond what Sholes and Glidden and others might have had in mind. There is a logic that inheres in the mechanism and the evolutionary chain of which it is a part.

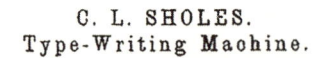

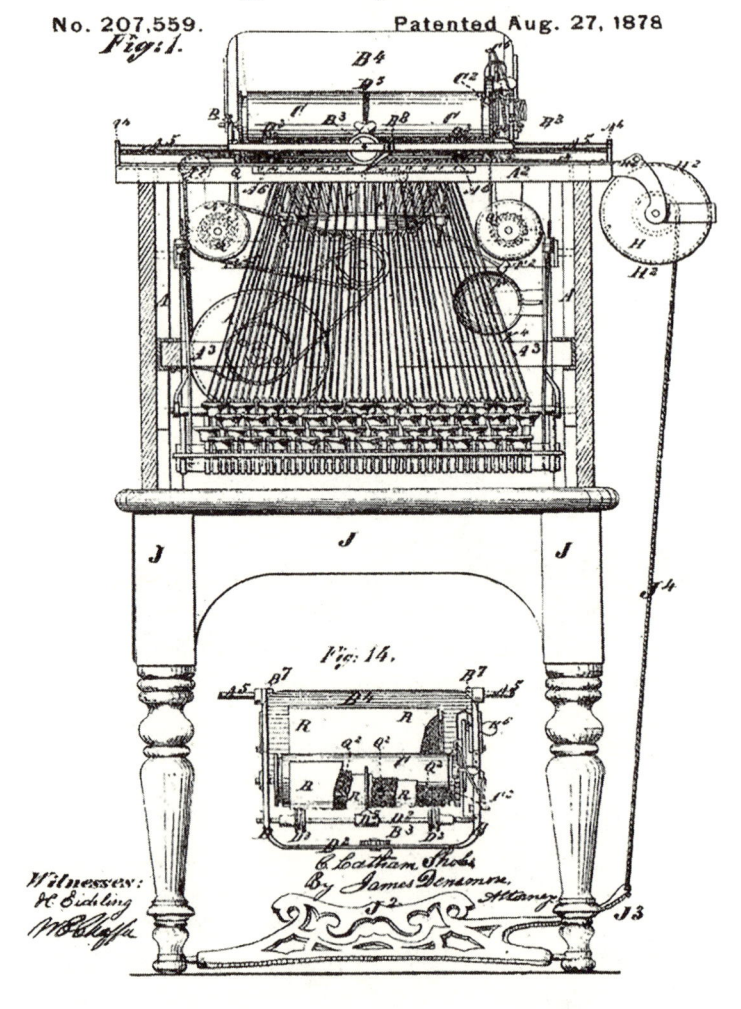

Figure 15.1. Sholes and Glidden Type-Writer.

Our hands continue to be shaped by QWERTY, but this is not to say only that we continue to be shaped by the humans who designed it. Much more than that is at work here. We cannot pin the whole thing on Christopher Latham Sholes, perhaps the first person to ever type the letters Q-W-E-R-T-Y. Indeed, our own continued reliance on QWERTY is how it keeps reproducing itself in the face of mounting evolutionary pressure. We, the contemporary users of QWERTY, are also its stock. Our work as writers, as composers, is also our work as the perpetuators of QWERTY's storied lineage. The keyboard layout came into being far in advance of the machines, techniques, and operators that would make the typewriter as we know it today possible. Indeed, Tenner writes, "The keyboard came into the world with no recommended technique" at all (198). It was composed with Morse operators and short handers in mind. There were no typists before the typewriter, before QWERTY: "Interestingly, most of the early designs had nothing to do with a desire to mechanise [sic] handwriting: instead, their purpose was to make reading possible for blind people" (Lundmark 13). Here we are struck with a staggering realization: *the typist is the child of QWERTY*.

Battle Tested

QWERTY's dominance, however, has been challenged at every turn: "even if the QWERTY is clearly the dominant artifact for typesetting, its status remained challenged for nearly its whole history, and numerous special projects, applications, and artifacts were proposed using alternative designs for textual input" (Bardini 246). August Dvorak was QWERTY's most formidable foe. It perhaps makes more sense to say that Dvorak remains a foe, for even though he died in 1975 his keyboard layout lives on. Dvorak was "convinced that the universal keyboard [QWERTY] was an obstacle to good technique" (Tenner 202). Dvorak's initial efforts were aimed at accommodating typists who only had one hand. But his most famous accomplishment is the Dvorak keyboard, patented in 1936, which has been the most serious threat to QWERTY's existence. Dvorak believed that the QWERTY keyboard put too much stress on the left hand and undue pressure on certain fingers. He also thought the home row was underutilized, that the typist was forced to "row hop" excessively, and that too many words could be typed with only the left hand (Noyes 267). While something like only a quarter of people in the world are left-handed, we might wonder about the jump in logic that suggests that the right hand should be doing more work (Holder). A right-handed person, though she writes with her right-hand, wears a watch on her left wrist. Perhaps typing is less like writing and more like telling time? Further, if we follow Dvorak's logic, what of all the left-handed people in the world? Are they merely human cruft that prevents faster typing speeds?

Dvorak's keyboard (the Dvorak Simplified Keyboard, or DSK) has had nearly a century to unseat QWERTY. Yet here stands QWERTY, a layout that reveals its dominance even in attempts to prop up the DSK. In a 1956 General Services Administration study, Earle Strong determined:

> [. . .] it took well over twenty-five days of four-hour-a-day training sessions for these typists to catch up to their old QWERTY speed. When the typists had finally caught up to their old speed, Strong began the second phase of

the experiment. The newly trained Dvorak typists continued training and a group of ten QWERTY typists began a parallel program to improve their skills. In this second phase, the Dvorak typists progressed less quickly with further Dvorak training than did QWERTY typists training on QWERTY keyboards. Thus, Strong concluded that Dvorak training would never be able to amortize its costs. (Liebowitz and Margolis 15–16)

As Stan Liebowitz and Stephen Margolis explain, the heralding of the DSK is based on shoddy research. Ergonomic studies show no evidence that Dvorak's layout is easier on the body than QWERTY, and competition among keyboard layouts was much more vigorous than the popular QWERTY myth lets on (9). Contrary to popular belief, the game was not rigged. QWERTY has won, fair and square.

QWERTY's fiercest foes continually underestimate the broad collective that supports our most famous and ubiquitous writing partner. In his detailed study of Douglas Engelbart, Thierry Bardini covers the contest between Engelbart and QWERTY in the 1960s. In his career-long efforts to "augment the human intellect," Engelbart sought out ways to make personal computing more efficient. He is perhaps best known for "the mother of all demos," in which he demonstrated the Graphical User Interface, the mouse, and (most importantly, for our purposes) his chord keyset. The latter was Engelbart's attempt to replace QWERTY, which he viewed as supremely inefficient. Engelbart hoped to free up one hand of the typist, and the chord keyset was his attempt to do so. Using a five key setup, the keyset mimicked the telegraph operator's interface. With 32 possible combinations (2^5), the five keys of the chord keyset allowed for the encoding of the Roman alphabet (Bardini 60). Typing with one hand freed up the other hand for Engelbart's most famous invention: the mouse.

In letters to Harold Wooster, one of the Air Force officials who supervised the research and helped determine how government funds would be spent on Engelbart's project, it is clear that Engelbart did not adequately respect his foe. Wooster believed that Engelbart was reinventing the wheel and that his chord keyset was a rehashing of technology that had already been usurped: "What you are proposing is essentially a telegraphic problem—at translation of finger motion into a code—and I suspect that the telegraphic art has thoroughly explored the pros and cons at each stage of its evolution—and that there is very little that is new that can be done with fingers and keys" (Wooster qtd. in Bardini 63). Further, Wooster believed that teaching users to use the keyset was an insurmountable challenge. Wooster's view of technological change was evolutionary, and he believed five-key devices were dead in the water. This view is interesting in that it offers a kind of "weak defense" of QWERTY, arguing that it is the result of inevitable technological progress. But this is once again not allowing for the complexity of QWERTY's lineage. The point is not that QWERTY is a lone

Figure 15.2. Engelbart's NLS, featuring the chord keyset, the mouse, and QWERTY.

wolf but that it has drawn a broad collective of supporters. QWERTY, though it has proven unstoppable, was never inevitable.

Engelbart's hubris was evident in his belief that QWERTY could be unseated by the chord keyset. According to Bardini, he was attempting to remake the human body rather than to develop an interface that worked well with it: "Engelbart did not want to accommodate his technology to the way people work—he wanted to use that technology to change the way people work, and to him, the chord keyset offered the best way to do that" (81). But Engelbart eventually succumbed, even if reluctantly. This is clearest as we watch his demo of the NLS system (oN-Line System). Once again, there stands QWERTY, right smack in the middle of Engelbert's workspace, sitting in between Engelbart's chord keyset and his mouse. It takes up an inordinate amount of space. Even as Engelbart tries his best to ignore its existence, it stares him right in the face. As he shows off the now mundane computational procedures of "cut," "copy," and "paste," he avoids QWERTY altogether.

Epilogue

Even as we twist and contort QWERTY (think of the ergonomic keyboards of the 1990s), it remains unstoppable. At every (re)turn, we have attempted to try to kill off our greatest writing companion, the one that never leaves our side.

Or, better, the one that sits beneath our hands, always at the ready. From competing layouts to brand new input interfaces to voice recognition software, we have tried to replace the QWERTY keyboard, which we see as an obstacle rather than as an integral part of our writing ecologies. We have even tried to attribute QWERTY's great acts to humans. In their corrective to Paul David's history of QWERTY and market forces (David's history, unsurprisingly, repeats a number of slanderous myths), the economists Liebowitz and Margolis explain that Frank McGurrin, a celebrity stenographer, is often seen as QWERTY's Michael Jordan:

> A watershed event in the received version of the QWERTY story is a typing contest held in Cincinnati on July 25, 1888. Frank McGurrin, a court stenographer from Salt Lake City, who was apparently one of the first typists to memorize the keyboard and use touch-typing, won a decisive victory over Louis Taub. Taub used the hunt-and-peck method on a Caligraph, a machine that used seventy-two keys to provide upper- and lower-case letters. According to popular history, the event established once and for all that the Remington typewriter, with its QWERTY keyboard, was technically superior. More important, the contest created an interest in touch-typing, an interest directed at the QWERTY arrangement. Reportedly, no one else at that time had skills that could even approach McGurrin's, so there was no possibility of countering the claim that the Remington keyboard arrangement was efficient. McGurrin participated in typing contests and demonstrations through the country and became something of a celebrity. His choice of the Remington keyboard, which may well have been arbitrary, contributed to the establishment of the standard. So, it was, according to the popular telling, that a keyboard designed to solve a short-lived mechanical problem became the standard used daily by millions of typists. (7–8)

Like Yasuoka and Yasuoka, we count Liebowitz and Margolis among QWERTY's allies, protecting it from false histories and from comforting tales of human triumph. McGurrin helped, but he is given too much credit, and he is not the only one. In 1869, E. Payson Porter, another of QWERTY's spokespersons, validated Christopher Latham Sholes with his touch-typing skill. In a demo that far predates Engelbart's, Porter was tasked with using a keyboard to type out incoming messages from telegraphers. As the dots and dashes arrived, Porter adroitly translated them into words using Sholes's invention. Other telegraphers were brought in to rush Porter and to test his speed, and he answered each challenge. The result of this demo was the adoption of Sholes's device: "A thorough trial of my ability to 'keep up' resulted so satisfactorily that the typewriter was taken into the operating room" (Porter, qtd. in Bardini 69). Porter positions himself as the hero of this story, proud of his ability to keep up with any telegrapher, but it is QWERTY who takes over the operating room.

A celebration of QWERTY calls us to pay attention to this nonhuman collaborator. Of course, if we pay too much attention to QWERTY, it gets in the way, and perhaps this is the case with any tool. Still, it might be worth allowing QWERTY to show itself now and again so that we remember how intricately it is threaded through our composing activities. One way to do this is to notice what each of our hands is doing in concert with QWERTY as we compose sentences. If the typist is using the home row on the QWERTY keyboard, the sentence you are reading requires the right hand to do most of the work, but not by much. But even this assumes all kinds of things about the typist: that she is using her right hand for the space bar or that she types the letter Y with her right hand. We know from a very unscientific study that the letter Y is not the sole purview of the right hand (Leard). Each performance of QWERTY is virtuosic.

However, our writing partner remains steadfast, shaping each word and sentence. We know, thanks to work in distributed and embodied cognition, that QWERTY is part of various cognitive systems. In a review of work on embodied cognition, Margaret Wilson explains how humans off-load certain tasks onto tools and other objects: "We make the environment hold or even manipulate information for us, and we harvest that information only on a need-to-know basis" (Wilson 626). While this account might risk transforming tools like QWERTY into what Heidegger would call "standing-reserve," the concept of off-loading at least reminds us that QWERTY plays a crucial role in the scene of writing. As Edwin Hutchins, a forerunner to Andy Clark, argues, "in watching people thinking in the wild, we may be learning more about their environment for thinking than what is inside them" (Hutchins 169). That is, the efficacy of environments and the tools that constitute them can and do shine forth. We need QWERTY to account for and understand our own cognitive abilities, and in so accounting QWERTY is unconcealed as an agent in its own right, and worthy of praise.

Takeshi Okadome offers what is, to our minds, the most important synopsis of the "problem" of QWERTY: "In order to optimize the human-keyboard interface, we should not force people to conform to a nonoptimal keyboard. Instead, we must build the best keyboard fit to people. However, at the present stage *we do not even know how people really are*, what they can perform best under what condition" (Okadome 31, emphasis added). We have too often assumed that the problem is QWERTY, this sometimes flat, sometimes curved, sometimes split, sometimes ergonomically contorted array of keys to which we are beholden as we compose. But do we even know anything about the human that sits "above" or hovers over QWERTY? Have we taken an account of the flaws and problems with our hands and wrists, with our fingertips or eyes? We must acknowledge these flaws, these uncertainties, because the exercise of our encomium, which is dutifully trifling and crushingly mundane, is a human exercise. This should not weary the audience too much. Just because we cannot go all the way does not mean we should not try.

Postscript: On the *Progymnasmata* and Rhetorical Ontologies

QWERTY's story is not one of jamming typewriters or celebrity typists. Neither is it a story of luck and stochastic technological shifts. It is not a three-act movie script, but is rather a complex story of an object that asserts itself over and over again, resisting attempts to eradicate it. For far too long we have treated encomia as exercises in epistemology—of a knowing subject coming to and describing a known object. Is it possible to compose and perform an encomium that does not do this? Is it worth it to try? It strikes us that we will have to do more here and not less. That is, critical distance is not the key to approaching objects but rather a strange sort of intimacy, a closeness born of familiarity wherein the object in itself is momentarily unconcealed before withdrawing.

To perform an encomium to an object, and a particularly mundane object at that, is to likewise compose a treatise on what it means to be able to act. If we are to truly praise QWERTY, we must imagine it as dynamic, unstable, emergent, and above all as active and maybe even agential. In short, how can we praise that which seemingly does not act without also rethinking what it is to act, and what it is to be? Encomia are always ontologies (or ontological). The benefit of an encomium of the mundane is to displace our own privileged place in an ecology. The elevation of a keyboard layout serves to flatten the universe of being. In this way, the encomium suggests itself as a viable and relevant methodology for researchers interested in tracing the ways everyday objects produce effects. In ways akin to actor-network theory—which, Bruno Latour argues, involves following the actors first and foremost—encomia provide a performative template for elevating the mundane in ways that attune us to their generative capacities, which remain irreducible to human intent or use. Encomia recount the lives of things, and they sit alongside Latour's method of "scientifiction" as ways to breathe life into nonhumans.

But we would go further still. Other *progymnasmata* exercises find their way into this conversation as well. Commonplaces, chreia, fables, and many other methods from the rhetorician's bag of tricks offer us ways to hover over the seemingly mundane, methods for accounting for an abundance of rhetorical actors and actions. Far beyond mere classroom trifles (here we could take issue with Gorgias's description of his famous *Encomium of Helen* as a *paignion*, a "child's toy" or "plaything"), the progymnasmata are worth returning to as we consider how to best follow actors through networks. We offer encomia in our account of QWERTY, but we would argue that an accompanying invective that attacks QWERTY and its various limitations would reveal more and different things about this device's lineage. The rhetorician has much to say about the methods emerging in new materialism, object-oriented ontology, and actor-network theory, and we hope that our demonstration here opens up more possibilities in this direction.

Afterword

A Crack in the Cosmic Egg, Tuning into Things

Thomas Rickert

A materialist turn is upon us in the humanities. Of course, one hesitates to say that: we have so many turns, every few years. It is, perhaps, part of the cycle of scholarship. History is rarely kind to such turns, seeing them instead as fodder for some new as yet unforeseen turn, or demonstrating that the new turn was not so new, nor perhaps really much of a turn. John Muckelbauer, in *The Future of Invention*, argues that such models—of turns, of transformations—are implicitly Hegelian, suggesting instead a different conception, one of rhythms, intensities. Thus, we might see interest in materiality and things, ontology and nonhumans, as less a turn than an ongoing realignment of intensities, an apparent shift in the pattern of relations, interests, foci, and terms. Nevertheless, this shift, characterized here as a return to things, would necessarily not be any simple return, for things would have to take part in what is happening. Put differently, the supposed object of inquiry—things—is itself part of the intricate web of relations giving rise to our contemporary foci. This renders things doubly rhetorical for our purposes. That is, things are not only rhetorical in the sense explored so well in the essays collected here, where we see things emerge as vital, active players in a wide spectrum of everyday activities, but also in the sense that things are involved in why we are considering them anew in the first place.

We might then say that a return to things is doubled, just as the rhetorical thing is doubled. A return to things that sees them as rhetorical renders them agential and at the same time elevates their status. This amounts to an epideictic to things, sometimes subtle, sometimes overt. Jeffrey Walker points out that such epideictic speech was part of rhetoric's origination in ancient Greece and included not only forms of praise and blame but also more elevated speech that oftentimes dealt with questions of high import, including philosophical issues, suitable for presentation (Walker 7). An investigation of the rhetorical thing is a subtle form of praise, then, and is itself rhetorical—and thus, the praise, since it must involve more than humans, is itself a form of things doing things with things.

One might object that this sounds like a sophism, in the pejorative sense. But I wonder if we cannot see similar projects already ongoing, including those outside academia, which would suggest that things are themselves somehow—and rhetorically—integral to their emergence in a new light. The rise of contemporary art movements such as glitch art suggests precisely this. Still, things emerge and participate in their ecological webs in accordance with what they are; anthropomorphizing things is not helpful. To respond to whatever is rhetorical about them must then need a kind of attunement. My wager is that glitch art is a good example of a trajectory that responds to and pursues such attunement. Glitch art is an awakening to the thing, in particular its complex participation in the social, equipmental, and environmental webs of contemporary life. It awakens by foregrounding the technologies and their roles in production and reproduction. Here, I would like to consider the recent work of Philip Stearns, whose project, *Evident Materials*, materially demonstrates the rhetoricity of technologies and material entities.

The *Augenblick*: the blink of an eye. In a flash something is revealed, is made. It leaves its imprint—residual ghosts of color and line and shape. The eye reveals the world that shapes the I, like a camera reveals the world for the film to show. This is an old trope. I can hear it on my 1980 Yes album, *Drama*: "I am a camera." We think it means that the world impresses itself upon us—that, through the senses, thing and world reveal themselves. We take shape within such revelation, make ourselves and are in turn made through this interplay.

The camera is a technology. Humans made it as an extension of the eye, one that takes what the world offers and reduplicates its image on film. But in the Yes song, the camera's essence in turn becomes a thought: I-ness is camera-like. One interpretation of this is that who we are is the internalization of symbols—a reification of a representational paradigm. But perhaps there is another way to understand it. There is an ancient tradition for the intermixture of thought and technical essence. We think that thought, such as philosophy, comes when we have time for reflection, leisure. We consider it, in this sense, an epistemological matter, something achieved via human enterprise wresting it from the world. But perhaps thought rather comes, as David Rothenberg suggests, in our forms of living which are also forms of transformation of the world (3). No wonder, then, that when we think, we look to technology, pulling from its forms and artifacts words to express the world. Hence the puzzlement over Heraclitus's famous cosmological statement: "They do not comprehend how, in differing, it [the cosmos] agrees with itself—a backward turning connection, like that of a bow and lyre" (Fr. B51). We see that the technologies of bow and lyre work via a tension, and this tension in turn characterizes the essence of the universe. In the technology, always at work, there is also a *logos* waiting to be spoken.[1] The word Heraclitus uses for bow is *bios*, which also means life. Another tension, between a thing and living life, or between what is human and what is nonhuman. But this tension, never relieved, nevertheless characterizes the cosmos itself.

Cosmology seems to speak grandly, but it is equally part of our everyday. The word, *logos*, conjoins with the world, *cosmos*. Artistry emerges within this conjoining. We are accustomed to understanding how it symbolizes, allegorizes, and affects. Certainly, art does this. But at the same time, as Rothenberg suggests, technology is inseparable from artifice, from the whole order of art. This comes as little surprise to those of a rhetorical bent, as rhetoric has ever wrestled with the question of art versus skill. But the point here is that artifice has a material dimension. As Heidegger says, art has to be more than a substratum for ideas, images, and feelings. The artly character of the art is inseparable from its material instantiation (*Poetry* 19–20). But we also thereby come back around to a materially ambient point: the thing takes part in its own expression. Epideictics to the material thing are already part of how we do things with things. And we see this point made materially in Stearns's artwork.[2]

Stearns's *Evident Materials* artwork is made by shooting electricity through film stock doused in various household chemicals. The process is itself striking. In a flash something is revealed, is made. Fifteen thousand volts of electricity flow into a piece of film, sparking, charring, marking. We have an assemblage of artist, equipment, and medium that bears the traces of those forces interacting with film, chemicals, atmosphere. We are asked to see the electricity as what Jane Bennett would call a "vital force," something active and dynamic assembled with other elements and orchestrated so as to leave particular traces (*Vibrant Matter* 24). The print shows these traces, both interior and exterior to its frame.

The print shows itself as a thing, a technical thing, accomplished through the orchestration and interaction of forces and materials. Whence comes the artly character of a thing? Heidegger would say art is "the truth of beings setting itself to work" (*Poetry* 36). By truth, Heidegger means the manifold disclosure that brings something to be what it is. What is disclosed here is the very dynamism of the process.[3] The material manifestation of the artwork emerges from a cradle of forces and materials, deeply interlocked and networked. As Graham Harman puts it, even the smallest item is "shipwrecked in an environment" of other things (*Towards* 25). In this sense, while the print may be a reproduction of a more originary material instantiation, nothing here is actually reproduced. As Paul Klee famously says, art does not reproduce, it makes visible. The art flows out, and in so flowing, lights up. As it was assembled from a variety of elements, so too its artly character now shows in how it assembles us as part of the work of its disclosure. We tend to forget that the artwork is a material thing, vital in its own right, that "throws its weight around in the world," orienting and shaping us in turn (Harman, *Towards* 25). It is not something that transcends its form, as if there were mundane materials here, artful meanings there. Its disclosive power is that of connection and entanglement: it gathers us viewers, the space around us, the words and beliefs that give art to us as something we seek, and the complex mystery of a world that grants us pathways and material for its making and circulation.

The artist, says Timothy Ingold, has developed a knowledge of substances. The artwork discloses this history of a long travelling with things and ideas. This would seem to mean that the artwork is finally the product of its creator. But when we assert this, we miss what the materials, in their quietude, light up. They illuminate how we are laced into a dense stitchwork of things that make us what we are. The *Augenblick* reveals a moment where a new disclosure can happen—that we ourselves, no different than the artist, are, as Ingold suggests, "following the materials" (*Being Alive* 213). The artwork does not reproduce, even as a reproduction. The artwork materializes a dynamic series of interactions that give us a glimpse of our story, that show us our deep interconnection with and interpenetration by media, technology, and tools, no less than the bustling social body itself. The artwork is evidence of our fundamental entanglement, given to us piecemeal and gradually, in layers, connections, and trajectories. It asks us to follow the materials, to reflect on the forces and flows momentarily stayed in the print even as they reach out and beyond.

If something lasts, if there is something secure about the object buoying it up amidst the flow that would dissolve such distinctions, it is, Ingold suggests, because of contrary forces of friction that materials exert on one another as they are more tightly interwoven (*Being Alive* 218). I like the specificity of Ingold's insight that thingness is a dynamic and not an inertia, but it might also remind us of Heraclitus: the cosmos, at variance with itself, also agrees with itself, like a bow or lyre. Thus, the artwork stammers a contradiction, offering itself as a simple thing when it is a kinetic complex of energy and matter, congruence and divergence, human and nonhuman. These polarities illuminate the conditions of possibility for who we are and how we live together as we do. Thus, as Heidegger will finally say, the artwork opens up a world (*Poetry* 42). The world it opens up is not a static one. It is not an image or a discourse. It is not a world at a remove, a representation. Nor is it only a world of sociality, of ideas, relations, mores, and feelings. It includes these things, but only as a continuation of the material world—from the shoes treading the floor of the building we inhabit to the phone in our hand connecting us to the family member in the car, from the satellites channeling our communications to the drones striking fear and hate overseas, from the medicine providing the sick with relief to the profits driving the corporate maker . . . and on it goes. Our dense ecology of life is telling us, if we can but catch a snip of its deep arcane speaking, that we are not everything, that all that we take for granted and ignore gets into us, becomes us, transforms us, even as we think we are in control.

The artist assembles the work as an orchestrator, driven by what is known and unknown, by joy and fear. The artist creatively responds to and coincides with the vital particularity of things: electricity, film, chemicals, equipment, intuitions, and ideas. But the things, rhetorical themselves, in turn spark us. When the human and nonhuman wantonly intermix, it introduces the nonhuman into art. Is this an irony? For it is the case that we so paradoxically understand *art* as a key marker for what makes the human *human*. Paleolithic cave and rock art the world over fascinates us all perhaps for this reason over all else. Artifice beyond the tool becomes the threshold whereby we enjoy the sense of humanness bequeathed us. But Lascaux and all the other sites are nothing without caves and darkness, shamanistic technics and trips into the transcendent, spirituality and a society, animals and ecology. Without, that is, a deep stitchwork of relations among bodies, consciousness, life, tools, technologies, and environments. If too often we think of artists, or even ourselves, as makers, we might see instead how making is also a response to the potentialities of materials. That is to say, Paleolithic peoples, no less than we, were finding the paths that the world opened up for them. Their artwork is an epideictic to things no less than anything else, and in so elevating, that artwork speaks its own rhetoricity. In this sense, across the millennia, that art attunes us still. Marker of the human, yes—but the human in a world, part of the world, inseparable from the world, beworlded and bethinged. The strangeness of their art is the strangeness this awakening still evokes.

In the *Augenblick* the materials offer a different trajectory for reflection and context. Film, as the medium for the photograph, we have always taken to reproduce the world for us, but here film projects otherwise—as a material link in a larger assemblage, bearing traces that open the world differently to us, opening a crack in the techno-biological ecology of modern life. It is both the closest and most obvious that we thereby neglect, and the farthest and most grandiose that we sneak upon with awe and fear. We dwell in this world, and in so dwelling, bedazzled by our everyday, we forget what is most plain before us, until perhaps we are drawn by the artwork to follow what is there. "I am a camera" becomes "We are an ecology"—of people, of things, of environs, of forces and material that elude us yet shape us.

The essays collected here are not artworks, at least in the populist sense. But they are artifice—they wield language in such fashion as to awaken us to what is most plain before us. It is to be hoped that they spark new conversations, as perhaps is the hope of all scholarly work. But there is, I think, another hope, that things might show up for us differently. However, this requires a further remark. Every realignment of scholarly energies and foci produces objections, digressions, and resistance. So too with interest in materialism. The attempt to spark a new attuning to things has been read by some as a turning away from the social and from social problems, including inequality, prejudice, and injustice. But nothing could be further from the truth. Rather, it is a deepening appreciation for society's material entanglement, and how its manifold forms of rhetoricity occasion us in ways we know and do not know. Which is to say, an appreciation for the rhetorical thing goes hand in hand with an appreciation for, or perhaps a humbleness concerning, what we cannot know, since ontology is never reducible to epistemology. And while there may be an ethic here, the larger point is that the challenge is not to single out a particular framework but to spur another sensitivity, a different attunement, and to crack open a few of the illusions of the certainty enwrapping our lives, by means of a new concreteness. This concreteness makes room by inviting the world back into who we are; or perhaps it simply awakens the world already in us, in a newly recursive manner. As Rothenberg suggests, this includes the explanatory power of what we construct (3). But this power can be extended, into the heart of whatever rhetoric, and perhaps even the human, might be. Thus, this concreteness opens up vistas themselves inseparable from our making and doing. We do not follow these vistas, exactly, but rather achieve them through our own participation in what gets cracked open, and what gets assembled. And what will have marked this collection, we hope, will be the paths still to be hollowed out, but perhaps aided by the plateaus raised up here.

Notes

1. Innumerable contemporary examples of technology becoming thought can be found, from the widespread idea that the brain functions in a computer-like manner to the Stooges' record I was listening to last night, where Iggy Pop proclaims that "she's got a TV eye me." The Heraclitus example, because of its age, further suggests that thought and technics are fundamentally entwined, and have always been so, but that idea cannot be further pursued here. However, it is explored in Bernard Stiegler's work, albeit quite differently than I sketch here; see *Technics and Time, 1: The Fault of Epimetheus*.

2. Visual examples of the *Evident Materials* series can be found online. There are some at the artist's website, with further links to follow: https://phillipstearns.wordpress.com/category/projects/installation/

3. Casey Boyle's essay on glitch art explores these ideas in even more detail, showing how "glitch is an ongoing practice of affirming the multiple relations available in any given moment of mediation; it is an ongoing practice of speculating 'what comes next'" (28). This "what comes next," as we shall see, directly applies here, and to this collection as a whole.

Works Cited

Adam, Barbara. *Time*. Cambridge, UK: Polity, 2004.
Ahmed, Sarah. "Orientations Matter." *New Materialisms: Ontology, Agency, and Politics*. Ed. Diana Coole and Samantha Frost. Durham: Duke UP, 2010. 234–57.
———. *Queer Phenomenology: Orientations, Objects, Others*. Duke UP, 2006.
Akrich, Madeline. "The De-Scription of Technical Objects." *Shaping Technology/Building Society: Studies in Sociotechnical Change*. Eds. Wiebe Bijker and John Law. Cambridge: MIT P, 1994. 205–24.
Alaimo, Stacy, and Susan Heckman, eds. *Material Feminisms*. Bloomington: Indiana UP, 2008.
American Diabetes Association. "Standards of Medical Care for Patients with Diabetes Mellitus (Position Statement)." *Diabetes Care 24* (2001): S33–S43.
Anderson, Leon. "Analytic Autoethnography." *Journal of Contemporary Ethnography* 35 (2006): 373–95.
Anderson, Robert S. "The Lacey Act: America's Premier Weapon in the Fight against Unlawful Wildlife Trafficking." *Public Law* 16.28 (1995): 27–85.
Anzaldúa, Gloria. *Borderlands : The New Mestiza=La Frontera*. San Francisco: Spinsters/Aunt Lute, 1987.
Arendt, Hannah. *The Human Condition*. Chicago: U of Chicago P, 1958.
Aristotle. Metaphysics. Trans. W. D. Ross. The Complete Works of Aristotle Vol. 2. Ed. Jonathan Barnes. Princeton: Princeton UP Bollingen Series LXXI 2. 1552–1728. Print.
———. *On Rhetoric: A Theory of Civic Discourse*, 2nd Ed. Trans. George A. Kennedy. New York: Oxford UP, 2007.
Arnold, Jeanne, Anthony Graesch, Enzo Ragazzini, and Elinor Ochs. *Life at Home in the Twenty-First Century: 32 Families Open Their Doors*. Los Angeles: Cotsen Institute of Archaeology P, 2012.
Atkinson, Paul. "Rescuing Autoethnography." *Journal of Contemporary Ethnography* 35 (2006): 400–403.
Azim, Eiman, Dean Mobbs, Booil Jo, Vinod Menon, and Allan L. Reiss. "Sex Differ-

ences in Brain Activation Elicited by Humor." *Proceedings of the National Academy of Science of the United States of America* 102.45 (2005): 16496–16501.

Babbitts, Judith. "Stereographs and the Construction of a Visual Culture in the United States." *Memory Bytes: History, Technology, and Digital Culture.* Ed. Lauren Rabinovitz and Abraham Geil. Durham: Duke UP, 2004. 126–49.

Bak, Meredith A. "Democracy and Discipline: Object Lessons and the Stereoscope in American Education, 1870–1920." *Early Popular Visual Culture* 10.2 (2012): 147–67.

Bakhtin, Mikhail. "Forms of Time and of the Chronotope in the Novel." *The Dialogic Imagination.* Austin: U of Texas P, 1981. 84–258.

Bandura, Albert, and Edwin A. Locke. "Negative Self-Efficacy and Goal Effects Revisited." *Journal of Applied Psychology* 88.1 (2003): 87.

Banfield, Ann. *The Phantom Table: Woolf, Fry, Russell, and Epistemology of Modernism.* New York: Cambridge UP, 2000.

Barad, Karen. *Meeting the Universe Halfway.* Durham: Duke UP, 2007.

———. "Posthuman Performativity: Toward an Understanding of How Matter Comes to Matter." *Signs* 28.3 (Spring 2003): 801–31.

Bardini, Thierry. *Bootstrapping: Douglas Engelbart, Coevolution, and the Origins of Personal Computing.* Stanford: Stanford UP, 2000.

Barikin, Amelia. *Parallel Presents: The Art of Pierre Huyghe.* Cambridge: MIT P, 2012.

Barnett, Scot. "Toward an Object-Oriented Rhetoric." *Enculturation* 7 (2010): n. pag. Web. 9 February 2013.

Baron, Dennis. "From Pencils to Pixels: The Stages of Literacy Technologies." *Passions, Pedagogies, and 21st Century Technologies.* Eds. Gail E. Hawisher and Cynthia L. Selfe. Logan: Utah State UP, 1999. 15–33.

Barthes, Roland. *Camera Lucida: Reflections on Photography.* Trans. Richard Howard. New York: Hill and Wang, 1981.

Bartholomae, David. "Inventing the University." *Cross-Talk in Comp Theory*, 2nd ed. Ed. Victor Villanueva. Urbana: NCTE, 2003. 623–53.

Barton, David. *Literacy: An Introduction to the Ecology of Written Language.* Oxford, UK; Cambridge: Blackwell, 1994.

Barton, David, Mary Hamilton, and Roz Ivanič. *Situated Literacies: Reading and Writing in Context.* New York: Routledge, 2000.

Bay, Jennifer, and Thomas Rickert. "New Media and the Fourfold." *JAC* 28.1–2 (2008): 207–44.

Becker, Howard S. "Stereographs: Local, National, and International Art Worlds." *Points of View: The Stereograph in America—A Cultural History.* Ed. Richard Earle. Rochester: The Visual Studies Workshop P, 1979. 89–96.

Belk, Russell W. "Possessions and the Extended Self." *Journal of Consumer Research* 15.2 (1988): 139–68.

Bennett, Jane. "The Force of Things: Steps Toward an Ecology of Matter." *Political Theory* 32.3 (2004): 347–72.

———. "Powers of the Hoard." *Animal, Vegetable, Mineral: Ethics and Objects.* Ed. Jeffrey Jerome Cohen. Washington, DC: Oliphaunt, 2012. 237–69.

———. *Vibrant Matter: A Political Ecology of Things*. Durham: Duke UP, 2010.
Benson, Thomas W. "Rhetoric as a Way of Being." *American Rhetoric: Context and Criticism*. Ed. Benson. Carbondale: Southern Illinois UP, 1989. 293–322.
Berkson, Joseph. "Tests of Significance Considered as Evidence." *Journal of the American Statistical Association* 37.219: 325–35.
Berlin, James A. *Rhetoric and Reality: Writing Instruction in American Colleges 1900–1985*. Carbondale: Southern Illinois UP, 1987.
Bernard-Donals, Michael. "Conflations of Memory or, What They Saw at the Holocaust Museum after 9/11." *CR: The New Centennial Review* 5.2 (2005): 73–106.
Bernard-Donals, Michael, and Richard R. Glejzer, eds. *Rhetoric in an Antifoundational World: Language, Culture, and Pedagogy*. New Haven: Yale UP, 1998.
Berthoff, Ann E. *Forming Thinking Writing: The Composing Imagination*. Montclair, NJ: Boynton/Cook, 1982.
———. *The Making of Meaning: Metaphors, Models, and Maxims for Writing Teachers*. Montclair: Boynton/Cook. 1981.
Berthoff, Ann E., and James Stephens. *Forming Thinking Writing*. 2nd ed. Portsmouth, NH: Boynton/Cook, 1988.
Biesecker, Barbara, and John Luis Lucaites, eds. *Rhetoric, Materiality, and Politics*. New York: Peter Lang, 2009.
Bitzer, Lloyd. "The Rhetorical Situation." *Philosophy and Rhetoric* 1.1 (1968): 1–14.
Blair, Carole. "Contemporary U.S. Memorial Sites as Exemplars of Rhetoric's Materiality." *Rhetorical Bodies*. Eds. Jack Selzer and Sharon Crowley. Madison: U of Wisconsin P, 1999.
Blair, Carole, Martha S. Jeppeson, and Enrico Pucci Jr. "Public Memorializing in Postmodernity: The Vietnam Veterans Memorial as Prototype." *Quarterly Journal of Speech* 77 (1991): 263–88.
Blair, Carole, and Neil Michel. "The Rhetorical Performances of the Civil Rights Memorial." *Rhetoric Society Quarterly* 30:2 (2000), 31–55.
Bogost, Ian. *Alien Phenomenology, or What It's Like to Be a Thing*. Minneapolis: U of Minnesota P, 2012.
———. "Seeing Things." *Ian Bogost, n.p.* Web. 14 September 2011.
Boyle, Casey. "The Rhetorical Question Concerning Glitch." *Computers and Composition*. 35 (2015): 12–29.
Boym, Svetlana. *The Future of Nostalgia*. New York: Basic Books, 2001.
Braidotti, Rosi. "The Politics of 'Life Itself' and the New Ways of Dying." *New Materialisms: Ontology, Agency, and Politics*. Eds. Diana Coole and Samantha Frost. Dunham: Duke UP, 2010. 201–18.
Brand, Alice Glarden. *The Psychology of Writing: The Affective Experience*. New York: Greenwood, 1989.
Brandt, Deborah. *Literacy in American Lives*. New York: Cambridge UP, 2001.
———. "Remembering Writing, Remembering Reading." *College Composition and Communication* 45.4 (1994): 459–79.
Brandt, Deborah, and Katie Clinton. "Limits of the Local: Expanding Perspectives on Literacy as a Social Practice." *Journal of Literacy Research* 34.3 (2002): 337–56.

Brewster, David. *The Stereoscope: Its History, Theory, and Construction.* Facsimile Ed. Hastings-on-Hudson, NY: Morgan and Morgan, 1971.

Brodkey, Linda. "Modernism and the Scene(s) of Writing." *College English* 49.4 (1987): 396–418.

Brooke, Collin Gifford. "Forgetting to Be (Post)Human: Media and Memory in the Kairotic Age." *JAC* 20.4 (2000): 775–95.

———. *Lingua Fracta: Towards a Rhetoric of New Media.* Cresskill, NJ: Hampton P, 2009.

Brummett, Barry. "Some Implications of 'Process' or 'Intersubjectivity': Postmodern Rhetoric." *Philosophy and Rhetoric* 9 (1976): 21–51.

Bryant, Levi. *The Democracy of Objects.* Ann Arbor: Open Humanities P, 2011.

Burke, Kenneth. "The Definition of Man." *Language as Symbolic Action: Essays on Life, Literature, and Method.* Berkeley: U of California P, 1966. 3–24.

Butler, Judith. *Excitable Speech: A Politics of the Performative.* New York: Routledge, 1997.

———. *Gender Trouble.* New York: Routledge, 1990.

Cahill, Larry. "His Brain, Her Brain." *Scientific American* 292.5 (2005): 40–47.

Callon, Michel. "Writing and (Re)writing Devices as Tools for Managing Complexity." *Complexities: Social Studies of Knowledge Practices.* Eds. Annemarie Mol and John Law. Durham: Duke UP, 2002. 191–217.

Callon, Michel, and Jean-Pierre Vignolle. "Breaking Down the Organization: Local Conflict and Societal Systems of Action." *Social Science Information* 16.2 (1977): 147–67.

Callon, Michel, and John Law. "Agency and the Hybrid Collectif." *South Atlantic Quarterly* 94.2 (1995): 481–507.

———. "On Interests and Their Transformation: Enrolment and Counter-Enrolment." *Social Studies of Science* 12.4 (1982): 615–25.

Callon, Michael, Pierre Lascoumes, and Yannick Barthe. *Acting in an Uncertain World: An Essay on Technical Democracy.* Cambridge: MIT P, 2011.

Campbell, Karlyn Kohrs. "The Ontological Foundations of Rhetorical Theory." *Philosophy and Rhetoric* 3 (1970): 97–108.

"Capital Bicycle Club Records." Washingtonia Collection. Public Library. Washington, DC.

Casselman, Anne. "Women Don't Understand." *Discover Magazine* 27.2 (2006): 14. Web. 01 July 2013.

Castells, Manuel. *The Rise of the Network Society (The Information Age: Economy, Society and Culture, Volume 1).* Malden, MA: Blackwell P, 1996.

Chaplin, Elizabeth. "The Photo Diary as an Autoethnographic Method." *The Sage Handbook of Visual Research Methods.* Eds. Eric Margolis and Luc Pauwels. London: Sage, 2011. 241–62.

Cherwitz, Richard A., and James Hikins. "Rhetorical Perspectivism." *Quarterly Journal of Speech* 69 (1983): 249–66.

Cherwitz, Richard A., and Thomas J. Darwin. "Toward a Relational Theory of Meaning." *Philosophy of Rhetoric* 28.1 (1996): 313–29.

Christakis, Nicholas A., and James H. Fowler. "The Spread of Obesity in a Large Social Network over 32 years." *New England Journal of Medicine* 357.4 (2007): 370–79.
Clark, Andy. *Natural-Born Cyborgs: Minds, Technologies, and the Future of Human Intelligence*. New York: Oxford UP, 2004.
Clemens, Samuel. SLC to Densmore, Yost and Company. 19 Mar. 1875. Web.
Cohen, Jacob. "The Earth Is Round (p < .05)." *American Psychologist* 49.12 (1994): 997–1003.
Coleman, Katie, et al. "Evidence on the Chronic Care Model in the New Millennium." *Health Affairs* 28.1 (2009): 75–85.
Condit, Celeste. "How Bad Science Stays That Way: Brain Sex, Demarcation, and the Status of Truth in the Rhetoric of Science." *Rhetoric Society Quarterly* 26.4 (1996): 83–109.
———. "Race and Genetics from a Modal Materialist Perspective." *Quarterly Journal of Speech* 94.4 (2008): 386–406.
Coole, Diana, and Samantha Frost. "Introducing the New Materialisms." *New Materialisms: Ontology, Agency, and Politics*. Eds. Coole and Frost. Durham: Duke UP, 2010. 1–43.
Coole, Diana, and Samantha Frost, eds. *New Materialisms: Ontology, Agency, and Politics*. Durham: Duke UP, 2010.
Cooper, Marilyn M. "The Ecology of Writing." *College English* 48.4 (1986): 364.
———. "Rhetorical Agency as Emergent and Enacted." *College Composition and Communication* 62 (2011): 420–49.
Cowley, Malcolm, ed. *Writers at Work: The Paris Review Interviews*, 1st Series. New York: Penguin, 1977.
Crary, Jonathan. *Techniques of the Observer: On Vision and Modernity in the Nineteenth Century*. Cambridge: MIT P, 1992.
Crick, Nathan. *Democracy and Rhetoric: John Dewey on the Arts of Becoming*. Columbia: U of South Carolina P, 2010.
Crowley, Sharon. *Toward a Civil Discourse: Rhetoric and Fundamentalism*. Pittsburgh: U of Pittsburgh P, 2006.
Csikszentmihalyi, Mihaly. "Why We Need Things." *History from Things: Essays on Material Culture*. Eds. Steven D. Lubar and David Kingery. Washington: Smithsonian Institution P, 1993. 20–29.
Csikszentmihalyi, Mihaly, and Eugene Rochberg-Halton. *The Meaning of Things: Domestic Symbols and the Self*. New York: Cambridge UP, 1981.
Darrah, William C. *The World of Stereographs*. Nashville: Land Yacht P, 1997.
Davis, Diane. "Creaturely Rhetorics." *Philosophy and Rhetoric* 44.1 (2009): 88–94.
———. *Inessential Solidarity: Rhetoric and Foreigner Relations*. Pittsburgh: U of Pittsburgh P, 2010.
Davis, Diane, and Michelle Ballif. "Guest Editors' Introduction: Pushing the Limits of the *Anthropos*." *Philosophy and Rhetoric* 47.4 (2014): 346–53.
De Castro, Eduardo Viveiros. "Exchanging Perspectives: The Transformation of Objects into Subjects in Amerindian Ontologies." *Common Knowledge* 10.3 (2004): 463–484.

238 / WORKS CITED

Deetz, James. *In Small Things Forgotten: The Archaeology of Early American Life.* Garden City, NY: Anchor Press/Doubleday, 1977.

Delanda, Manuel. *A New Philosophy of Society: Assemblage Theory and Social Complexity.* New York: Continuum, 2006.

Deleuze, Gilles. *Cinema 2: The Time-Image.* Trans. Hugh Tomlinson and Robert Galeta. Minneapolis: U of Minnesota P, 1989.

———. *Difference and Repetition.* Trans. P. Patton. New York: Columbia UP, 1995.

Deleuze, Gilles, and Felix Guattari. *A Thousand Plateaus.* Trans. Brian Massumi. Minneapolis: U of Minnesota P, 1987.

Delicath, John W., and Kevin Michael Deluca. "Image Events, the Public Sphere, and Argumentative Practice: The Case of Radical Environmental Groups." *Argumentation* 17 (2006): 315–33.

de Romilly, Jacqueline. *Magic and Rhetoric in Ancient Greece.* Cambridge: Harvard UP, 1975.

Derrida, Jacques. *Dissemination.* Trans. Barbara Johnson. Chicago: U of Chicago P, 1981.

———."Signature, Event, Context." *Margins of Philosophy.* Trans. Alan Bass. Chicago: U of Chicago P, 1982. 307–30.

———. *Specters of Marx: The State of Debt, the Work of Mourning, and the New International.* Trans. Peggy Kamuf. New York: Routledge, 2006.

———. *Writing and Difference.* Trans. Alan Bass. Chicago: U of Chicago P, 1980.

Despret, Vinciane. "The Becomings of Subjectivity in Animal Worlds." *Subjectivity* 23 (2008): 123–39.

———. "The Body We Care For: Figures of Anthropo-zoo-genesis." *Body and Society* 10 (2004): 111–34.

——— "Sheep Do Have Opinions." *Making Things Public: Atmospheres of Democracy.* Eds. Bruno Latour and Peter Weibel. Cambridge: MIT P, 2005. 360–68.

Dewey, Ryan. "Human Cognition and Lamb 86 at Alinea—An Encounter with Basic Human Categorization." *Kitchen Cognition.* Web. 13 Sept. 2013.

Diamond, Jared. "The Curse of QWERTY | DiscoverMagazine.com." *Discover Magazine.* Web. 13 Sept. 2013.

Dickinson, Greg, Carole Blair, and Brian L. Ott, eds. *Places of Public Memory: The Rhetoric of Museums and Memorials.* Tuscaloosa: U of Alabama P, 2010.

Dobrin, Sidney I., and Christopher J. Keller. *Writing Environments.* Albany: SUNY P, 2005.

———. *Natural Discourse Toward Ecocomposition.* Albany: SUNY P, 2002.

Dodge, Pryor. *The Bicycle.* Flammarion: New York, 1997.

Duncan, Margot. "Autoethnography: Critical Appreciation of an Emerging Art." *International Journal of Qualitative Methods* 3.4 (2004): 28–39.

Eagly, Alice H., and Wendy Wood. "Feminism and the Evolution of Sex Differences and Similarities." *Sex Roles* 64.9–12 (2011): 758–67.

Earle, Edward W. "The Stereograph in America: Pictorial Antecedents and Cultural Perspectives." *Points of View: The Stereograph in America—A Cultural History.* Ed. Edward W. Earle. Rochester: The Visual Studies Workshop P, 1979. 9–21.

———, ed. *Points of View: The Stereograph in America—A Cultural History*. Rochester: The Visual Studies Workshop P, 1979.
Edbauer, Jenny. "Unframing Models of Public Distribution: From Rhetorical Situation to Rhetorical Ecologies." *Rhetoric Society Quarterly* 35.4 (2005): 5–24.
Ehses, Hanno H. J. "Representing Macbeth: A Case Study in Visual Rhetoric." *Design Issues* 1.1 (1984): 53–63.
Ellis, Shelley E., et al. "Diabetes Patient Education: A Meta-Analysis and Meta-Regression." *Patient Education and Counseling* 52.1 (2004): 97–105.
Emig, Janet A. *The Composing Processes of Twelfth Graders*. Urbana: NCTE, 1971.
Enoch, Jessica. "Finding New Spaces for Rhetorical Research." *Rhetoric Review* 30.2: 115–17.
Epp, Amber M., and Linda L. Price. "Family Identity: A Framework of Identity Interplay in Consumption Practices." *Journal of Consumer Research* 35.1 (2008): 50–70.
———. "The Storied Life of Singularized Objects: Forces of Agency and Network Transformation." *Journal of Consumer Research* 36.5 (2010): 820–37.
"Fact Sheet: BRAIN Initiative." 02 April 2013. Web. 01 June 2013.
Fahnestock, Jeanne. "Accommodating Science: The Rhetorical Life of Scientific Facts." *Written Communication* 3.3 (1986): 275–96.
———. *Rhetorical Figures in Science*. Oxford: Oxford UP, 1999.
Farrell, Thomas. "Knowledge, Consensus, and Rhetorical Theory." *Quarterly Journal of Speech* 62 (1976): 1–14.
Fausto-Sterling, Anne. *Sexing the Body: Gender Politics and the Construction of Sexuality*. New York: Basic Books, 2000.
Finders, Margaret J. *Just Girls: Hidden Literacies and Life in Junior High*. New York: Teachers College P, 1997.
Fine, Cordelia. "From Scanner to Sound Bite: Issues in Interpreting and Reporting Sex Differences in the Brain." *Current Directions in Psychological Science* 19.5 (2010): 280–283.
Finnegan, Cara. "Recognizing Lincoln: Image Vernaculars in Nineteenth Century Visual Culture." *Rhetoric and Public Affairs* 8 (Spring 2005): 31–58.
Fish, Stanley. *Doing What Comes Naturally: Change, Rhetoric, and the Practice of Theory in Literary and Legal Studies*. Durham: Duke UP, 1989.
Fisher, R. A. "Studies in Crop Variation." *Journal of Agricultural Science* 11 (1921): 107–35.
Fiumara, Gemma Corradi. *The Other Side of Language: A Philosophy of Listening*. London: Routledge, 1990.
Fleming, David. "Becoming Rhetorical: An Education in the Topics." *The Realms of Rhetoric: Inquiries into the Prospects for Rhetoric Education*. Eds. Deepika Bahri and Joseph Petraglia. Albany: SUNY P, 2003. 93–116.
Foss, Sonja K., and Cindy L. Griffin. "Beyond Persuasion: A Proposal for an Invitational Rhetoric." *Communication Monographs* 62.1 (1995): 2–18.
Foucault, Michel. "What Is an Author?" *The Essential Foucault*. Eds. Paul Rabinow and Nikolas Rose. New York: The New Press, 2003. 377–91.

Fowles, Jib. "Stereography and the Standardization of Vision." *Journal of American Cultures* 17.2 (Summer 1994): 89–93.
Fuss, Diana. *The Sense of an Interior: Four Rooms and the Writers That Shaped Them.* New York: Routledge, 2004.
Gagarin, Michael. "Did the Sophists Aim to Persuade?" *Rhetorica* 19.3 (2001): 275–91.
Gardner, Howard. "Keyboards." *Evocative Objects: Things We Think With.* Ed. Sherry Turkle. Cambridge, MA: MIT P, 2011.
Garsten, Bryan. *Saving Persuasion: A Defense of Rhetoric and Judgment.* Cambridge: Harvard UP, 2006.
Gere, Ann Ruggles "Kitchen Tables and Rented Rooms: The Extracurriculum of Composition." *College Composition and Communication* 45.1 (1994): 75–92.
Gingerenzer, Gerd. "Surrogates for Theories." *Theory and Psychology* 8.2 (1998): 195–204.
Glassie, Henry H. *Folk Housing in Middle Virginia: A Structural Analysis of Historic Artifacts.* Knoxville: U of Tennessee P, 1975.
Glenn, Cheryl. *Rhetoric Retold: Regendering the Tradition from Antiquity through the Renaissance.* Carbondale: Southern Illinois UP, 1997.
Goodman, Steven. "Toward Evidence-Based Medical Statistics. 2: The Bayes Factor." *Annals of Internal Medicine* 130 (1999): 1005–1013.
Gordon, Beverly. "American Denim: Blue Jeans and Their Multiple Layers of Meaning." *Dress and Popular Culture.* Eds. Patricia A. Cunningham and Susan Voso Lab. Bowling Green: Bowling Green State U Popular P, 1991.
Graham, S. Scott. "Agency and the Rhetoric of Medicine: Biomedical Brain Scans and the Ontology of Fibromyalgia." *Technical Communication Quarterly* 18.4 (2009): 376–404.
———. *The Politics of Pain Medicine: A Rhetorical-Ontological Inquiry.* Chicago: U of Chicago P, 2015.
Graham, S. Scott, and Brandon Whalen. "Mode, Medium, and Genre: A Case Study in New Media Design Decisions." *Journal of Business and Technical Communication* 22.1, 65–91. 2008.
Graham, S. Scott, and Carl G. Herndl. "Multiple Ontologies in Pain Management: Towards a Postplural Rhetoric of Science." *Technical Communication Quarterly* 22.2 (2013): 103–25.
Graves, Heather Brodie. "Rhetoric and Reality in the Process of Scientific Inquiry." *Rhetoric Review* 14.1 (1995): 106–25.
Green, Bill. *Water, Ice, and Stone: Science and Memory of the Antarctic Lakes.* New York: Crown, 1995.
Green, Harvey. "'Pasteboard Masks': The Stereograph in American Culture 1865–1910." *Points of View: The Stereograph in America—A Cultural History.* Ed. Edward W. Earl. Rochester: The Visual Studies Workshop P, 1979. 109–15.
Gross, Alan G. *Starring the Text: The Place of Rhetoric in Science Studies.* Carbondale: Southern Illinois UP, 2006.
Gross, Allen, and Keith, William, eds. *Rhetorical Hermeneutics: Invention and Interpretation in the Age of Science.* SUNY P, 1999.

Grosz, Elizabeth. *Architecture from the Outside: Essays on Virtual and Real Space*. Cambridge: MIT P, 2001.
Gruber, David, and Jordynn Jack, Lisa Keranen, John M. McKenzie, and Matthew B. Morris. "Rhetoric and the Neurosciences: Engagement and Exploration." *POROI: The Project on Rhetoric of Inquiry* 7.1 (2011): 1–12.
Gruber, David R. "Mirror Neurons in Group Analysis 'Hall of Mirrors': Translation as a Rhetorical Approach to Neurodisciplinary Writing." *Technical Communication Quarterly*, forthcoming.
Gur, Ruben C., Lyn Harper Mozley, David Mozley, Susan M. Resnick, Joel S. Karp, Abass Alavi, Steven E. Arnold, and Raquel E. Gur. "Sex Differences in Regional Cerebral Glucose Metabolism During a Resting State." *Science* 267.5197 (1995): 528–31.
Hacking, Ian. *Historical Ontology*. Cambridge: Harvard UP, 2002.
Hallenbeck, Sarah. *Pope Manufacturing Company Handlebars, 1896*. Hagley Museum. Wilmington, Delaware. Photograph. 23 June 2008.
Halpern, Diane F. "How Neuromythologies Support Sex Role Stereotypes." *Science* 330 (2010): 1320–21.
Halpern, Diane F., Camila P. Benbow, David C. Geary, Ruben C. Gur, Janet Hyde, and Morton Ann Gernsbacher. "The Science of Sex Differences in Science and Mathematics." *Psychological Science in the Public Interest* 8.1 (2007): 1–51.
Halpern, Diane F., Lise Eliot, Rebecca S. Bigler, Richard A. Fabes, Laura D. Hanish, Janet Hyde, Lynn S. Liben, and Doreen Kimura. "Sex Differences in the Brain." *Scientific American* 12 (2002): 32–37. Web. 01 July 2013.
Halpern, Diane F., Lise Eliot, Rebecca S. Bigler, Richard A. Fabes, Laura D. Hanish, Janet Hyde, Lynn S. Liben, and Carol Lynn Martin. "The Pseudoscience of Single-Sex Schooling." *Science Magazine* 333 (2011): 1706–1707.
Haraway, Donna. *Simians, Cyborgs, and Women*. London: Routledge, 1991.
———. *When Species Meet*. Minneapolis: U of Minnesota P, 2008.
Harding, Sandra. *The Science Question in Feminism*. Ithaca: Cornell UP, 1986.
Hariman, Robert, and John Louis Lucaites. *No Caption Needed: Iconic Photographs, Public Culture, and Liberal Democracy*. Chicago: U of Chicago P, 2007.
Harman, Graham. *Guerilla Metaphysics: Phenomenology and the Carpentry of Things*. Chicago: Open Court, 2005.
———. "Latour Litanies and Gibbon." *Object-Oriented Philosophy*. 15 Dec. 2009. Web. 13 Sept. 2013.
———. "Phenomenology and the Theory of Equipment." *Towards Speculative Realism: Essays and Lectures*. Alresford: Zero Books, 2010.
———. *Prince of Networks: Bruno Latour and Metaphysics*. Melbourne: re.press, 2009.
———. *The Quadruple Object*. Alresford: Zero Books, 2011.
———. *Towards Speculative Realism: Essays and Lectures*. Alresford: Zero Books, 2010.
Hawhee, Debra. "Technology, Objects, and Things in Heidegger." *Cambridge Journal of Economics* 34 (2010): 17–25.
———. "Toward a Bestial Rhetoric." *Philosophy and Rhetoric* 44.1 (2009): 81–87.

Hawk, Byron. *A Counter-History of Composition: Toward Methodologies of Complexity.* Pittsburgh: U of Pittsburgh P, 2007.

———. "Reassembling Post-Process: Toward a Posthuman Theory of Public Rhetoric." *Beyond Post-Process.* Eds. Sidney I. Dobrin, J. A. Rice, and Michael Vastola. Logan: Utah State UP, 2011. 75–93.

Hawkins, Gay. *The Ethics of Waste: How We Relate to Rubbish.* Lanham: Rowman and Littlefield, 2006.

Hayles, N. Katherine. "Hyper and Deep Attention: The Generational Divide in Cognitive Modes." *Profession 2007* (2007): 187–99.

Heidegger, Martin. *Being and Time.* Trans. John Macquarrie and Edward Robinson. New York: Harper and Row, 1962.

———. *Being and Time.* Trans. Joan Stambaugh. Albany: SUNY Press, 2010.

———. *Poetry, Language, Thought.* Trans. Albert Hofstadter. New York: Harper and Row, 1971.

———. "The Thing." *Poetry, Language, and Thought.* Trans. Albert Hofstadter. New York: Harper and Row, 1971.

Herndl, Carl. "Rhetoric of Science as Non-Modern Practice." *Professing Rhetoric: Selected Papers from the 2000 Rhetoric Society of America Conference.* Eds. Frederick Antczak, Cinda Coggins, and Geoffrey Klinger. Mahwah: Lawrence Erlbaum, 2002. 215–22.

Hesse, Doug, Nancy Sommers, and Kathleen Blake Yancey. "Evocative Objects: Reflections on Teaching, Learning, and Living in Between." *College English* 74.4 (2012): 325–50.

Hodder, Ian. *Entangled: An Archaeology of the Relationships between Humans and Things.* West Sussex: Wiley-Blackwell, 2012.

Holder, M. K. "Why Are More People Right-handed?" *Scientific American.* Web. 13 Sept. 2013.

Holmes, Oliver Wendell. "The Stereoscope and the Stereograph." *Atlantic Monthly* 3.20 (1859): 738–48. Cornell U Library, Making of America. Web. 06 Jan. 2007.

———. "Sun-Painting and Sun-Sculpture." *Atlantic Monthly* 8.45 (1861): 13–29. Cornell U Library, Making of America. Web. 06 Jan. 2007.

Hopkins, Rob. "Who We Are." *Transition Network.* Web. 10 May 2012.

Hunt, Scott A., and Natalia Ruiz Junco. "Introduction to Two Thematic Issues: Defective Memory and Analytical Autoethnography." *Journal of Contemporary Ethnography* 35 (2006): 371–72. Web.

Hutchins, Edwin. *Cognition in the Wild.* Cambridge: MIT P, 1995.

Ingold, Tim. *Being Alive: Essays on Movement, Knowledge, and Description.* New York: Routledge, 2011.

———. "Bindings Against Boundaries: Entanglements of Life in an Open World." *Environment and Planning A* 40 (2008): 1796–1810.

"Injurious Wildlife Species; Listing the Bighead Carp (*Hypophthalmichthys nobilis*) as Injurious Fish." 50 CFR 16. 2011.

"Interpretive Chronology—Stereos, American History, and Popular Culture 1850–

1914." *Points of View: The Stereograph in America—A Cultural History*. Ed. Edward W. Earle. Rochester: The Visual Studies Workshop P, 1979. 24–87.

Ivanic, Roz. *Writing and Identity: The Discoursal Construction of Identity in Academic Writing*. Amsterdam; Philadelphia: John Benjamins, 1998.

Jack, Jordynn. "Acts of Institution: Embodying Feminist Rhetorical Methodologies in Space and Time." *Rhetoric Review* 28.3 (2009): 285–303.

Jack, Jordynn, and Gregory Appelbaum. "'This is Your Brain on Rhetoric': Research Directions for Neurorhetorics." *Rhetoric Society Quarterly* 40.5 (2010): 411–37.

Jameson, Frederic. *Postmodernism, Or, The Cultural Logic of Late Capitalism*. Durham: Duke UP, 1991.

Jarratt, Susan. *Rereading the Sophists: Classical Rhetoric Refigured*. Carbondale: Southern Illinois UP, 1991.

Johnson, Nan. *Gender and Rhetorical Space in American Life: 1866–1910*. Carbondale: Southern Illinois UP, 2002.

Jones, Taylor. *Dear Photograph*. New York: William Morrow, 2012.

Kant, Immanuel. *Critique of Pure Reason*. Trans. Werner S. Pluhar. Indianapolis: Hackett, 1996.

Keeling, Diane, and Daniel H. Kim. "Turning on the Posthuman." National Communication Association. Orlando. 17 November 2012. Lecture.

Kelly, Ashley R. and Kate Maddalena. "Harnessing Agency for Efficacy: 'Foldit' and Citizen Science." *POROI* 11.1 (2015): 1–20.

Kelly, Casey. "Women's Rhetorical Agency in the American West: The New Penelope." *Women's Studies in Communication* 32.2 (2009): 203–231.

Kennedy, George A. *Comparative Rhetorics: An Historical and Cross-Cultural Introduction*. New York: Oxford UP, 1997.

———. "A Hoot in the Dark: The Evolution of General Rhetoric." *Philosophy and Rhetoric* 25.1 (1992): 1–21.

King, Magda. *A Guide to Heidegger's* Being and Time. Ed. John Llewelyn. Albany: SUNY P, 2001.

Kittler, Friedrich A, Geoffrey Winthrop-Young, and Michael Wutz. *Gramophone, Film, Typewriter*. Stanford: Stanford UP, 1999.

Kleine, Robert E., Susan Schultz Kleine, and Jerome B. Kernan. "Mundane Consumption and the Self: A Social-Identity Perspective." *Journal of Consumer Psychology* 2.3 (1993): 209–235.

Kleine, Susan Schultz, and Stacey Menzel Baker. "An Integrative Review of Material Possession Attachment." *Academy of Marketing Science Review* 1.1 (2004): 1–39.

Kleine, Susan Schultz, Robert E. Kleine III, and Chris T. Allen. "How Is a Possession 'Me' or 'Not Me'?: Characterizing Types and an Antecedent of Material Possession Attachment." *Journal of Consumer Research* (1995): 327–43.

Koh, Howard K., et al. "A Proposed 'Health Literate Care Model' Would Constitute a Systems Approach to Improving Patients' Engagement In Care." *Health Affairs* 32.2 (2013): 357–67.

Krementz, Jill. *The Writer's Desk*. New York: Random House, 1996.

Krueger, Joachim. "Null Hypothesis Significance Testing: On the Survival of a Flawed Method." *American Psychologist* 56.1 (2001): 16–26.

Lakatos, Imre. "Falsification and the Methodology of Scientific Research Programmes." *The Methodology of Scientific Research Programmes: Imre Lakatos' Philosophical Papers (Vol. 1)*. Cambridge: Cambridge UP, 1978.

Lanham, Richard. *A Handlist of Rhetorical Terms*, 2nd ed. Berkeley: U of California P, 1991.

Larenov, Sergey. *Link to the Past*. Web. 16 April 2014.

Latour, Bruno. "From Realpolitik to Dingpolitik or How to Make Things Public." *Making Things Public: Atmospheres of Democracy*. Eds. Bruno Latour and Peter Weibel. Cambridge: MIT P, 2005. 4–31.

———. "On Actor-Network Theory: A Few Clarifications." *Soziale Welt* 47.4 (1996): 369–81.

———. "On Interobjectivity." *Mind, Culture, and Activity* 3.4 (1996): 228–45.

———. *Pandora's Hope: Essays on the Reality of Science Studies*. Cambridge: Harvard UP, 1999.

———. *Politics of Nature: How to Bring the Sciences into Democracy*. Trans. Catherine Porter. Cambridge: Harvard UP, 2004.

———. *Reassembling the Social: An Introduction to Actor-Network-Theory*. New York: Oxford UP, 2005.

———. *We Have Never Been Modern*. Trans. Catherine Porter. Cambridge: Harvard UP, 1999.

———. "A Well-Articulated Primatology: Reflections of a Fellow Traveler." *Primate Encounters: Models of Science, Gender, and Society*. Eds. Shirley C. Strum and Linda Marie Fedigan. Chicago: U Chicago P, 2000. 358–81.

———. "Why Critique Has Run Out of Steam: From Matters of Fact to Matters of Concern." *Critical Inquiry* 30.2 (2004): 225–48.

Latour, Bruno, Graham Harman, and Peter Erdélyi. *The Prince and the Wolf: Latour and Harman at the LSE*. Winchester, UK: Zero, 2011.

Latour, Bruno, and Paulo Fabbri. "The Rhetoric of Science: Authority and Duty in an Article from the Exact Sciences." *Technostyle* 16.1. 115–34. 2000.

Latour, Bruno, and Peter Weibel. *Making Things Public: Atmospheres of Democracy*, Cambridge: MIT Press, 2005. 14–41.

Latour, Bruno, and Steve Woolgar. *Laboratory Life: The Construction of Scientific Facts*. Princeton: Princeton UP, 1986.

Law, John. *Aircraft Stories: Decentering the Object in Technoscience*. Durham: Duke UP, 2002.

———. "Objects, Spaces, Others." The Centre for Science Studies. 2000. Web. 21 July 2013.

Law, John, and Annemarie Mol. "The Actor-enacted: Cumbrian Sheep in 2001." *Material Agency: Towards a Non-Anthropocentric Approach*. Eds. Lambros Malafouris and Carl Knappett. New York: Spring, 2008. 55–77.

Leard, Jefferson (jtleard). "@jamesjbrownjr so I Space Seemingly Mostly with the

Right, but Because of This I Type y with Left and Shift Exclusively Left." 9 July 2013. Web. 13 Sept. 2013.

Leff, Michael. "In Search of Ariadne's Thread: A Review of the Recent Literature on Rhetorical Theory." *Central States Speech Journal* 29 (1978): 145–52.

Liebowitz, Stan J., and Stephen E. Margolis. "The Fable of the Keys." *Journal of Law and Economics* 33.1 (1990): 1–25.

Lien, Marianne, and John Law. "Emergent Aliens: On Salmon, Nature, and their Enactment." *Ethnos: A Journal of Anthropology* 76.1 (2011): 65–87.

Lippi-Green, Rosina. *English with an Accent: Language, Ideology, and Discrimination in the United States*. London: Routledge, 1997.

Lockton, Dan, David Harrison, and Neville Stanton. "Design with Intent: Persuasive Technology in a Wider Context." *Persuasive Technology: Third International Conference, PERSUASIVE 2008, Oulu, Finland, 4–6 June 2008*. Eds. Harri Oinas-Kukkonen, Per Hasle, Marja Harjumaa, Katarina Segerståhl, Peter Øhrstrøm. New York: Springer, 2008.

Lubar, Steven D., and W. D. Kingery. *History From Things: Essays on Material Culture*. Washington, DC: Smithsonian Institution P, 1993.

Lundmark, Torbjörn. *Quirky Qwerty: The Story of the Keyboard Your Fingertips*. Coogee: NewSouth Publishing, 2002.

Lunsford, Andrea, ed. *Reclaiming Rhetorica: Women in the Rhetorical Tradition*. Pittsburgh: U of Pittsburgh P, 1995.

Lynch, John. "Articulating Scientific Practice: Understanding Dean Hamer's 'Gay Gene' Study as Overlapping Material, Social, and Rhetorical Registers." *Quarterly Journal of Speech* 95.4 (2009): 435–56.

Lynch, Kevin. *What Time Is This Place?* Cambridge: MIT P, 1972.

Lynch, Michael. "Discipline and the Material Form of Images: An Analysis of Scientific Visibility." *Social Studies of Science* 15.1 (1985): 37–66.

Lynch, Paul. "Composition's New Thing: Bruno Latour and the Apocalyptic Turn." *College English* 74.5 (2012): 458–76.

Mahiri, Jabari, and Amanda J. Godley, "Rewriting Identity: Social Meanings of Literacy and 'Re-Visions' of Self." *Reading Research Quarterly* 33.4 (1988): 416–33.

Malin, Jo, and Victoria Boynton. *Herspace: Women, Writing, and Solitude*. New York: Haworth, 2003. Print

Manovich, Lev. *The Language of New Media*. Cambridge: MIT P, 2001.

Marback, Richard. "Unclenching the Fist: Embodying Rhetoric and Giving Objects Their Due." *Rhetoric Society Quarterly* 38.1 (2008): 46–65.

Markus, Hazel, and Paula Nurius. "Possible Selves." *American Psychologist* 41.9 (1986): 954–69.

Marston, Sallie, John Paul Jones, and Keith Woodward. "Human Geography without Scale." *Transactions of the Institute of British Geographers* 30.4 (2005): 416–32.

Massey, Doreen. *For Space*. London: Sage, 2005.

Mazis, Glen A. *Humans, Animals, Machines: Blurring Boundaries*. Albany: SUNY P, 2008.

McCarthy, Sarah J., and Elizabeth Mirr Moje. "Identity Matters." *Reading Research Quarterly* 37.2 (2002): 228–38.

McCracken, Grant. "Culture and Consumption: A Theoretical Account of the Structure and Movement of the Cultural Meaning of Consumer Goods." *Journal of Consumer Research* (1986): 71–84.

McGee, Michael Calvin. "A Materialist's Conception of Reality." *Explorations in Rhetoric: Studies in Honor of Douglas Ehninger*. Ed. Ray E. McKerrow. Glenview, IL: Scott Foresman, 1982. 23–48.

McLuhan, Marshall, and Quentin Fiore. *The Medium is the Massage: An Inventory of Effects*. Berkeley: Ginko, 2001.

Mead, Kurt. *Dragonflies of the North Woods*. 2nd ed. Duluth, MN: Kollath + Stensaas, 2009.

Miller, Daniel. *Material Cultures: Why Some Things Matter*. Chicago: U of Chicago P, 1998.

Mitchell, Don. *The Right to the City: Social Justice and the Fight for Public Space*. New York: Guillford, 2003.

Mitchell, W. J. T. *Picture Theory*. Chicago: U of Chicago P, 1994.

———. "Visual Literacy or Literary Visualcy?" *Visual Literacy*. Ed. James Elkin. London: Routledge, 2007. 11–30.

Mobbs, Dean et al. "Humor Modulates the Mesolimbic Reward Centers." *Neuron* 40 (2003): 1041–48.

Mol, Annemarie. *The Body Multiple: Ontology in Medical Practice*. Durham: Duke UP, 2003.

———. "Ontological Politics: A Word and Some Questions." *Actor Network Theory and After*. Eds. John Law and John Hassard. Oxford: Blackwell, 1999. 74–89.

Mol, Annemarie, and John Law. "Embodied Action, Enacted Bodies: The Example of Hypoglycaemia." *Body and Society* 10.2–3 (2004): 43–62.

Mollison, Bill. *Permaculture: A Designer's Manual*. Tyalgum, AU: Tagari, 1988.

Mon Pere, Claudia: "Car, Kitchen, Canyon: Mother Writing." *Herspace: Women, Writing, and Solitude*. Eds. Jo Malin and Victoria Boynton. New York: Haworth, 2003. 165–78.

Morton, Timothy. *The Ecological Thought*. Cambridge: Harvard UP, 2010.

———. *Ecology Without Nature: Rethinking Environmental Aesthetics*. Cambridge: Harvard UP, 2009.

———. "Sublime Objects." *Speculations* II (2011): 207–27.

Mountford, Roxanne. *The Gendered Pulpit: Preaching in American Protestant Spaces*. Carbondale: Southern Illinois UP, 2003.

Muckelbauer, John. "Domesticating Animal Theory." *Philosophy and Rhetoric* 44.1 (2009): 95–100.

———. *The Future of Invention: Rhetoric, Postmodernism, and the Problem of Change*. Albany: SUNY P, 2009.

Mudry, Jessica J. *Measured Meals: Nutrition in America*. Albany: SUNY P, 2009.

Naas, Michael. *Turning: From Persuasion to Philosophy*. Amherst: Humanities P, 1995.

Nickerson, Raymond S. "Null Hypothesis Significance Testing: A Review of an Old and Continuing Controversy." *Psychological Methods* 5.2 (2000): 241–301.
Norris, Susan L., et al. "Self-Management Education for Adults with Type 2 Diabetes: A Meta-analysis of the Effect on Glycemic Control." *Diabetes Care* 25.7 (2002): 1159–71. 5 USC. Sec. 553. 2000.
Noyes, Jan. "The QWERTY Keyboard: A Review." *International Journal of Man-Machine Studies* 18.3 (1983): 265–81.
Núñez, Rafael. "Inferential Statistics in the Context of Empirical Cognitive Linguistics." *Methods in Cognitive Linguistics*. Eds. Monica González-Márquez, Irene Mittelberg, Seana Coulson, and Michael J. Spivey. Philadelphia: John Benjamins, 2007. 87–118.
Okadome, Takeshi. "A Performance Evaluation on DSK and Qwerty Keyboards." *International Journal of Computer Processing of Oriental Languages* 20.01 (2007): 15–35.
Olomu, Ade. "Implementing Change in Practice in Federally Qualified Community Health Centers: The Office-Guidelines Applied to Practice (Office-GAP) Model." *Journal of General Internal Medicine* 28.1 (Supplement, June 2013): 103.
"Our History." *Little Free Library*. 25 Oct. 2013. Web. 09 Jan. 2014.
Oyserman, Daphna, Deborah Bybee, and Kathy Terry. "Possible Selves and Academic Outcomes: How and When Possible Selves Impel Action." *Journal of Personality and Social Psychology* 91.1 (2006): 188.
Oyserman, Daphna, Larry Gant, and Joel Ager. "A Socially Contextualized Model of African American Identity: Possible Selves and School Persistence." *Journal of Personality and Social Psychology* 69.6 (1995): 1216.
Packer, Martin. *The Science of Qualitative Research*. Cambridge: Cambridge UP, 2011.
Pappas, Stephanie. "Obama Announces Huge Brain-Mapping Project." *LiveScience*, 02 April 2013. Web. 01 July 2013.
Passman, R. H. "Providing Attachment Objects to Facilitate Learning and Reduce Distress: Effects of Mothers and Security Blankets." *Developmental Psychology* 13.1 (1977): 25.
Passman, Richard H., and J. S. Halonen. "A Developmental Survey of Young Children's Attachments to Inanimate Objects." *The Journal of Genetic Psychology: Research and Theory on Human Development* 134: 2 (1979): 165–78.
Perelman, Chaim, and L. Olbrechts-Tyteca. *The New Rhetoric: A Treatise on Argumentation*. South Bend: U of Notre Dame P, 1969.
Petroski, Henry. *The Pencil: A History of Design and Circumstance*. New York: Knopf, 1990.
Phelps, Louise Wetherbee. *Composition as a Human Science: Contributions to the Self-Understanding of a Discipline*. Oxford: Oxford UP, 1988.
Pickering, Andrew. *The Cybernetic Brain: Sketches of Another Future*. Chicago: U of Chicago P, 2010.
———. *The Mangle of Practice: Time, Agency, and Science*. Chicago: U of Chicago P, 1995.
Pink, Sarah. *Situating Everyday Life: Practices and Places*. Los Angeles: Sage, 2012.
Plato. *Gorgias*. Trans. James H. Nichols Jr. Ithacca: Cornell UP, 1998.

Ploeger, Joanna S. *The Boundaries of the New Frontier: Rhetoric and Communication at Fermi National Accelerator Laboratory*. Columbia: U of South Carolina P, 2009.

Pope Bicycle and Tricycle, 1885. Advertisement. 15 April 2009. Web.

Poster, Carol. "Being and Becoming: Rhetorical Ontology in Early Greek Thought." *Philosophy and Rhetoric* 29.1 (1999): 1–14.

Prelli, Lawrence J., ed. *Rhetorics of Display*. Columbia: U of South Carolina P, 2006.

Prior, Paul, and Jody Shipka. "Chronotopic Lamination: Tracing the Contours of Literate Activity." *Writing Selves, Writing Societies: Research from Activity Perspectives* (2003): 180–238. Web.

Prown, Jules David. "Style as Evidence." *Winterthur Portfolio* 15.3 (1980): 197.

———. "The Truth of Material Culture: History or Fiction?" *History from Things: Essays on Material Culture*. Ed. Steven D. Lubar and W. David Kingery. Washington: Smithsonian Institution P, 1993.

Pruchnic, Jeff. "Neurorhetorics: Cybernetics, Psychotropics, and the Materiality of Persuasion." *Configurations* 16.2 (2008): 167–197.

Queen, Mary. "Transnational Feminist Rhetorics in a Digital World." *College English*. 70.5 (2008): 34–57.

Quintilian. *Institutes of Oratory*. Ed. Lee Honeycutt. Trans. John Selby Watson. 2006. Iowa State. Web. 15 April 2014.

Racine, Eric, Ofek Bar-Illan, and Judy Illes. "fMRI in the Public Eye." *National Review of Neuroscience* 6.2 (2005): 159–64.

Ratcliffe, Krista. *Rhetorical Listening: Identification, Gender, Whiteness*. Carbondale: Southern Illinois UP, 2005.

Reid, Alex. "What Is Object-Oriented Rhetoric?" *Itineration*, 28 November 2012. Web. 9 February 2013.

Renders, Carry M., et al. "Interventions to Improve the Management of Diabetes in Primary Care, Outpatient, and Community Settings: A Systematic Review." *Diabetes Care* 24.10 (2001): 1821–33.

Reyes, Mitchell G. "The Rhetoric in Mathematics: Newton, Leibniz, the Calculus, and the Rhetorical Force of the Infinitesimal." *Quarterly Journal of Speech* 90.2 (2004): 163–188.

Reynolds, Nedra. *Geographies of Writing: Inhabiting Places and Encountering Difference*. Carbondale: Southern Illinois UP, 2004.

Rheinberger, Hans-Jörg. *An Epistemology of the Concrete: Twentieth-Century Histories of Life*. Durham: Duke UP, 2010.

———. "Valuing Things: The Public and Private Meanings of Possessions." *Journal of Consumer Research* (1994): 504–21.

Rice, Jeff. *Digital Detroit: Rhetoric and Space in the Age of the Network*. Carbondale: Southern Illinois UP, 2012.

———. "Noetic Writing: Plato Comes to Missouri." *Composition Studies* 39.2. (2011): 9–28.

Rice, Jenny. *Distant Publics: Development Rhetoric and the Subject of Crisis*. Pittsburgh: U of Pittsburgh P, 2013.

Richins, Marsha L. "Special Possessions and the Expression of Material Values." *Journal of Consumer Research* (1994): 522–33.

Rickert, Thomas. *Ambient Rhetoric: The Attunements of Rhetorical Being*. Pittsburgh: U of Pittsburgh P, 2013.

Rivers, Nathaniel A. "Rhetorics of (Non)Symbolic Cultivation." *Ecology, Writing Theory, and New Media: Writing Ecology*. Ed. Sidney Dobrin. New York: Routledge, 2012. 34–50.

———. "Some Assembly Required: The Latourian Collective and the Banal Work of Technical and Professional Communication." *Journal of Technical Writing and Communication* 38.3 (2008): 189–206.

Rothenberg, David. *Hand's End: Technology and the Limits of Nature*. Berkeley: U of California P, 1993.

Rozeboom, William. "The Fallacy of the Null-Hypothesis Significance Test." *Psychological Bulletin* 57.5 (1997): 416–28.

Sarkar, Urmimala, Lawrence Fisher, and Dean Schillinger. "Is Self-Efficacy Associated with Diabetes Self-Management Across Race/Ethnicity and Health Literacy?" *Diabetes Care* 29.4 (2006): 823–29.

Schatzki, Theodore R. *The Site of the Social: A Philosophical Account of the Constitution of Social Life and Change*. University Park: Pennsylvania State UP, 2002.

Schiavo, Laura Burd. "From Phantom Image to Perfect Vision: Physiological Optics, Commercial Photography, and the Popularization of the Stereoscope." *New Media, 1740–1915*. Eds. Lisa Gitelman and Geoffrey B. Pingee. Cambridge: MIT P, 2003. 113–37.

Schlereth, Thomas J. *Material Culture Studies in America*. Nashville: American Association for State and Local History, 1982.

Schmidt, Frank L. and John Hunter. "Eight Common but False Objections to the Discontinuation of Significance Testing in the Analysis of Research Data." *Understanding and Using Statistics in Psychology*. Eds. Jeremy Miles and Philip Banyard. Thousand Oaks: Sage, 1997.

Schneirov, Matthew. *The Dream of a New Social Order: Popular Magazines in America 1893 – 1914*. New York: Columbia UP, 1994.

Scott, J. Blake. "Extending Rhetorical-Cultural Analysis: Transformations of Home HIV Testing." *College English* 65.4 (2003): 349–67.

Scott, Robert L. "On Viewing Rhetoric as Epistemic." *Central States Speech Journal* 18 (1967): 9–16.

Scult, Allen. "Aristotle's *Rhetoric* on Ontology: A Heideggerian Reading." *Philosophy and Rhetoric* 32.2 (1999): 146–59.

Selzer, Jack. "Habeas Corpus: An Introduction." *Rhetorical Bodies*. Eds. Jack Selzer and Sharon Crowley. Madison: U of Wisconsin P, 1999. 3–15.

Selzer, Jack, and Sharon Crowley, eds. *Rhetorical Bodies*. Madison: U of Wisconsin P, 1999.

Shapin, Steven, and Simon Schaffer. *Leviathan and the Air-pump: Hobbes, Boyle and the Experimental Life*. Princeton: Princeton UP, 1985.

Shaver, James P. "What Statistical Significance Testing Is, and What it Is Not." *Journal of Experimental Education* 61.4 (1993): 293–316.

Shaviro, Steven. "Kant, Deleuze, and the Virtual." *The Pinocchio Theory*. 09 May 2007. Web. 15 June 2009.

———. *Without Criteria*. Cambridge: MIT P, 2009.

Shea, Elizabeth Parthenia. *How the Gene Got its Groove: Figurative Language, Science, and the Rhetoric of the Real*. Albany: SUNY P. 2008.

Sholes, Christopher. "Improvement in Type-Writing Machines." 1878 : n. pag.

Shove, Elizabeth, Matthew Watson, Martin Hand, and Jack Ingram. *The Design of Everyday Life*. New York: Berg, 2007.

Silverman, Robert J. "The Stereoscope and Photographic Depiction in the 19th Century." *Technology and Culture* 34.4 (1993): 729–56.

Simons, Herbert W., ed. *The Rhetorical Turn: Invention and Persuasion in the Conduct of Inquiry*. Chicago: U of Chicago P, 1990.

"Since This Old Cap Was New." *All the Year Round* 2.30 (1859): 76–80.

Smith, Caroline Minna. "Women as Cyclers." *Outing*. Vol VI, Issue 3 (1885): 317–21. LA 84. Web. 11 October 2011.

Southall, Thomas. "White Mountain Stereographs and the Development of a Collective Vision." *Points of View: The Stereograph in America—A Cultural History*. Ed. Edward W. Earle. Rochester: The Visual Studies Workshop P, 1979. 97–108.

Spalding Men's and Women's Safety Bicycles, 1908 Hagley Museum. Wilmington, Delaware.

Spinuzzi, Clay. *Network: Theorizing Knowledge in Telecommunications*. New York: Cambridge UP, 2008.

———. *Tracing Genres through Organizations*. Boston: MIT P, 2003.

Springsteen, Karen. Facebook post. 23 September 2013. Web.

Stamp, Jimmy. "Fact of Fiction? The Legend of the QWERTY Keyboard." *Smithsonian Magazine*. Web. 13 Sept. 2013.

Stengers, Isabelle. *Thinking with Whitehead: A Free and Wild Creation of Concepts*. Trans. Michael Chase. Cambridge: Harvard UP, 2011.

"Stereoscope, The." *Godey's Lady's Book* (Oct. 1852): 45. American Periodicals Series. Web. 15 Aug. 2013.

"Stereoscope Free." *Evening World* 5 July 1905: 3. Library of Congress. Web. 15 Aug. 2013.

"Stereoscope and View Offer." *National Tribune* 14 Nov. 1907: 6. Library of Congress. Web. 15 Aug. 2013.

Stern, Joanna. "AT&T Slammed on Twitter and Facebook for Sept. 11 Marketing Move." *ABC News*. 11 September 2013. Web. 15 April 2014.

Stewart, Kathleen. "Atmospheric Attunements." *Environment and Planning D: Society and Space* 29 (2011): 445–53.

———. *Ordinary Affects*. Durham: Duke UP, 2007.

———. "Weak Theory in an Unfinished World." *Journal of Folklore Research* 45.1 (2008): 71–82.

Stiegler, Bernard. *Technics and Time, 1: The Fault of Epimetheus*. Trans. Richard Beardworth and George Collins. Stanford UP, 1998.

Stooges, The. *Funhouse*. Elektra Records, 1970. LP.

Stormer, Nathan. "Articulation: A Working Paper on Rhetoric and Taxis." *Quarterly Journal of Speech* 90 (2004): 257–84.

Syverson, Margaret. *The Wealth of Reality: An Ecology of Composition*. Carbondale: Southern Illinois UP, 1999.

Tampio, Nicholas. "Multiplicity." *Encyclopedia of Political Theory*, 2010. SAGE Publications. 30 Aug. 2010. Web. 15 April 2014.

Tenner, Edward. *Our Own Devices: How Technology Remakes Humanity*. Random House Digital, 2009. *Google Scholar*. Web. 13 Sept. 2013.

Terranova, Tiziana. *Network Cultures: Politics for the Information Age*. London: Pluto Press, 2004.

Teston, Christa B., Scott S. Graham, Raquel Baldwinson, Andrea Li, and Jessamyn Swift. "Public Voices in Pharmaceutical Deliberations: Negotiating Benefit in the FDA's Avastin Hearing." *Journal of Medical Humanities* 35.2 (2014): 149–70.

Thompson, Charis. "When Elephants Stand for Competing Philosophies of Nature: Amboseli National Park, Kenya." *Complexities in Science, Technology, and Medicine*. Eds. John Law and Annemarie Mol. Durham: Duke UP, 2001. 166–90.

Toulmin, Stephen. *The Uses of Argument*. Cambridge: Cambridge UP, 2003.

Trachtenberg, Alan. *Reading American Photographs: Images as History, Mathew Brady to Walker Evans*. New York: Hill and Wang, 1989.

Transition Network. Web. 10 May 2012.

Trimbur, John. "Composition and the Circulation of Writing." *College Composition and Communication* 52.2 (2000): 188–219.

Turkle, Sherry. *Evocative Objects: Things We Think With*. Cambridge: MIT P, 2007.

Underwood, Bert and E. Underwood. "New Woman Wash Day." 1901. Web. 20 May 2013.

Van Deusen, Richard. "Public Space Design as Class Warfare: Urban Design, the 'Right to the City,' and the Production of Clinton Square, Syracuse, NY." *GeoJournal* 58.2–3 (2002): 149–58.

Vatz, Richard. "The Myth of the Rhetorical Situation." *Philosophy and Rhetoric* 6.3 (1973): 154–61.

Verbeek, Peter-Paul. *What Things Do: Philosophical Reflections on Technology, Agency, and Design*. University Park: Pennsylvania State UP, 2005.

Villanueva, Victor. *Bootstraps: From an American Academic of Color*. Urbana: NCTE, 1993.

Virilio, Paul. "The Third Interval: A Critical Transition." *Rethinking Technologies: A Reader in Architecture Theory*. Eds. William W. Braham and Jonathan A. Hale. Minneapolis: U of Minnesota P, 2004. 358–66.

Vivian, Bradford. *Being Made Strange: Rhetoric Beyond Representation*. Albany: SUNY P, 2004.

———. "In the Regard of the Image." *JAC* 27 (2007): 471–504.

———. *Public Forgetting: The Rhetoric and Politics of Beginning Again.* University Park: The Pennsylvania State UP, 2010.

Wagner, Jon. "Seeing Things: Visual Research and Material Culture." *The Sage Handbook of Visual Research Methods.* Eds. Eric Margolis and Luc Pauwels. London: Sage, 2011. 72–95.

Walker, Jeffrey. *Rhetoric and Poetics in Antiquity.* New York: Oxford UP, 2000.

Wallendorf, Melanie, and Eric J. Arnould. "'My Favorite Things': A Cross-Cultural Inquiry into Object Attachment, Possessiveness, and Social Linkage." *Journal of Consumer Research* (1988): 531–47.

Weber, Dennis. "X and Y Brains." *Scientific American* 293.3 (2005): 14–15. Web. 01 July 2013.

Whatmore, Sarah. *Hybrid Geographies: Natures Cultures Spaces.* Thousand Oaks: Sage Publications Ltd, 2001.

Whitehead, Alfred North. *The Concept of Nature.* Amherst: Prometheus, 2004.

———. *Modes of Thought.* New York: Free P, 1938.

———. *Process and Reality,* corrected edition. Eds. David Ray Griffin and Donald W. Sherburne. New York: Free P, 1978.

———. *Science and the Modern World.* New York: Free P, 196.

Wickman, Chad. "Rhetoric, *Techne,* and the Art of Scientific Inquiry." *Rhetoric Review* 31.1 (2012). 21–40.

Wilde, Oscar. *The Decay of Lying.* Whitefish, MT: Kessinger Publishing, 2004.

Willard, Frances. *A Wheel Within A Wheel: How I Learned to Ride the Bicycle.* Chicago: Women's Temperance Publishing Association, 1895.

Wilson, Margaret. "Six Views of Embodied Cognition." *Psychonomic Bulletin and Review* 9.4 (2002): 625–36.

Winner, Langdon. *The Whale and the Reactor: A Search for Limits in an Age of High Technology.* Chicago: U of Chicago P, 1989.

Wittgenstein, Ludwig. *Philosophical Investigations,* 3rd ed. Trans. G. E. M. Anscombe. New York: Macmillan, 1958.

"Women's, Men's Brains Respond Differently to Hungry Infant's Cries." *Medical Xpress.* n.p. 07 May 2013. Web. 01 July 2013.

Woolf, Virginia. *A Room of One's Own.* San Diego: Harcourt Brace Jovanovich, 1989.

Wyche-Smith, and Susan Lee. "The Magic Circle: Writers and Ritual." Dissertation. University of Washington, 1988.

———. "Time, Tools, and Talismans." *The Subject Is Writing: Essays by Teachers and Students.* Ed. Wendy Bishop. Portsmouth: Boynton/Cook, 1993.

Wynn, James. "Arithmetic of the Species: Darwin and the Role of Mathematics in his Argumentation." *Rhetorica* 27.1 (2009): 76–97.

Wysocki, Anne. "Opening New Media to Writing: Openings and Justifications." *Writing New Media: Theory and Applications for Expanding the Teaching of Composition.* Eds. Anne Wysocki et al. Logan: Utah State UP, 2004.

Yagelski, Robert P. "A Thousand Writers Writing: Seeking Change Through the Radical Practice of Writing as a Way of Being." *English Education* (2009): 6–28.

Yaneva, Albena, and Bruno Latour. "Give Me A Gun And I Will Make All Buildings

Move: An ANT's View Of Architecture." *Explorations in Architecture: Teaching, Design, Research*. Ed. Reto Geiser. Basel: Birkhäuser. (2008): 80–89.

Yasuoka, Koichi. *The Truth of QWERTY*. 16 Aug. 2006. Web. 13 Sept. 2013.

Yasuoka, Koichi, and Motoko Yasuoka. "On the Prehistory of QWERTY." *ZINBUN* 42 (2011): 161–174.

Yes. *Drama*. Atlantic Records, 1980. LP.

Young, Richard E., Alton L. Becker, and Kenneth L. Pike. *Rhetoric: Discovery and Change*. New York: Harcourt, 1970.

Zachry, Mark. "An Interview with Bonnie A. Nardi." *Technical Communication Quarterly* 15.4 (2006): 483–503.

Zarefsky, David. "Four Senses of Rhetorical History." *Doing Rhetorical History: Concepts and Cases*. Ed. Kathleen J. Turner. Tuscaloosa: U of Alabama P, 2008. 19–32.

Zickefoose, Julie. *The Bluebird Effect: Uncommon Bonds with Common Birds*. Boston: Houghton Mifflin Harcourt, 2012.

Contributors

Cydney Alexis is Assistant Professor of English and Director of the Writing Center at Kansas State University. Her research focuses on the material culture of writing—those material goods and practices that support writers in their trade. Her research unveils the consumer and family rituals around material goods that support literacy development in young children and their connection to adult writing identity practice.

Scot Barnett is Assistant Professor of English at Indiana University. His current research focuses on the intersections among rhetorical history and theory, digital media, and object-oriented ontology. His writing has appeared in several collections as well as in the journals *Enculturation* and *Kairos*. His book *Rhetorical Realism: Rhetoric, Ethics, and the Ontology of Things* is forthcoming from Routledge (Studies in Rhetoric and Communication).

Casey Boyle is Assistant Professor in the Department of Rhetoric and Writing at the University of Texas-Austin. His research focuses on digital rhetoric, composition theory, and media studies. His work has appeared in *Computers and Composition*, *Kairos*, and *Philosophy and Rhetoric*, as well as in the edited collections *Rhetoric and the Digital Humanities* and *Thinking with Latour in Rhetoric and Composition*. He is also completing a book manuscript, *Rhetoric as a Posthuman Practice*, which examines the role of practice and ethics in digital rhetoric.

James J. Brown Jr. is Assistant Professor of English and Director of the Digital Studies Center at Rutgers University-Camden. His research focuses on digital rhetoric and software studies, and he is the author of *Ethical Programs: Hospitality and the Rhetorics of Software* (University of Michigan Press, 2015), which examines the ethical and rhetorical underpinnings of networked software environments.

Marilyn M. Cooper is Emerita Professor of Humanities at Michigan Technological University. She has published "Rhetorical Agency as Emergent and Enacted" (*College Composition and Communication [CCC]*, 2011), as well as "Mo-

256 / CONTRIBUTORS

ments of Argument: Agonistic Inquiry and Confrontational Cooperation" (*CCC*, 1997), for which she won the Richard Braddock Award along with coauthors Dennis A. Lynch and Diana George. She is currently completing a book entitled *The Animal Who Writes*, which proposes a vision of writing as not just a social practice but an embodied and enworlded behavior that is especially important to—but not limited to—human animals.

Kristie S. Fleckenstein is Professor of English and Director of the Graduate Program in Rhetoric and Composition at Florida State University. She is the recipient of the 2005 CCC Outstanding Book of the Year Award for *Embodied Literacies: Imageword and a Poetics of Teaching* (SIUP, 2003), and the 2009 W. Ross Winterowd Award for Best Book in Composition Theory for *Vision, Rhetoric, and Social Action in the Composition Classroom* (SIUP, 2009). Her research interests include feminism and race, especially as both intersect with material and visual rhetorics.

S. Scott Graham is the Director of the Scientific and Medical Communications Laboratory and a faculty member in the English Department at the University of Wisconsin-Milwaukee. His research is devoted to exploring deliberation among technical experts and public stakeholders in scientific and medical policy. He has just finished a book on pain medicine and new materialist methods for rhetorical inquiry entitled *The Politics of Pain Medicine: A Rhetorical-Ontological Inquiry* (University of Chicago Press, 2015).

Laurie Gries is Assistant Professor at the University of Colorado, where she teaches courses in rhetoric, writing, theory, and new media. Her work has appeared in *Computers and Composition, Composition Studies, JAC, Rhetoric Review*, and several edited collections. Her book *Still Life with Rhetoric: A New Materialist Approach for Visual Rhetorics* was published by Utah State University Press in 2015.

Sarah Hallenbeck is Assistant Professor of English at the University of North Carolina-Wilmington, where she teaches courses in professional writing and rhetoric. Her work has appeared in *Technical Communication Quarterly, Rhetoric Society Quarterly, Advances in the History of Rhetoric*, and *Rhetoric Review*, and she is currently completing a book manuscript titled *Nineteenth-Century Women Write the Bicycle*.

William Hart-Davidson is Associate Dean for Graduate Education in the College of Arts and Letters; Associate Professor in the Department of Writing, Rhetoric and American Cultures; and a senior researcher at the Center for Research on Writing in Digital Environments at Michigan State University. His recent scholarly work includes a volume, coedited with Jim Ridolfo, titled *Rhetoric and the Digital Humanities* and published by the University of Chicago Press (2015).

Kim Lacey is Assistant Professor of English at Saginaw Valley State University, where she teaches writing and gender studies. Her writing has appeared in the *Journal of Evolution and Technology, Rhetoric Society Quarterly, Bad Subjects,* and *The Information Society.*

Brian J. McNely is Director of Undergraduate Studies in the Department of Writing, Rhetoric, and Digital Studies at the University of Kentucky. He studies everyday genres, technologies, objects, and practices of communication using qualitative methodologies and visual research methods.

John Muckelbauer teaches rhetorical theory at the University of South Carolina. Some speculate that his first book, *The Future of Invention: Rhetoric, Postmodernism, and the Problem of Change,* may have been the cause of the Wall Street financial crisis of 2008. At the moment, he is seriously at work on a book on style in the work of Nietzsche, Derrida, and Deleuze. Seriously.

Jodie Nicotra is Associate Professor of English at the University of Idaho. She has published articles on digital rhetorics, rhetorical theory, and the thought of Kenneth Burke in (among other places) *Rhetoric Society Quarterly, Rhetoric Review,* and *CCC.* Her textbook *Becoming Rhetorical: A Toolbox for Analyzing and Creating Written, Visual, and Multimodal Compositions* will be available in 2016 from Cengage. She is currently working on a book manuscript, tentatively titled *The Microbial Imaginary: Attuning to the Rhetorics of Tiny Life.*

Jason Palmeri is Associate Professor of English and Director of Composition at Miami University in Oxford, Ohio. He is the author of *Remixing Composition: A History of Multimodal Writing Pedagogy* (SIUP 2012). Most recently, Jason has been refining his object-oriented pedagogy while teaching food and travel writing in Italy.

Thomas Rickert is Professor of English at Purdue University. He has published two books and over twenty articles. His first book, *Acts of Enjoyment: Rhetoric, Žižek, and the Return of the Subject* (University of Pittsburgh Press), was published in 2007. His second book, *Ambient Rhetoric: The Attunements of Rhetorical Being* (University of Pittsburgh Press), was published in 2013. He has begun a third book tentatively called *A Prehistory of Rhetoric.*

Nathaniel A. Rivers is Assistant Professor of English at Saint Louis University. His current research addresses new materialism's impact on public rhetorics such as environmentalism and urban design. He is at work on a book project currently titled *The Strange Defense of Rhetoric.* Together with Paul Lynch, he edited *Thinking with Bruno Latour in Rhetoric and Composition* (SIUP 2015), which explores the impact of Bruno Latour on rhetoric and composition. His work has appeared in *CCC, Kairos, Technical Communication Quarterly, Journal of Technical Writing and Communication, Enculturation,* and *Present Tense.*

Kevin Rutherford is a doctoral candidate in English (Composition and Rhetoric) at Miami University. Although he only began to fully realize it during his doctoral work, rhetoric's connection to ontology has always been lurking in the background of his research. In his work he attempts to connect the ontological character and practical applications of thinking in technical communication, game studies, and composition pedagogy.

Donnie Johnson Sackey is Assistant Professor of English at Wayne State University. His research centers on the dynamics of environmental public policy deliberation, environmental justice, and environmental cultural history. Sackey is currently a co-investigator on a project funded by the Center for Urban Responses to Environmental Stressors. The project investigates the ecological impact of airborne petroleum coke on vulnerable populations in Detroit, Dearborn, MI, and Windsor, ON.

Christa Teston is Assistant Professor of English at The Ohio State University. In much of her work, Christa investigates how, in an effort to manage uncertainty, humans partner with text, images, sound, and statistics in rhetorically inventive ways. Her research has appeared in *Written Communication, Technical Communication Quarterly, Present Tense*, and the *Journal of Medical Humanities*.

Katie Zabrowski is a doctoral candidate with an emphasis in rhetoric and composition in the English Department at Saint Louis University. Her interests in new materialism and object-oriented ontology guide her research in rhetoric and inform her approach to writing pedagogy. Her current research positions *cookery* as a rich analogy for rhetoric. By way of this analogy, she explores hospitality at the level of ontology, tracing the activities of generosity and relationality at the ontological, disciplinary, and institutional levels.

Index

Page numbers in italics refer to illustrations.

Achatz, Grant, 55, 62, 63
actor-network theory, 6, 7–8, 10, 98, 120, 121, 224
actualization, 161, 163
Adrià, Ferran, 62
Ahmed, Sarah, 8
Akrich, Madeline, 203
Alinea, 55, 57, 63. *See also* Lamb 86 (Alinea)
Allen, Chris T., 86
Alliance for the Great Lakes, 71
Althing, 5
ambient rhetoric, 28n2, 116–17, 141, 142
American Rivers, 71
American Water Operators, 71
analysis of variance (ANOVA), 49
Anderson, Leon, 145–46
Andrés, Jose, 62
animal activity, and rhetoric, 39
antimetabole, 201, 210
antithesis, 201–3, 210
Aquatic Invasive Species Summit Proceedings Conference, 72–73
Aristotelian paradigm of rhetoric: division of rhetoric into deliberative, forensic, and epideictic, 31–32; formal and juridical notion of rhetoric, 31–32, 35; importance of intentionality, 34–35; privileging of speech over writing, 33–34
art, as material thing, 228–29

articulation, 199, 211n2
artistic proofs, 5
assemblages: assemblage thinking, 143–45, 186–87; attunement to, 191, 194–96; composition as, 101–2, 106–7; cookery as, 60; and enactments of ideologies, 48; and habits of experience, 18–19; and Little Free Library, 151; as material commonplaces, 200; and object-oriented ontology (OOO), 97, 98; and permaculture, 192–93; rulemaking as, 71, 72; and Transitional Network, 194, 196; and trash, 13, 188–90
atherosclerosis, as body multiple, 164–65
attachment, 94n1
attunements, 227; to assemblages, 191; as a matter of respect, 24–25; and momentary intensities, 140, 143; worldish, 140, 145–47
Augenblick, 227, 229, 230
Augustine, St., 103
autoethnography, 145–46
awakening, 18
Azim, Eiman, "Sex Differences in Brain Activation Elicited by Humor," 44, 45

Babbitts, Judith, 130, 131
Bahktin, Mikhail, 166
Bak, Meredith A., 131, 133–34, 137

260 / INDEX

Ballif, Michelle, 1–2
Bandura, Albert, 78
Barad, Karen, 8, 47–49, 199
Bardini, Thierry, 214, 220
Barthe, Yannick, 48
Barthes, Roland, theory of the *punctum*, 141, 147
Bartholomae, David, 200
Becker, Alton. See *Rhetoric: Discovery and Change* (Young, Becker, and Pike)
becoming: networks of, 169n4; ontological notion of as it relates to visual-material rhetoric, 155, 157–61, 166; and possessions, 86, 92–93
Belk, Russell, "Possessions and the Extended Self," 86
Benhabib, Seyla, 21
Bennett, Jane: assemblage thinking, 186; on hoarders, 191; and thing-power, 126, 159; on 2003 North American blackout, 186–87; vibrant materialism, 108; *Vibrant Matter*, 191; "vital force," 228
Benson, Thomas W., 9
Bergson, Henri, 173, 179, 180
Berkson, Joseph, 51
Berlin, James, 96, 107
Bernard-Donals, Michael, 185
Berthoff, Ann E., 96–98; composition as assemblage, 101–2; critique of positivism, 99; *Forming Thinking Writing*, 99–102; *The Making of Meaning*, 99; pedagogical emphasis on dialogic observation and empathy with nonhuman objects, 100; pedagogical use of metaphor as tool of ontological investigation, 100; rhetorical ontology, 99–102; and usefulness of scientific study to ontological investigation, 99, 101
bicycling, for women, late nineteenth century: cartoons lampooning women's bicycling, 207–8; Frances Willard on, 197–99, 201, 211; handlebar options for male and female riders, 206, *207*; impact on women's dress reform, 198; and material commonplaces about gender order, 200–11; and "New Woman, 198, 210; "The New Woman Wash Day," 208, *209*; ordinary bicycle for men and tricycle for women, articulating gender differences (antithesis), 201–3, 204, 209; and performative agency, 198–99; Pope advertisement reinforcing distinctions between men and women, *203*; Safety Bicycle articulating gender differences in degree (gradatio), 204–6, *205*, 210; "skirt-guards," 204, 206; small man/robust woman in bloomers on Safety Bicycle, articulating reversals of gender roles (antimetabole), 206–9, 211n3; tricycles, 202
Biesecker, Barbara, 126
bighead carp: addition to list of injurious fish by US Fish and Wildlife Service (Service), 72; in aquaculture, 73–76, *74*; and issue of living or dead, 75; technical objects that form invasive identity, 76; in the wild, 75
Big versus Little Rhetoric debates, 30
Bitzer, Lloyd, 141
black box formation, 121
Blair, Carole, 94n5, 185, 186
Blumenthal, Heston, 62
Bogost, Ian: *Alien Phenomenology*, 55, 57, 58, 61, 63, 108, 172; appraisal of lists, 58; and carpentry, 64; comparison of ontographs and exploded view diagrams, 59–60; concept of metaphor to describe vicarious causation, 98; on correlationism, 64, 66n2; distinction between definition and description, 64; focus on distinction and disjunction, 59; on Latour litanies, 101–2; the "meanwhile," 172; modification of Heideggerian thing theory, 113; and object-oriented ontology (OOO), 58–59; on ontography, 172; and philosophical creativity, 60; "Seeing Things," 172; on thing-oriented ontologies, 120
Bol, Todd, 139
Boyle, Casey, 231n3

Boym, Svetlana, 173, 181, 182
Braidotti, Rosi, 8
Brain Research through Advancing Innovative Neurotechnologies (BRAIN) project, 42
brain sex science: accommodation of for popular audiences, 43, 44–46; article titles in popular science magazines displaying assumption that human brains are dimorphic, 44–45; and null hypothesis significance testing (NHST), 43, 49–52; Touminian trace of claims, data, and backing between and among accommodated and unaccommodated scientific findings, 45–46
Brand, Alice Glarden, 94n6
Brandt, Deborah, 94n6
Brewster, David: lenticular stereoscope, 132, 133; redesign of Wheatstone stereotype, 128; *The Stereoscope*, 128
Brooke, Collin, 158
Brooks, Rick, 139
Brown, Bill, 1, 4
Bryant, Levi: *Democracy of Objects*, 114; and endostructure and exostructure, 114, 117–18; and flat ontology, 97–98; and "hegemonic fallacy," 110; modification of Heideggerian thing theory, 113; theory of information, 115–16; virtual proper being, 170n9
Burke, Kenneth, 39, 127–28
Butler, Judith, 8

Callon, Michael, 48, 69, 70
Campbell, Karlyn Kohrs, 9
Capital Bicycle Club, 201, 204
carpentry, 64
Casselman, Anne, "Women Don't Understand," 44–46
Chaplin, Elizabeth, 146
Cherwitz, Richard, 47–48, 49
chord keyset, 220–21
Chorost, Michael, 23, 24
chronotopes, 165–66

"Chronotopic Lamination" (Prior and Shipka), 94n2, 166
Cintron, Ralph, 10
circulation: and acquisition of thing-power, 157, 166, 168; and rhetorical transformation, 157–61
circulatory intensities, 140–41, 142, 147–53
Clark, Andy, 215, 223
co-construction, 56
Code of Federal Regulations (CFR), 71–72
cognitive mapping, 177–78
collectif, 70
College of Human Medicine, Michigan State University, 78
communication, transmission theory of, 116
composition: and agency of everyday things in act of, 96; as assemblage, 101–2; history of as object assemblage, 106–7
composition studies: counter-history of, 96; and object-oriented ontology (OOO), 12, 96–97
concrete, epistemology of, 109
Condit, Celeste: critique of bad brain sex science, 42, 43–44, 46, 49, 52; and suasive capacity of language, 47
constitution, as ontological process, 140, 145
cookery: as assemblage, 60; as flat ontography, 57, 60–61, 64; as generative process, 60, 62; "new," as ontographical, 63, 64; "new," statement on, 62–63; and philosophical creativity, 60
Coole, Diana, 108, 109, 118, 126, 127, 135
correlationism, 60, 64, 66n2
Crary, Jonathan, 127, 138
Crick, Nathan, 155
Crowley, Sharon, 126, 159

Darwin, Charles, use of mathematics in arguments about the origin of species, 49–50
Darwin, Thomas, 47–48, 49
David, Paul, 222
Davis, Diane, 1–2
Dear Photograph/Dear Photograph images:

affect, 173; as form of place-based collocation, 172–73; image that launched, 175; importance of medium, 175, 176; and the "meanwhile," 172, 173, 177, 179; recapturing time, 178–80; shaping of memory through things, time, places, and affective response, 172; siblings on steps, 180–81; symbolic nature of standing in same place as someone else, 173–75; as temporal pastiche, 172, 177–78; third memory, 177; vertical stacking of past and present to illustrate change, 179; virtual time available within actual time, 180
Deetz, James, 85
Deleuze, Gilles, 70, 164, 193; *Cinema 2*, 178; distinctions between differentiation and differenciation, 170n10; monist perspective of the virtual, 170n9; theory of time, 173
deliberative rhetoric, 31–32, 34
Densmore, Amos, 212, 214
Derrida, Jacques: hauntology, 180; on privileging of speech over writing in West, 33
Despret, Vinciane, 21, 26
Dewey, John, 155
diabetes health maintenance, secondary therapies: caregiver-to-patient interaction, 80; group visits focusing on evidence-based therapies, 79; mobile phone messaging (SMS), 79; patterns of information flow among patients and care providers, 80; peer interactions, 80; two-way interaction between caregivers and patients, 80; writing devices, 11, 79–81
difference, spurious ways in which sex differences are reported, 51
digital photographs, 174
digital remixing, 157
digital rhetoricians, 6
Ding: Harman on, 114–15; Heidegger's distinction from *Gegenstand*, 112–13, 119; Heidegger's understanding of gathering together of beings and ideas, 5, 12

disclosive ambience, 141–43
Discover Magazine, 45
divergence, 18
dragonflies, 18
Dubuffet, Jean, 195
Dvorak (August) Simplified Keyboard (DSK), 219–20

Eagly, Alice, 54n1
Earle, Edward, 129
Edbauer Rice, Jenny, 142, 159, 185
Ehses, Hanno H. J., 200
electronic texts, 157
Ellis, S. E., 81
embodied cognition, 223
emergence, representational, 116
encomium, as methodology for tracing ways in which everyday objects produce effects, 224
endostructure, 115
Engelbart, Douglas, oN-Line System (NLS) of chord keyset, mouse, and QWERTY, 220–21
Enoch, Jessica, 199
enthymemes, 5
environmentalist movement, 37
epideictic rhetoric, 32, 34–35, 226
epiphenomena, 118
epistemic fallacy, 111, 112
epistemology, distinction from ontology, 8
ergonomic keyboards, 221
everyday rhetoric, 36–38
exostructure, 115
exploded view diagrams, 59–60

Fahnestock, Jeanne, 44; on antimetabole, 207; on antithesis, 202
Fahnestock-Toulminian analysis, 45–46, 53
Fairey, Shepard, Obama Hope image, 156, 161, 165, 169n2. *See also* Obama Hope image
Fausto-Sterling, Anne, 42
Federal Register (FR), 71
feminist new materialism, 6–7, 8

fibromyalgia, 47
Fine, Cordelia, 51
Finland, Waste Act of 1993, 190
Finnegan, Cara, 157, 199
Fisher, R. A., "Studies in Crop Variation," 53
Fiumara, Gemma Corradi, 20, 23, 28
flat ontology: cookery as, 57, 60–61, 64; litanies and, 58; and object-oriented ontology (OOO), 97–98, 101, 103
Fleming, David, 155
Flower, Linda, 107
forensic rhetoric, 31, 34
Foucault, Michel, 121
FourSquare, 174
four-world problem, of new materialism, 111–17, 112
Fowles, Jib, 132
Free Humanity, 164
Frost, Samantha, 108, 109, 118, 126, 127, 135
functional magnetic resonance imaging (fMRI), 45, 46, 53
Fuss, Diana, 94n7

Garcia, Mannie, "Obama Photo," 165, 169n2
Gardner, Howard, 213
Garsten, Bryan: on respect for actual opinions of audience, 21; view of persuasion, 17–20, 28n2
gaze, 159
gendering, through object relations, 200, 210
Gigerenzer, Gerd, 52
Glassie, Henry, 83
glitch art, 227
Goodman, Steven, 51
Gorgias: *Encomium of Helen*, 224; on the nonexistent, 9
gradatio, 201, 210
Graham, S. Scott: "Agency and the Rhetoric of Medicine," 47; *The Politics of Pain Medicine*, 121
Grand, Sarah, coining of term "New Woman," 198
Graphical User Interface (mouse), 220
Green, Bill, 17, 27–28, 29n5

Greenpeace, 165
Grosz, Elizabeth, 1, 4, 8
group means, and logical fallacy, 51
Guattari, Felix, 193
Gur, Rubin, 43

habits, surrounding management of waste, 188–89
habits of experience, 18–19, 25
Hacking, Ian, 3
Haraway, Donna: "A Cyborg Manifesto," 8; on respect, 24–25, 28
Harding, Sandra, 44
Hariman, Robert, 157
Harman, Graham, 8, 186, 228; and actor-network theory, 120; asymmetrical theory of object relations, 7; on correlationism, 66n2; on independence of objects, 98; on inherent limits of exploration, 65; and lists, 58; modification of Heideggerian thing theory, 113; notion of carpentry, 60, 64; object-oriented ontology, 8, 13n1, 14n2, 108; *Prince of Networks*, 185; and problem of access, 110; *The Quadruple Object*, 113–14; on relations between objects as "vicarious causation," 98; and reverse-Cartesian lobotomy, 115; *Towards Speculative Realism*, 228, 229
Hart-Davidson, William, 78, 82
Hawhee, Debra, 2, 185
Hawk, Byron, 96, 104
Hawkins, Guy, *The Ethics of Waste*, 188
Hayles, N. Katherine, 134
Heidegger, Martin, 8; on art, 228, 229; *Being and Time*, 113, 142–43; concept of "standing-reserve," 223; concept of *Zuhandenheit* ("readiness-to-hand"), 186; concepts of thrownness, worldliness, and attunement, 141, 142–43; and *Ding*, 5, 12, 112–13, 119; distinction of thing from object, 13n1; hammer example, 113; notion of disclosure, 142; "The Thing," 4–5, 21, 23, 24, 119; thing theory, 112–13, 118; *Weltlichkeit*, 154n2

heliotropism, 39–40
Heraclitus, 227–28, 229, 231n1
Herndl, Carl G., 121
Hesse, Hermann, 4
Hidalgo, Fred, 163
hoarders, 191
Holmes, Oliver Wendell: encouragement of deep attention to stereoscopic views, 135, 136; Holmes-Bates Stereoscope, 129, *131*; on rapid movement of stereograph cards, 134, 136; "Stereoscope," 125, 128; on stereoscope and the printed word, 138; on stereoscope's appearance of reality, 130, 132–33; on stereoscope's concentration of user's whole attention, 131; "stereoscopic trip," 136–37
Holmgren, David, 192
Hooke, Robert, *Micrographia*, 127
Hopkins, Rob, 194
Hunt, Scott, 145
Hunter, John, 52
Hutchins, Edwin, *Cognition in the Wild*, 48, 223
Huyghe, Pierre, *Third Memory*, 177
hyper attention, and stereograph, 134–37

iconographic tracking, 160
identity, and possessions, 86, 94n3
ideographic methodologies, 153n1
Illinois Black Chamber of Commerce, 71
images: new media images, 157, 160, 161; single, and multiple, 157–68; virtual and actual, 161–64. *See also* Obama Hope image
incommensurable beings, 18
industrialized farming, bad design of, 193
inferential statistical analyses, 49, 53
infinitesimal, idea of, 49
Ingold, Timothy, 144, 229
Instagram, 174, 176
intent, as nonconscious process, 22
invasive species, making of by political entities, 71–73

Jack, Jordynn, and pedagogy of sight, 126–27
Jameson, Frederic, and "cognitive mapping," 177–78
Johnson, Barbara, 4
Jones, Taylor, 174
Junco, Natalia Ruiz, 145

Kang, Jiyeon, 157
Kantianism, 144
Keller, Thomas, 62
Kelly, Ashley R., 121
Kelly, Casey, 198
Kennedy, George, 39
Kernan, Jerome B., 86
keyboard. *See* QWERTY keyboard layout
King, Magda, 154n2
Kingery, David, 83
Kittler, Friedrich, *Gramophone, Film, Typewriter*, 217
Klee, Paul, 228
Kleine, Robert E., 86
Kleine, Susan Schultz, 86
Krueger, Joachim, 51

Lacey Act, 73; amendment of in 2008, 75–76; effect on how fishermen perform their identities, 75; effect on ontological status of Asian carp, 81; joined with Black Bass Act of 1926, 75; use of to frame bighead carp as invasive, 74–75
Lakatos, Imre, 52
Lamb 86 (Alinea): as description of relational possibilities, 64; and material rhetoricity, 65–66; as occasion of carpentry, 64–65; as ontograph, 55, 57, 64; resemblance to exploded view diagrams, 60; as a rhetorical litany, 58, 59
Larenkov, Sergey, *Link to the Past*, 177
Lascoumes, Pierre, 48
Latour, Bruno, 4, 22, 186; actor-network theory, 98, 121, 224; critique of modernist epistemology, 110; and demarcation of facts from artifacts, 47; *Dingpolitik*, 109;

"From Matters of Fact to Matters of Concern," 118–19; and idea of things as gatherings, 5; litanies, 58, 59, 101–2; and networks, 70; on new ways of listening, 21; *Pandora*, 28; on postmodernism, 110; *Reassembling the Social*, 27, 106; "scientification," 224; and shift from metaphysics to ontology, 111; speed bump example, 36–37; and symmetrical models of relationality, 7–8

Law, John, 69, 70, 77, 81
Lefebvre, Henri, 170n8
Leibniz, Gottfried Wilhelm, 49, 50
Liebowitz, Stan, 220, 222
Lippi-Green, Rosina, 20–21
listening, habits of, 20–21; and speech protheses, 26–27; between strange strangers, 20, 23
litanies: and flat ontology, 58, 59; Latour and, 58, 59, 101–2
Little Free Library, autoethnographic study of: circulations, disclosures, and attunements in rhetorical situatedness, 153; constitution and attunements to worldishness, 149–52; current holdings, December 12, 2012, 148; data on book circulation patterns, fieldnotes, and photographs, 146–47; looking down street toward an eagle's perch, 152; and suasive circulations, 148–49; worldishness through circulatory intensities, 147, 153
Little Free Library movement: establishment of, 139–40; placard and credo, 139
Locke, Edwin, 78
Lubar, Steven D., 83
Lucaites, John, 126, 157
Lynch, Kevin, *What Time is This Place?*, 173, 177–78

Maddalena, Kate, 121
magnetic resonance imaging (fMRI), 45, 46, 53
Malin, Brenton J., 127, 138

Margolis, Stephen, 220, 222
Markus, Hazel, 87
Massey, Doreen, 139
material commonplaces, 200–201
material culture scholarship, 84, 86, 94n3, 94n5
materialisms. *See* new materialisms
materiality: and ontology, 109; rhetoric of, and handheld stereoscope, 126, 127, 131–34
materials: making as response to potentialities of, 230; relation to semiotic, 47
mathematics, as rhetorical ontology, 49
Mazis, Glen, 23–24
McGee, Harold, 62
McGee, Michael Calvin, 126
McGurrin, Frank, 222
McLuhan, Marshall, 148, 176
medical imaging devices, 48
Meillassoux, Quentin, 66n2
Meisel, Stefan, 162
memory, and community meaning-making, 173
memory-image, 180
Mercieca, Jennifer, 167
Merleau-Ponty, Maurice, 23–24
metaphorism, 98
metaphysical fallacy, 111–17, 117; and four-world problem, 111–12
Missouri Dairy Association, 71
Mitchell, W. J. T., 161
Mol, Annemarie, 122n1; *The Body Multiple: Ontology in Medical Practice*, 48, 164–65; cross-ontological calibration, 109; "Embodied Action, Enacted Bodies, 77, 81; empirical philosophy, 165; idea of "ontological politics," 9; multiple ontologies, 108, 119; "single multiple" images, 164
molecular gastronomy, 62–63
Mollison, Bill: example of chickens, 193; *Permaculture: A Designer's Manual*, 192
monuments, as rhetorical agents, 6
Morton, Timothy: on ecological thought, 17;

"Sublime Objects," 116; theory of mediation, 116
Moses, Robert, 1
Muckelbauer, John, *The Future of Invention*, 226
multiple ontologies, 10, 108, 109, 119
multiplicity, 70, 157, 163–65, 169n3
museums, as rhetorical agents, 6

Naas, Michael, 39–40
Nardi, Bonnie, 147
Natural Resource Defense Council, 71
natural rhetoric, 38–40
Nature Magazine, 45
Never Forget, AT&T Twitter advertisement, 176
"new cookery," statement on, 62–63
new materialisms, 10; and agency, 159; and becoming, 160; democracy of things, 155; and diagnostic consensus of two-world problem, 109–10; and efforts to circumnavigate the epistemic fallacy, 113; feminist, 6–7, 8; four-world problem of, 111–17, 112; impossibility of knowing all forces at work in given event, 187; *New Materialisms: Ontology, Agency, and Politics* (Coole and Frost), 109, 126; object-oriented, 120–21; recent work on, 186–87; rejection of rhetorical, 108, 117–18, 122n1; rhetoric friendly, 121; and thing theory, 114; vibrant, 108, 109, 147
New Materialisms: Ontology, Agency, and Politics (Coole and Frost), 109
new media images: and rhetorical divergence, 157; rhetorical transformation and distributed ontology, 160, 161, 166–67; virtual-action constitution, 161
Newton, Isaac, 49, 50
"New Woman," 198, 210
Nickerson, Raymond, 50–51, 52
nonartistic proofs, 5
nongovernmental organizations, and making of invasive species, 71
nonhuman subjectivity, 69–71
Norris, Susan L., 81

nostalgia, 173, 181
noumena and phenomena, separation between, 111, 117–18
null hypothesis significance testing (NHST), 43; critiques of, 52, 53; difference, spurious ways in which sex differences are reported, 51; frequently used method of data collection and analysis in scientific publications, 46; group means, and logical fallacy, 51; null, 50–51; production of fallacious or misleading findings, 49, 50–52; reification and magnification of small differences, 50, 53; as rhetorical ontology, 48–52; significance, problems with determining, 51
Nurius, Paula, 87

Obama, Barack, 42
Obama Hope image: Beacon by OVO, 162; as body multiple, 165; designed by Shepard Fairey, 156; flux in location, form, medium, genre, and activity, 158; in a Los Angeles mural, 163–64; Obama biscuits, 166; Obama for Presidente poster, 161, 163; Obama in Ghana bag, 162; parodies of ("Obamicons"), 165, 167; remixes of in France and Germany, 165; rhetorical transformation, 12, 157–68; serious roles around world, 167–68; *Yes, We Scan* (Rene Walter), 169. *See also* single, multiple images, rhetorical transformation of
object dependency, writers and, 83–84
object-oriented ontology (OOO), 7, 10, 109; Bogost and, 58–59; compared to thing-oriented ontologies, 120; composition studies and, 12, 96–97; concept of flat ontology, 97–98; and engagement of human and nonhuman objects on equal ontological grounds, 97; essences of objects only in relation to other things, 98; Harman and, 8, 13n1, 14n2, 108; and object assemblage, 97, 98; as rhetorical methodology, 97–98; and unknowability of objects, 97

Okadome, Takeshi, 223
Ong, Walter, 30
oN-Line System (NLS), *221*
ontography, 55–56, 59
ontology: emphasis on relational being, 8–9; multiple ontologies, 10, 108, 109, 119; rhetorical ontologies, 2–3, 8–11, 46–52, 99–102; thing-oriented ontologies, 109, 118–21. *See also* flat ontology; object-oriented ontology (OOO)
outernet, 169n7
Oyserman, Daphna, 87

Packer, Martin, 140, 145
particle-wave-field heuristic, 98, 103–5
Pearson, Karl, 51
permaculture: attunement as design, 191–94; and cooperation, 192–93; design in terms of assemblage rather than hierarchies, 192; intentional design, 192
persuasion: and entertaining of new possibilities, 23; "everyday" instances of, 36–38; of plants, 39–40; and politeness, 19–20, 26–27, 28n2; Rickert on, 28n2; speculative thought as, 18
PhotoFunia-generated montage of Pimp Obamico, 167, *168*
Pickering, Andrew: on correspondence epistemology, 118; and "ontological theatre," 10, 13, 108
Pike, Kenneth. See *Rhetoric: Discovery and Change* (Young, Becker, and Pike)
pilcrow, 63
Pink, Sarah, 144
places, as events, 139
plants, persuasiveness of, 39–40
Plato: alignment of flattery with the feminine, 56, 57, 61; *Gorgias*, 56, 57–58; *The Phaedrus*, 33; rhetoric as cookery, 56–57, 58, 61–62; rhetoric as distraction from objectivity, 57–58; rhetoric as ornamentation or deceptive flattery, 56
politeness, and persuasion, 19–20, 26–27, 28n2

Porter, E. Payson, 222–23
possessions, and identity, 86, 94n3
possible self, and goods used to enact possibilities, 87
Poster, Carol, 9
postmodernism, 110
prehension, unity of, 23, 25
Prelli, Lawrence, *Rhetorics of Display*, 126
Prior, Paul, 93, 94n2, 166
progymasmata exercises, 224
propositions, 18
Protagoras, 155, 169n1
Prown, Jules David, 84
Psychology Today, 45
public memorials, 6, 185
punctum, 141, 147
pure memory, 180

Quintilian, *Institutes of Oratory*, 5–6
QWERTY keyboard layout: and American Morse Code, 217; attacks on, 212; challenges to status, 219–22; design as result of "stochastic" forces, 214; and Dvorak keyboard, 219–20; encomium of, 13, 224–25; lineage, 215–19; and Mark Twain, 216; merging with humans, 215; myths about history of, 213–14; ontological similarity to human continual construct, 214–15; patented in 1878, 212–13; preceded typewriter, 213–14, 219; and touch-typing, 222

Reinberger, Hans-Jörg, 108
Reiss, Allan L., "Humor Modulates the Mesolimbic Reward Centers," 45
Remington & Sons, Sholes and Glidden Type-Writer, 217, *218*
Remington Standard Type-Writer No. 2, 216
respect, 24–25
reverse-Cartesian lobotomy, 112, 114–17
"Review of Information Concerning Bighead Carp (*Hypophthalmichthys nobilis*)," 74
Reyes, Mitchell, and mathematics, 49
rhetoric: ambient, 28n2, 116–17, 141,

142; and animal activity, 39; Aristotelian paradigm of, 31–32, 33–35; Big versus Little Rhetoric debates, 30; defined as epistemic practice in past, 3; deliberative, 31–32, 34; epideictic, 32, 34–35, 226; everyday, 36–38; forensic, 31, 34; and gathering of people and things around matters of interest, 5; history, 168; implicit paradigms of, 30–40; as knowledge-making art, 3; as mode of attunement to thrownness, entanglement, and worldishness, 143; and monuments and museums as agents of, 6; "natural," 38–40; Plato on, 56–57, 58, 61–62; rhetorical theory, 1–2, 6; rise and fall of in conjunction with rise and fall of democratic forms of government in the West, 32–33; as symbolic action with material effects, 128; visual, 156, 158–59, 166. *See also* rhetorical ontology; rhetorical situatedness

Rhetoric: Discovery and Change (Young, Becker, and Pike), 96–98, 103–6

Rhetoric, Materiality, and Politics (Biesecker and Lucaites), 126

Rhetorical Bodies (Selzer and Crowley), 126

rhetorical ecological model, 159

rhetorical ontology, 2–3, 8–11; Berthoff and, 99–102; and null hypothesis significance testing (NHST), 48–52; in science, 46–49

rhetorical situatedness: attunement to, 140–41, 142; and worldish things, 143

rhetorical transformation, of a new media image, 12, 156, 157–68

Rice, Jeff, 156, 170n8

Rice, Jenny, 29n4

Rickert, Thomas: and ambience, 23; ambient rhetoric, 28n2, 116–17, 141, 142; *Ambient Rhetoric*, 118, 122n2; on insufficiency of intent and consciousness to account for rhetoric, 21–22; modification of Heideggerian thing theory, 113; and reverse-Cartesian lobotomy, 117; rhetorical understanding of kairos for exploration of space-time, 121; theory of situatedness, 142; use of terms "worldliness" or "worldly," 154n2

Rogers, Carl, 37

Rothenberg, David, 227, 228, 231

Rotman, Brian, *Mathematics as Sign: Writing, Imagining, Counting*, 49

Rozeboom, William, 52

rulemaking, 72

Sackey, Donnie Johnson, 72, 73, 81

Salem Witch Trial Memorial, 185

Schatzki, Theodore, 70–71

Schiavo, Laura, 138

Schmidt, Frank, 52

science, bad: Condit's critique of, 42, 43–44, 46, 49, 52; ontological problem of, 48

science, rhetorical ontologies in, 46–48

science magazines, popular, article titles displaying assumption that human brains are dimorphic, 44–45

Scott, Robert L., 3

Scult, Andrew, reading of Aristotle's *Rhetoric*, 9

self-efficacy, as causal determinant of motivation and performance, 78

self-extension, through possessions, 86

Selzer, Jack, 3–4, 94n5, 126

sex differences vs. gender, 54n1

Shannon, Claude Elwood, 116

Shaver, James, 52

Shaviro, Steven, 161, 170n8

Shins, The, "Saint Simon," 212

Shipka, Jody, 93, 94n2, 166

Shole and Glidden Type-Writer, 216, 217, 222

Sholes, Christopher, 212, 214, 218

Shove, Elizabeth, 143

significance, problems with determining in NHST, 51

single, multiple images, rhetorical transformation of, 157–68; acquisition of thing-power with circulation in time and space, 157, 166, 168; chronotopic perspectives on, 165–67; from nonmodern perspective, 160–61

sites, as occurrences created via event relations, 70–71
Smith, Caroline Minna, 204
Snapchat, 174
Socrates, condemnation of writing, 33
Sommers, Nancy, 4
speculative thought, as persuasion, 18
speech, privileging of over writing, 33–34
speech prostheses, 21, 26–27
Spinoza, Baruch, 193
Spinuzzi, Clay, 145, 185
Stamp, Jimmy, 216, 217
stasis deliberation, 121
"Statement on the 'New Cookery'," 62–63
Stearns, Philip, *Evident Materials*, 227, 228, 231n2
Stengers, Isabelle, 18, 19, 21, 23
stereoscope, parlor: classroom use of, 133–34, 137; disembodiment of vision, 129–34; first mass production and dissemination of representational photographs, 129; handheld quality of, 131–34; materiality, rhetoric of, 126, 127, 131–34; materiality of artifact and user acting on each other in reciprocal feedback loop, 130; and new materialist ontology, 125–26; pervasiveness in nineteenth-century American culture, 127–29; as rhetorical agent of vision, 12, 126–28; rhetorical work of size and shape and content of cards, 135; standardization of stereographs, 134–35; stereographs' argument for hyper attention, 134–37
Stewart, Kathleen, 140, 144–45
Stormer, Nathan, 199
Strong, Earle, 219–20
syllogisms, 5
Syverson, Margaret, and co-construction, 56, 66n1

Taub, Louis, 222
Tenner, Edward, 214, 219
Terranova, Tiziana, 169n7
Teston, Christa B., 121
texts, organizing work of, 70

thingectomy, 112–14, 115, 117–19
thing-oriented ontologies, 109, 118–21
thing-power, 5, 126, 157, 159, 166
things: as active agents, 2; challenge to understandings of rhetoric, 1, 4; gathering power of, 3–6; relations between, 6–8; renewed importance of in humanities and social sciences, 1; as suasive and agential, 4
thing theory, 4, 10, 121; and cult of the z-axis, 114; Harman's analysis of, 113–15; Heidegger's, 112–13, 118; and reverse-Cartesian lobotomy, 114–15
thought, and technology, 227, 231n1
Title IX, impact on collegiate classrooms and athletics, 210
touch-typing, 222
Toulmin, Stephen, 37
Toulminian traces, 45–46, 53
Trachtenberg, Alan, 129
Transitional Network: deliberate rhetorical action through attunement to assemblages, 194, 196; emphasis on dissolution, 195; practical community preparation for change, 194, 195; principles of permaculture, 194; role as nurturer and facilitator, 194–95; Sandpoint, Idaho, Transition Initiative, 195–96
transmission models of delivery, 116, 158
trash, and assemblage rhetoric, 13, 188–90
trophic pyramid, 192
Tumblr, 174
Turkle, Sherry, 4, 83–84, 92
Twain, Mark, and QWERTY keyboard, 216
two-world problem, 109–10, 117
Typewriter Trust, 213

US Fish and Wildlife Service: addition of bighead carp to list of injurious fish, 72; conflict with fish farmers via writing, 73–77; Document No. 03-23745, 75, 76; limited engagement with local, state, and regional agencies, 73; search for science-based information in regard to invasive species, 72–73

Vatz, Richard, 141
Vaughn, Justin, 167
vibrant materialisms, 108, 109, 147
Vietnam Veterans Memorial, as rhetorical agent, 6
virtual image, divergent and multiple actualizations, 163
vision, intersection with rhetoric and materiality, 126
visual autoethnography, 146
visual rhetoric: and freeze-framing, 158–59; and rhetorical transformation, 156; theory of founded on ontological notion of becoming, 166
Viveiros de Castro, Eduardo, 9–10
Vivian, Bradford, 173
Vogel, Hermann, 129

Wagner, Jon, 146
Walker, Jeffrey, 226
Walter, Rene, *Yes, We Scan*, 169
waste. See trash and assemblage rhetoric
Weaver, Warren, 116
Wheatstone, Charles, invention of stereoscope, 125, 128
Whitehead, Alfred North, 18, 170n8; "actual entity," 21; *Modes of Thought*, 26, 27; notion of the unity of a prehension, 23, 25; and transformation of habits, 20; on Wordsworth, 22–23
Wickman, Chad, 46
Wikipedia, 158
Wilde, Oscar, 22
Willard, Frances: on impact of bicycle on American women, 197–98, 201, 211; *A Wheel Within a Wheel: How I Learned to Ride the Bicycle*, 197, 199
Williamson, Richard, 107
Wilson, Margaret, 223
Wittgenstein, Ludwig, 21, 22
"Woman Question," 211n1
women: "New Woman," 198, 210. See also bicycling, for women, late nineteenth century
Wood, Wendy, 54n1

Woolf, Virginia, 83
Woolgar, Steve, 47
Wooster, Harold, 220
Wordsworth, William, 22–23
worldish attunements, 140, 145–47
worldishness, 141–43, 154n2; Little Free Library and, 147, 149–52, 153
writing, material culture of, 84–93; and writing identity, 85, 86–87, 93. See also writing habitat
writing devices: effective mediational functions of, 78; following rulemaking notices, 72; and performance of bighead carp, 71–77; role in assembling organizations, 69; use of in clinical setting, 77–79 (*See also* diabetes health maintenance, secondary therapies)
writing habitat: connection of space with specific writing task or genre, 90; mobile writing practices, 87–92, 89; "scene of writing," 84–85; and writers' relationships with material goods and rituals that support their work, 83, 84; writing desk, 86–87, 93; writing spaces, 87–93
Writing in Digital Environments (WIDE) research center, Michigan State University, 77
writing technologies, 186
Wyche, Susan, 94n2
Wynn, James, 49–50
Wysocki, Anne, 186

Yagelski, Robert P., *Writing as a Way of Being*, 10
Yancey, Kathleen Blake, 4
Yasuoka, Koichi, 213, 216, 222
Yasuoka, Motoko, 213, 216, 222
Yes, Drama, 227
Young, Richard. See *Rhetoric: Discovery and Change* (Young, Becker, and Pike)

Zarefsky, David, 167
z-axis, cult of, 114
Zickefoose, Julie: *The Bluebird Effect*, 25–26; and listening to strangers, 25–26, 28; use of speech protheses, 26